The
Doctrine
Of
Reconciliation
&
Reconciliation
By The
Blood of Christ

The
Doctrine
Of
Reconciliation

Arthur W. Pink

&

Reconciliation
By The
Blood of Christ

Thomas Goodwin

Sovereign Grace Publishers, Inc.
P.O. Box 4998
Lafayette, IN 47903

Printed In the United States of America

THE DOCTRINE OF RECONCILIATION.

INTRODUCTION

Three considerations have influenced us in the selection of this theme. First, a desire to preserve the balance of Truth. In order to do this it is desirable that there should be an alternation between and a proportionate emphasis upon both the objective and the subjective sides of the Truth. After we had completed our exposition of the doctrine of Justification we followed the same with a series on the doctrine of Sanctification: the former treats entirely of the righteousness which Christ has wrought or procured for His people, being something wholly outside of themselves and independent of their own efforts; whereas the latter speaks not only of the perfect purity which the believer has in Christ, but also of the holiness which the Spirit actually communicates to the soul and which is influential on his conduct. Then we took up the doctrine of Predestination which is concerned entirely with the sovereignty of God, and therefore we followed that with a series of man's Impotency and the Saint's Perseverance, where the principal emphasis was upon human responsibility. It will be well for us now to turn our attention back again to the Divine operations and the wondrous provisions of Divine grace for the recovery of rebels against God.

Second, because of a felt need of again bringing conspicuously before our readers "the cross of our Lord Jesus Christ." It is His sacrificial work which is prominent, yea, dominant in the reconciling of God to His people. It was by the shedding of Christ's precious blood that God was placated and His wrath averted. It was by Christ's being chastised that peace has been made for us. And it is by the preaching of the Cross that our awful enmity against God is slain and that we are moved to abandon our vile warfare against Him. As it is upwards of twelve years since we completed the rather lengthy series of articles we wrote upon the Atonement, under the title "The Satisfaction of Christ," it seems high time that we once more contemplated the greatest marvel and miracle of all history, namely, the Lamb of God being slain for the redemption of sinners. The doctrine of reconciliation has much to do with what took place at Calvary, yea apart from that no reconciliation with God had been possible. It is therefore a subject which should warm the hearts of the saints and bow them in adoration at the feet of the Redeemer.

Third, because it treats of an aspect of the Gospel which receives scant attention in the modern pulpit. Nor has it ever, so far as we have been able to ascertain, been made very prominent. This doctrine has failed to command the notice which it merits even from God's own servants and people. Far less appears to have been preached on it than on either justification or sanctification. For one book written on this subject probably fifty have been published on either of the others. Why this should be is not easy to explain: it is not because it is more obscure or intricate. In our judgment, much to the contrary. Certainly it is of equal inportance and value, for it treats of an aspect of our relationship and recovery to God as essential as either of the others. Our need of justification lies in our failure to keep the Law of God; of sanctification, because we are defiled and polluted by sin, and therefore unfit for the presence of the Holy One; our reconciliation, because we are alienated from God, rebels against Him, with no heart for fellowship with Him. Though the terms justify and sanctify occur more

1

frequently in the New Testament than does "reconcile," yet the correlative "God of peace" and other expressions must also be duly noted.

Not only has this doctrine been more or less neglected, but it has been seriously perverted by some and considerably misunderstood by many others. Both Socinians (who repudiate the Tri-unity of the Godhead and the Atonement of Christ) and Arminians deny the twofoldness of reconciliation, declaring it to be only on one side. They insist that it is man who is alienated from God, and so in need of reconciliation, that God never entertained enmity toward His fallen creatures, but has ever sought their recovery. They argue that since it was man who made the breach by departing from his Maker, he is the one who needs to be reconciled and restored to Him. They refuse to allow that sin has produced any change in God's relationship or attitude unto the guilty, yea, so far from doing so that His own love moved Him to take the initiative and provide a Saviour for rebels, and that He now beseeches them to throw down the weapons of their opposition, assuring them of a Father's welcome when they return unto Him.

Such is the view of the Plymouth Brethren. In his work *"The Ministry of Reconciliation"* C. H. Machintosh (one of the most influential of their early men) declares: "We often hear it said that 'the death of Christ was necessary in order to reconcile God to man.' This is a pious mistake, arising from inattention to the language of the Holy Spirit and indeed to the plain meaning of the word *'reconcile.'* God never changed, never stepped out of His normal and true position. He abides faithful. There was, and could be, no derangement, no confusion, no alienation, so far as He was concerned; and therefore there could be no need of reconciling Him to us. In fact it was exactly the contrary. Man had gone astray; he was the enemy, and needed to be reconciled...Wherefore, then, as might be expected, Scripture never speaks of reconciling God to man. There is no such expression to be found within the covers of the New Testament." This is something he calls a "point of immense importance," and consequently all who have succeeded him in that strange system have echoed his teaching: how far it is removed from the Truth will be shown in the articles that follow.

Some hyper-Calvinists are also much confused on this doctrine. Through failing to see that God's being reconciled to sinners who believe concerns His official relationship and not His essential character, they have demurred at the expression *"a reconciled God,"* supposing it connotes some charge within Himself. They argue that since God has loved His elect with an everlasting love (Jer. 31:3) and that since He changes not (Mal. 3:6), it is wrong for us to suppose that reconciliation to anything more on our side only. They insist that to speak of God's being reconciled unto us implies an alteration either in His affections or purpose, and that neither of these can stand with His immutability. To speak of God's first loving His people, then hating then, and then again loving them, appears to them as imputing fickleness to Him. So it would be if these predictions of God were made of Him considered in the same character and relationship. But they are not. As their Father God has loved His people with an unalterable love, but as the Moral Governor of this world and the Judge of all the earth He has a legal enmity against those who trample His Law beneath their feet.

The following question was submitted to Mr. J. C. Philpot: — "What is meant by 'a reconciled God,' an expression which some of the Lord's children, even great and good men, have made use of? I believe that the Lord Jehovah from all eternity foresaw the fall, and provided means to save those whom He had chosen in Christ, consistent with all His attributes, holiness, justice, etc. Now, as love was the moving cause, how can the word *'reconcile'* be correctly used in respect of God? Does it not imply a change? If it does, how can it be correctly used in reference to God?" His answer to this appears in the March 1856 issue of *"The Gospel Standard,"* and though it will make a rather lengthy quotation, yet we might be doing him an injustice not to give it in full.

"We do not consider the expression *'A reconciled God'* strictly correct. The language of the New Testament is not that God is reconciled to us, but that we are reconciled to God. *'And all things are of God, who has reconciled us unto Himself by Jesus Christ, and has given to us the ministry of reconciliation – that God was in Christ reconciling the world to Himself, not imputing their trespasses to them; and that He has committed to us the word of reconciliation. Now we are ambassadors for Christ, as though God did beseech you by us. We beg you in Christ's stead, be reconciled to God.'* (2 Cor. 5:18-20). And again *'And, having made peace through the blood of His cross, it pleased the Father to reconcile all things by Him unto Himself – by Him, whether things in earth or things in Heaven. And you, who were once alienated and enemies in your mind by wicked works, yet now He has reconciled in the body of His flesh through death to present you holy and unblameable and unreprovable in His sight,'* (Col. 1:20-22). See also Rom. 5:10.

"The very nature of God, His very being and essence, is to be unchanging and unchangeable, as James beautifully speaks: *'With Him there is no variableness, neither shadow of turning.'* But reconciliation on God's part to us, would seem to imply a change of mind, an alteration of purpose in Him, and is therefore, so far, inconsistent and incompatible with the unchangeableness of the Divine character. It is also, strictly speaking, inconsistent, as our correspondent observes, with the eternal love of God, and seems to represent the atonement as influencing His mind, and turning it from wrath to love, and from displeasure to mercy and grace. Now, the Scripture represents the gift of Christ, and consequently the sufferings and blood-shedding for which and unto which He was given, not, as the procuring cause, but as the gracious effect of the love of God. *'Herein is love, not that we loved God, but that He loved us, and sent His Son to be a propitiation for our sins'* (1 John 4:10). See also John 3:16, Rom. 8:32, 1 John 4:9.

"But though the Scripture speaks of reconciliation, not of God to man, but of man to God, and that through the blood of the cross alone (Col. 1:20); yet it holds forth, in the plainest, strongest language, a real and effective *'sacrifice,' 'atonement,'* and *'propitiation,'* offered to God by the Lord Jesus; all which terms express or imply an actual satisfaction rendered to God for sin, and such a satisfaction, as that without it there could be no pardon. It is especially needful to bear this in mind, because the Socinians and other heretics who deny or explain away the atonement, insist much on this point, that the Scripture does not speak of a reconciled God. Therefore, though we do not believe that the atonement produced a change in the mind of God, so as to turn Him from hatred to love, for He loved the elect with an everlasting love, (Jer. 31:3), or that it was a price paid to procure His favor, still, there was a sacrifice offered, a propitiation made, whereby, and whereby alone, sin was pardoned, blotted out, and forever put away.

"By steadily bearing these two things in mind, we shall be the better prepared to understand in what reconciliation through the blood of the cross consists. Against the persons of the elect there was, in the mind of God, no vindictive wrath, no penal anger (Isa. 27:4); but there was a displeasure against their sins, and so far with them for their sins. So God was angry with Moses (Deut. 1:37), with Aaron (Deut. 9:20), with David (2 Sam. 11:27; 1 Chron. 21:7), with Solomon (1 Kings 11:9) for their personal sins, though all of them were in the covenant of grace, and loved by Him with an everlasting love. Thus the Scriptures speak of the anger and wrath of God, and of that wrath being turned away and pacified (Isa. 12:1; Ezek. 16:63), which it could only be by the blood of the Lamb.

"Again, sin is a violation of the justice of God, a breaking of His holy Law, an offence against His intrinsic purity and holiness, which He cannot pass by. Adequate satisfaction must, therefore, be made to His offended justice, or pardon cannot be granted. Now, here we see the necessity and nature of the sufferings and obedience, blood-shedding and death of the Lord Jesus, as also why reconciliation was needed, and what reconciliation effected. By the active and passive obedience of the Son of God in the flesh, by His meritorious life and death, by His offering Himself as a sacrifice for sin, a full and complete satisfaction was rendered to the violating justice of God, the Law was perfectly obeyed and everlasting righteousness brought in. Satisfaction being rendered to His infinite justice, now God can be *just and yet the Justifier of him which believes in Jesus.'* Now the jarring perfections of mercy and justice are harmonized and reconciled, so that mercy and truth meet together, righteousness and peace kiss each other. Now God can not only be gracious, but *'faithful and just to forgive us our sins and to cleanse us from all unrighteousness.'* There is, then, no such reconciliation of God as to make Him love those whom He did not love before, for He loved the elect from all eternity in Christ, their covenant—head. But a breach being made by the fall, and sin having, as it were, burst in to make a separation between God and them (Isa. 59:2), that love could not flow forth till satisfaction was made for sin, and that barrier removed, which it was in one day (Zech. 3:9). And not only so, but the persons of the elect were defiled with sin (Ezek. 16:5,6), and therefore needed washing, which they were in the blood of the Lamb (Rev. 1:5, etc.). In this way not only was the reconciliation of the Church effected, but she, the bride and spouse of Christ, was brought near unto God, from whom sin had separated her.

"But reconciliation has a further aspect. It comprehends our reconciliation to God not merely as a thing already effected by the blood-shedding of God's dear Son, but as a present experience in the soul. The apostle says *'By whom we have now received the atonement'* (Rom. 5:11); and again, *'we pray you, in Christ's stead, be reconciled to God'* (2 Cor. 5:20), that is, by receiving into your hearts the reconciliation already made by His blood. It is with reference to this experience that much is spoken in the Scriptures which has led to the idea of *'a reconciled God.'* Thus the Church complains of God's being angry with her (Isa. 12:1), of being *'consumed by His anger and troubled by His wrath'*(Ps. 90:7), of His *'shutting up in anger His tender mercies'* (Ps. 77:9), and again of His *'turning away from the fierceness of His anger and causing it to cease'* (Ps. 85:3,4), of His '*not keeping anger forever*'(Ps. 103:9), of His being pacified (Ezek. 16:63) of His '*anger being turned away*' (Ps. 78:38; Hos. 14:4). All these expressions are the utterance of the Church's experience. When God's anger is sensibly felt in the conscience He is viewed as angry, and His wrathful displeasure is dreaded and deprecated; when He manifests mercy this anger is felt to be removed, to be turned away; and it is now as if He were reconciled to the sinner.

"Putting all these things together we seem to arrive at the following conclusions: (1) That it is not God who is reconciled to the Church, but that it is the Church which is reconciled to God. (2) That this reconciliation was effected by the incarnation, obedience, sacrifice and death of the Lord Jesus. (3) That till this reconciliation be made experimentally known the awakened conscience feels the anger of God on account of sin. (4) That when the atonement is received and the blood of Christ sprinkled on the conscience, then the soul is really and truly reconciled to God."

What satisfaction this reply gave to the original inquirer, or how lucid it appears to our readers (even after a second or third perusal), we know not, but to us it seems a strange medley, lacking in perspecuity and betraying confusion of thought in the mind of its composer. First, Mr. Philpot considered that the language of the New Testament does not warrant the expression "*A reconciled God.*" Second, he felt that to affirm a reconciliation on God's part to us would imply an alteration of purpose in Him and as though the Atonement changed His mind "*From displeasure to mercy and grace.*" Then he evidently feared he was coming very close to the ground occupied by the Socinians; so, third, he allowed that the work of Christ was both a "*sacrifice*" and a "*propitiation.*" But "*a propitiation*" is the very thing which is needed to conciliate one who is offended! To aver there was "*rendered to God for sin an actual satisfaction, and such a satisfaction as that without which there could be no pardon,*" is only another way of saying that God was alienated and needed placating before He could be reconciled to His enemies.

In his next paragraph he virtually or in effect contradicts what he had advanced in the previous one, for he expressly declares "Against the persons of the elect there was in the mind of God no vindictive wrath, no penal anger." Then wherein lay the need of a "*propitiation?*" "*Penal*" means "*relating to punishment.*" if there was no judicial anger on God's part as Governor and Judge and if His elect were not exposed to the punishment of the Law because of their sins, then why the sacrifice of Christ for them? Clearly Mr. P. felt the shoe pinching him there, for in his next paragraph he brings in the violation of the justice of God and the "*satisfaction*" this required. Yet toward the end he wavers again by saying "sin having, as it were, burst in to make a separation between God and them." Why such hesitating qualification? Sin did cause a breach on both sides, and the one Party needed to be "*propitiated,*" and the other "*converted*" before the breach could be healed. Our purpose in quoting form C.H. Machintosh and J.C. Philpot (whose writings served to mould the views of many thousands) is to demonstrate the need for a Scriptural exposition of this doctrine.

We are glad to say that in his last years Mr. Philpot was granted a clearer grasp of the truth, as appears from his helpful exposition of Eph. 2.

CHAPTER I.

ITS DISTINCTIONS.

Before taking up our subject in a positive and constructive manner it seems advisable that we should endeavor to remove a misapprehension under which a number of our readers are laboring, and which requires to be cleared up before they will be in a fit condition to weigh without bias and thus be enabled to receive what we hope to present in later articles. It is for their special benefit this one is composed, and we trust that other friends will kindly bear with us if they find it rather wearisome to follow a labored discussion of that which presents no difficulty to them. To enter into a consideration of this particular point at such an early stage in the series will oblige us to somewhat infringe upon other aspects of our subject which will be taken up later, but, this appears necessary if we are to "clear the decks for action," or to change the figure, if we are to rid the ground of superfluous incumbrances and fit it for a sowing of the seed.

That which presents a difficulty to those who have been brought up in some Calvinistic circles is, how can God be said to be reconciled to His elect, seeing that He has loved them with an everlasting and unchanging love? Much of our opening article was devoted to a particular answer to such an inquiry, but as we deem that answer far from being a satisfactory one, we shall here confine ourself to its elucidation. To us it appears that the explanation furnished by Mr. Philpot was confused and faulty, and that is was so through failure to distinguish between things that differ – therefore the title we have accorded this article. If we are to avoid becoming hopelessly muddled on this point, we must discriminate sharply between what the elect are as viewed only in the eternal purpose of God, and what they are in themselves by nature. And further, we must carefully differentiate between God considered as their Father and God considered as the Moral Governor and Judge of all mankind.

That it may appear we do not advance anything in the remainder of this article which clashes with or deviates from the teaching of sound theologians in the past, we will make brief quotations from four of the best-known Puritans. "We are actually justified, pardoned and reconciled when we repent and believe. Whatever thoughts and purposes of grace God may have towards us from eternity, we are under the fruits of sin till we become penitent believers" (T. Manton). In his treatise on *"The Work of the Holy Spirit in our Salvation"* Thos. Goodwin points out: "There are two different states or conditions which the elect of God, who are saved, pass through, between which regeneration is the passage. The one is their first state in which they are born: a state of bondage to sin, and obnoxious to instant damnation while they remain in it...The other of grace and salvation, therefore opposite to the former state."

God does hate His elect in some sense before their actual reconciliation. God was placable before Christ, appeased By Christ. But until there be such conditions which God has appointed in the creature, he has no interest in this reconciliation of God, and whatever person he be in whom the condition is not found, he remains under the wrath of God, and therefore in some sense under God's hatred" (Stephen Charnock, vol. 3, p. 345). When writing on *"The Satisfaction of Christ"* John Owen said: "This then is what we ascribe to the death of Christ, when we say that as a sacrifice we were reconciled to God or that He made reconciliation for us. Having made God our Enemy by sin, Christ by His death turned away His anger, appeased His wrath, and brought us into favor again with God." How far Mr. Philpot digressed from the teaching of these men we must leave his friends to judge for themselves. But we appeal now to an infinitely higher authority, namely, the Word of God.

Nothing is more plainly taught in Scripture than that all men without exception are before actual regeneration in a like state and condition, and occupy the same standing or status before the Divine Law. Whatever distinguishing design God has purposed in Himself to afterward effect as a change in His own elect by the operations of His free grace, until those operations take place they are in precisely the same case as the non-elect. *"We have before proved both Jews and Gentiles that they are all under sin"* — guilty, beneath sentence of condemnation. *"There is none righteous, no not one"* — not one who has met the requirements of the Divine Law. *"That every mouth may be stopped and all the world may become guilty before God"* — that is, obnoxious to the Divine Judgment. *"There is no difference for all have sinned and come short of the glory of God"* (Rom. 3:9, 10, 19, 22, 23). The condition and position of every one relative to the Law is one and the same before his regeneration and justification, and the decree of God concerning any difference that is yet to be made in some in nowise modifies that solemn fact. This is one chief reason why the Gospel is to be preached to every creature.

The Scriptures are equally explicit in describing the effects and consequences of lying under God's wrath. Before conversion the elect equally with the non-elect are in a state of alienation from God (Eph. 4:18), and therefore none of their services or performances can be acceptable to Him. He will receive naught at their hands: *"he who turns away his ear from hearing the Law* (an in the case with every unregenerate soul), *even his prayer is a hateful thing"* (Prov. 28:9). They are all under the power of the Devil (Col. 1:13), who rules at his pleausre in the children of disobedience (Eph. 2:2). They are *"without Christ . . . having no hope, and without God in the world"* (Eph. 2:12). They are under the curse or condemning power of the Law (Gal. 3:13). They are *"children in whom is no faith"* (Deut. 32:20) and therefore utterly unable to do a single thing which can meet with God's approval, for *"without faith it is impossible to please God"* (Heb. 11:6). They are therefore *"ready to perish"* (Deut. 26:5).

"He who does not the Son shall not see life, but the wrath of God abides upon him" (John 3:36). What could be plainer than that? Is not an elect soul an unbeliever until the moment God is pleased to give faith unto him? Assuredly: then equally sure is it that he is also under the wrath of God so long as he remains an unbeliever. Not only so, but the Word of God solemnly declares that the elect are *"by nature the children of wrath even as others"* (Eph. 2:3), and no Papish priest can make them otherwise by sprinkling a few drops of "holy water" upon them. But *"children of wrath"* they could not be had they come into this world in a justified and reconciled state. No person can be in two contrary states at the same time, obnoxious to wrath, and yet God at peace with him, under the guilt of sin and yet justified. Wrath is upon them from the womb (because of their sinning in Adam), and that wrath remains on them so long as they continue unbelievers. Though they were (in God's purpose) in Christ from eternity, that did not prevent them being in Adam in time and suffering the penal effects of this fall.

There is an appointed hour in their earthly history when the elect pass from under the penal wrath of God and are justified by Him and reconciled to Him. Justification is an act of God, an act in time, an external act. It is an act of God in a way of judicial process – His declaration as supreme Judge. It is opposed to condemnation, the granting a full discharge therefrom (Rom. 8:33-35). It is not an internal decision in God, which always remains in Him, and effects change in the status of the person justified; but is a temporal act of His power which makes a relative change in the person's standing before Him. It is upon the person's believing in Christ that God justifies him and that he passes from a state of guilt and alienation to one of righteousness and reconciliation: he that believes on Him is not condemned (that is, he is justified), but he that believes not is condemned already (John 3:18). *"He who believes on Him that sent Me but has everlasting life* (by regeneration), *and shall not come into condemnation, but is passed from death unto life"* – that is, the life of justification (John 5:24).

If persons are justified in a proper sense by faith, then they are not justified from eternity, for we believe in time, not eternity. That we are justified by faith, is the doctrine of the Gospel, as is apparent from the whole current of God's Word. To cite but one verse: *"Knowing that a man is not justified by the works of the Law, but by faith of Jesus Christ, even we have believed in Jesus Christ,"* (Gal. 2:16). That the apostle is there speaking of being justified in the sight of God, and not merely in the court of conscience, is beyond all doubt to any that will duly and fairly consider the scope of the Holy Spirit in that passage. Being justified by faith in Jesus Christ is there placed in opposition to being *"justified by the works of the Law"* which shows that something more fundamental than our own assurance is in view. *"By the deeds of the Law shall no flesh be justified in His sight"* (Rom. 3:19) makes it clear that none can obtain sentence of acquittal in the court of Divine adjudication by their own deeds. It is before God and not in the believer's consciousness that justification takes place.

"And the Scripture foreseeing that God would justify the heathen through faith, preached before the Gospel unto Abraham, saying, In you shall all nations be blessed" (Gal. 3:8). It is to be noted that there are two words here which lie directly against justification before believing: that God would justify the heathen – which must needs respect time to come; and *"shall all nations be blessed"* or justified – a *"shall be"* cannot be put for a thing already done. To this agrees *"in the Lord shall all the seed of Israel be justified"* (Isa. 45:25): by union with Christ through faith shall they be pronounced righteous. Again; *"For as by one man's disobedience many were made sinners, so by the obedience of One shall many be made righteous"* (Rom. 5:19). Upon which the Puritan Wm. Bridge said, "It is remarkable that when the Holy Spirit speaks of Adam's sin condemning his posterity, He speaks of it as already past; but when He speaks of Christ's righteousness for the justification of sinners He changes to the future tense – as if He purposely designed to prevent our thoughts running after justification before believing."

What has been said above about the justification of God's elect upon their believing, holds equally good concerning His reconciliation to them when they throw down the weapons of their warfare against Him. Not only was their reconciliation decreed from everlasting but peace was actually made by Christ when He shed His blood (Col. 1:20); nevertheless, reconciliation itself is not effected until the Holy Spirit has so wrought within them as to bring about their conversion. This is conclusively established by the following passages: *"For if, when we were enemies we were reconciled to God by the death of His Son, much more being reconciled, we shall be saved by His life. And not only so, but we also joy in God through our Lord Jesus Christ, by whom we have now received the reconciliation"* (Rom. 5:10,11) – that *"now"* would be meaningless if we were reconciled only in the eternal decree of God: what God decreed for us is here received by us! So again, *"And you that were sometime alienated and enemies in your mind by wicked works, yet NOW has He reconciled"* (Col. 1:21).

It would obviate considerable misunderstanding if it were clearly perceived that the everlasting love of God toward His elect is mainly an act of His will, the exercise of His good pleasure, the purpose of His grace, whereby He determined to do certain things for them and instate them in glory in His own good time and way. But that purpose effects nothing for them nor puts anything into them – for these there must be external acts of God's power making good His purpose. From all eternity God determined to make this earth, yet six thousand years ago it did not exist! He had ordained a final Day of Judgment but it has not yet arrived. God has purposed that in and through Christ He will justify and save certain persons, but they are not thereby justified because God has purposed it. It is true they will be in due time, but not before they have been enabled to believingly appropriate the atoning work of Christ in their behalf. We must therefore draw a line between the absolute certainty of the fruition of anything God has eternally purposed, and its actual accomplishment or bringing it to pass in His appointed time.

What has been pointed out in the last paragraph should make it easier for the reader to grasp that God's eternal love unto His own (which is an imminent act of His will or good pleasure, entirely within Himself) does not exempt them from coming beneath His anger (which is not any passion in God, but the outward visitation of His displeasure– because of sin; nor does it prevent their lying beneath the dispensations of His judicial wrath, until by some interpositions of His grace in time, when He actually changes their personal state (by regeneration) and legal status (by justification), freeing them from condemnation and instating them into His favor. In other words, much may occur in the interval between God's eternal purpose and the actual working out of the same – though nothing which can in anywise jeopardise His purpose, and nothing that was not foreseen when He framed it.

But it is objected by hyper-Calvinists, If the elect were not justified in Christ from all eternity then when God pronounces them just there is an alteration in His will and love toward them. Not so, God is no more mutable because He justifies His people in time, than He is because He regenerates them in time. God is no more chargeable with change of purpose when He produces a change in a person's standing upon his believing, than He is when He produces a change in a person's condition by the miracle of the new birth. All the change is in the creature. Though God absolutely decrees, and that from everlasting, to regenerate, to justify and to reconcile all His chosen, with the alteration of His governmental attitude toward them which that involves, yet this argues not the least shadow of change in God HImself when at the predestinated hour that great change is effected. Do but distinguish between the grace decreeing and the power of God executing, and all is plain. *"Whom He did predestinate, them He also called, and whom He called, them He also justified"* (Rom. 8:30) — the calling and justifying are the fruits of His electing love.

But again it is objected, the elect are designated *"sheep"* before they believe (John 10:16), and in God's esteem they are then in a justified state. Answer: they are called *"sheep"* according to the immutability of the Divine decree, which cannot be frustrated, and on that account God calls *"things which are not as though they were"* (Rom. 4:17), nevertheless, that verse affirms they *"are not"* that is, they have no actual existence. They are *"sheep"* in the purpose of God, but not so as touching the accomplishment of the same until they are regenerated. Paul was a sheep in the decree of God even when he was wolflike in preying upon the flock of Christ. Surely none will say he was actually a sheep while he was *"breathing out threatenings and slaughter against the disciples of the Lord"* (Acts 9:1). From the decree of God we may safely conclude the certainty of its accomplishment; but to argue that a thing is actually accomplished because Diviniely forordained is a most foolish and dangerous way of reasoning.

The love of God's purpose and good pleasure has not the least inconsistency with those hindrances to the peace and friendship of God which sin has interposed, for though the holiness of His Law, the righteousness of His government and the veracity of His Word, stood in the way of His taking a sinner into friendship and fellowship with Himself, until full satisfaction has been made to His broken Law and insulted Majesty; nevertheless His love determined and His wisdom devised a way where His sovereign good will should recover His people, and that, without sullying the Divine character to the slightest degree, yea, in magnifying those attributes which sin had affronted. God's love has proven efficacious by the means He devised *"that His banished one may not be cast out from Him"* (2 Sam. 14:14).

From all that has been pointed out above it should be quite evident that this doctrine of reconciliation does not teach that God loved and hated His elect at the same time and in the same respect. He loved them in respect of the free purpose of His sovereign will; but His wrath was upon them in respect of His violated Law and provoked justice by their sin. But His love gave Christ to satisfy for their sins and to redeem them from the curse of the Law, and in due time He sends His Spirit to regenerate them, which lays the foundation for their conversion and restoration to Him.

The following distinctions must, then, be kept steadily in mind:

1. Between God's looking upon His elect in the purpose of His grace and as under the sentence of His Law: though the elect are born under the dispensation of His wrath, yet it is not executed upon them personally.

2. Between there being no change in God and a change in His outward dealings with us.

3. Between God's purpose concerning His elect in eternity and the accomplishment of that purpose in a time state.

4. Between God's viewing the elect in Christ their Covenant—Head and as the depraved descendents of fallen Adam. In the one cause, as *"His dear children"* in

the other; as being *"by nature the children of wrath."*

5. Between God's unchanging love for us as our Father, and His official displeasure as our moral Governor and Judge. This distinction is illustrated in the case of Christ. He was the Beloved of the Father and never ceased to be so, yet Divine wrath was visited upon Him at the cross. He was dealt with not as the Son (as such) but as the Surety of His guilty people, by the Father, not as such, but as the supreme Judge.

CHAPTER II.

ITS NEED.

The word reconciliation means to unite two parties who are estranged. It denotes that one has given offence and the other has taken umbrage or is displeased by it, in consequence of which there is a breach between them. Instead of friendship there is a state of hostility existing, instead of amity there is enmity, which results in separation and alienation between them. This it is which makes manifest the need for peace to be made between the estranged parties, that the wrong may be righted, the cause of the displeasure be removed, the ill-feeling cease, the breach be healed and reconciliation accomplished. The parties at variance are man and God. Man has grievously offended the Most High. He has cast off allegiance to Him, revolted from Him, despised His authority, trampled upon His commandments. The enormity of such an offence it is impossible for us to fully conceive. The heinousness of it can only be measured by the exalted dignity of the One against whom it is committed. It has been committed against the Almighty against One who is infinite in majesty, infinite in excellency, infinite in His sovereign rights over the creature of His own hands; and therefore it is an offence of infinite magnitude and turpitude.

The original offence was committed by Adam in Eden, but that fearful transgression can only be rightly understood as we recognise that Adam acted there not as a private individual but as a public person. He was Divinely constituted to be not only the father but also the federal head of the human race. He stood as the legal representative of all mankind, so that in the sight of the Divine Law what he did they did, the one transacting on the behalf of the many. The whole human race was placed on probation in the person of the first man. His trial was their trial. While he stood they stood. While he retained the approbation of God and remained in fellowship with Him, they did the same. Had he survived the trial, had he fitly discharged his responsibility, had he continued in obedience to God, his obedience had been reckoned to their account, and they had entered into the reward which had been bestowed upon him. Contrariwise, if he failed and fell, they failed and fell in him. If he disobeyed God his disobedience is imputed unto all those whom he represented and the just but fearful curse pronounced upon him falls likewise on all for whom he transacted.

What has just been pointed out by us above, was amplified at some length in our articles on the Adamic Covenant, which appeared in this magazine some ten years ago, but as many of our present readers have never seen them it will be necessary for us now to give a brief summary of what was then said. The legal relation between Adam and his posterity may be illustrated thus. God did not deal with mankind as with a field of corn, where each stalk stands upon its own individual root; but He dealt with it as a tree, all the branches of which have one common root and trunk. If you strike with an axe at the root of a tree, the whole tree falls — not only the trunk, but also the branches and even the twigs on the branches. All wither and die. So it was with Adam in Eden. God permitted Satan to lay the axe at the root of humanity and when he fell all his posterity fell with him. At one fatal stroke Adam was severed from communion with his Maker, and as the consequence *"death passed upon all men."* This is not a theory of human speculation but a fact of Divine revelation.

12

That Adam was the federal head of the human race, that he did act and transact in a representative character, and that the judicial consequences of his act was imputed to all those for whom he stood, is clearly taught in Rom. 5. *"Wherefore as by one man sin entered into the world, and death by sin, and so death passed upon all men, in whom all sinned"* (v. 12). *"Through the offence of one many be dead"* (v. 15). *"The judgment was by one to condemnation...By one man's offence death reigned...By the offence of one judgment came upon all men to condemnation...By one man's offence many were made sinners"*(vers. 16,17,18,19). Such repetition and emphasis intimates the basic importance of the truth here revealed and also hints at our slowness or rather reluctance to receive the same. The meaning of these declarations is too plain for any unprejudiced mind to misunderstand. It pleased God to deal with the human race as represented in and by Adam. *"In Adam all die"* (1 Cor. 15:22). There is the plainly-revealed fact, and they who deny it make God a liar.

Here, then, we learn what is the formal ground of man's judicial condemnation before God. The popular idea of what it is which renders man a sinner in the sight of Heaven is altogether inadequate and erroneous. The prevailing conception is that a sinner is one who commits and practices sin. It is true that this is the character of the sinner, but it certainly is not that which primarily constitutes him such before the Divine Law. The truth is that every member of our race enters into this world a guilty sinner, alienated from God, before ever he commits a single transgression. It is not only that he possesses a depraved nature but that he is directly *"under condemnation"* the curse of the broken Law resting upon him, and from God he is *"estranged from the womb"* (Ps. 58:3). We are legally constituted sinners neither by what we are nor by what we are doing, but by the disobedience of our federal head, Adam. Adam acted not for himself alone, but for all who were to spring from him, so that his act, was forensically, our act.

Here also is the only key which satisfactorily opens to us the meaning of human history and explains the universal prevalence of sin. The human race is suffering for the sin of Adam, or it is suffering for nothing at all. There is no escape from that alternative. This earth is the scene of a grim and awful tragedy. In it we behold misery and wretchedness, strife and hatred, pain and poverty, disease and death on every side. None escape the fearful entail. That *"man is born unto trouble as the sparks fly upward"* is an indisputable fact. But what is the explanation of it? Every effect must have a previous cause. If we are not being punished for Adam's sin, then, coming into this world we are *"children of wrath"* (Eph. 2:3), beneath the Divine judgment, corrupt and defiled, on the broad road which leads to destruction, for nothing at all! Who would contend that this was better, more satisfactory, more illuminative, than the Scriptural explanation of our ruin? Gen. 3 alone explains why human history is written in the ink of blood and tears.

The objection that such an arrangement is unjust is invalid. The prinicple of representation is a fundamental one in human society. The father is the legal head of his children during their minority. What he does binds the family. A business house is held responsible for the transactions of its agents. Every popular election illustrates the fact that a constituency will act through its representative and be bound by his acts. The heads of a state are vested with such authority that the treaties they make are binding upon the whole nation. This principle is so basic it cannot be set aside. Human affairs could not continue nor society exist without it. This is the method by which God has acted all through. The sins of the fathers are visited upon the children. The posterity of Canaan were cursed for the single transgression of their parent (Gen. 9), the whole of his family stoned for Achan's sin (Josh 7). Israel's high priest acted on behalf of the whole nation. One acting for others is a basic principle both of human and Divine government.

Finally, let it be pointed out that the sinner's salvation is made to depend upon this very same method. Beware, then, my reader, of quarrelling with the justice of this principle of representation – the one standing for the many. On this principle we were wrecked, and by this principle only can we be rescued. If on the one hand, the disobedience of the first Adam was the judicial ground of our condemnation, on the other hand the obedience of the last Adam is the legal basis on which God justifies sinners. The substitution of Christ in the place of His people, the imputation of their sins to Him and of His righteousness to them, is the central fact of the Gospel. But the principle of being saved by what Another has done is only possible on the ground that we were lost through what another did. The two stand or fall together. If there had been no Covenant of Works there would have been no Covenant of Grace. If there had been no death in Adam there had been no life in Christ. The Christian knows that such an arrangement is just because it is part of the revealed ways of Him who is infinitely holy and righteous.

Here, then, is the Divinely-revealed fact: *"by the offence of one judgment came upon all men to condemnation"* (Rom. 5:19). Here is cause of humiliation which few think about. We are members of an accursed race, the fallen children of a fallen parent, and as such we enter this world *"alienated from the life of God"* (Eph. 4:18), exposed to His judicial displeasure. In the day that Adam fell the frown of the Most High came upon His children. The holy nature of God abhorred the apostate race. The curse of His broken Law descended upon all of Adam's posterity. It is only thus we can account for the universality of human depravity and suffering. The corruption of human nature which we inherit from our first parents is a great evil, for it is the source of all our personal sins. For God to allow this transmission of depravity is to inflict a punishment. But how can God punish all, unless all were guilty? The fact that all do share in this common punishment is proof that all sinned in Adam. Our depravity and misery are not, as such, the infliction of the Creator, but are the retribution of the Judge.

If we now repeat some of the statements made above it is that the reader may not form a wrong conception or draw a false conclusion. We are very far from teaching here that the human race is suffering for an offence in which they had no part, that innocent creatures are being condemned for the action of another which could not fairly be laid to their account. Let it be clearly understood that God punishes none for Adam's sin (if considering him as a private person), but only for his own sin in Adam. The whole human race had a federal standing in Adam. Not only was each of us seminally in his loins when God created him, but each of us was legally represented by him when God made with him the Covenant of Works. Adam acted and transacted in that Covenant as a public person, not simply as a private individual, but as the surety and sponsor of his race. The very fact that we continue breaking the Covenant of Works and disobeying the Law of God demonstrates our oneness with Adam under the Covenant. Our complicity with Adam in his rebellion is evidenced every time that we personally sin against God.

It is nothing short of downright hypocrisy for us to murmur against the justice of this arrangement of constitution while we follow in the steps of Adam. If we have nothing to do with him and are not in bondage through him, why do we not repudiate him — refuse to sin, break the chain, stand out in opposition to him, and be holy? This brings us to the second chief count in the fearful indictment against us. We take sides with Adam. We perpetuate his evil course. We make him are exemplar. The life of the unregenerate is one unbroken curse of rebellion against God. There is no genuine submission to Him, no concern for His glory, no disinterested love for Him. Self-will is our governing principle and self-pleasing our goal. Whatever religious deference may apparently be shown God, it is rendered out of self-interest — either to curry favor with Him, or to appease His anger. The things of time and sense are preferred before Him, the lies of Satan are heeded rather than the Word of Truth, and instead of humbling ourselves before Him because of our original offence in Eden, we multiply transgressions against Him.

However unpalatable it may be to proud flesh and blood the fact is that the natural man is engaged in a warfare against God. He hates the things God loves, and loves the things He hates. He scorns the things God enjoins and pursues the things He has forbidden. He is a rebel against the Divine government, refusing to be in subjection to the Divine will. The moment his own will is crossed by the dispensations of Providence he murmurs. He is unthankful for the mercies of which he is the daily recipient, and less mindful of the Hand that so freely ministers to him than the horse or the mule to the one who feeds him. He continually growls at his lot, constantly grumbles at the weather, and is a stranger to contentment. In short *"the carnal mind is emnity against God and is not subject to the Law of God, neither indeed can be"* (Rom. 8:7). *"The natural man does not receive the things of the Spirit of God, for they are foolishness unto him"* (1 Cor. 2:14) — contrary to his corrupted mind, at variance with his vitiated desires. *"There is none that seeks after God"* (Rom. 3:11).

There is then a breach — a real, a broad, a fearful breach — between God and man. In the very nature of the cause it cannot be otherwise. That breach has been made by sin. God is holy, so holy that He is *"of purer eyes than to behold evil and can not look on iniquity"* (Hab. 1:13). Sin has given infinite offence unto God, for it is that *"abominable thing"* which He hates (Jer. 44:4). Sin is a species of spiritual anarchy, a defiance of the triune Jehovah. It is a saying in actions *"Let us break Their bands, and cast away Their cords from us"* (Ps. 2:3) — let us disregard the Divine laws and be lords of ourselves. Not only is sin highly obnoxious to the infinitely-pure nature of God, but it is flagrant affront to His government, being rebellion against it, and therefore as the moral Rector of the universe He declares His displeasure against the same *"For the wrath of God is revealed from heaven against all ungodliness and unrighteousness of men"* (Rom. 1:18) — an open display of which was made of old when the flood swept the earth clean of His enemies.

Here then is the black background which discovers to us the need for reconciliation. *"your iniquities have separated between you and your God, and your sins have hid His face from you"* (Isa. 59:2). He is displeased with us and His justice cries out for our destruction. *"They rebelled and vexed His Holy Spirit; therefore He was turned to be their Enemy"* (Isa. 63:10). Unspeakably solemn is that, the terrible import of which is utterly beyond our powers to conceive. That the great I am, the Creator and Sustainer of the universe has become man's *"Enemy"* so that His anger burns against him. This was evidenced at the beginning, for right after God had arraigned the guilty culprits in Eden, we are told that *"He drove out the man. And He placed cherubims at the east of the garden of Eden, and a flaming sword which turned every way – to keep the way of the tree of life"* (Gen. 3:24). Man was now cut off from access to the One whom he had so grievously offended and turned to be his Enemy. And man is also at enmity with Him.

How little is it realized that there is an immeasureable gulf between God and sinner. And little wonder that so few have even the vaguest idea of the same. All human religion is an attempt to gloss over this fearful fact. And with exceedingly rare exceptions the religion of present-day Christendom is but a studied effort to hide the awful truth that man has forfeited the favor of God and is barred from His holy presence, yea that *"the Lord is far from the wicked"* (Prov. 15:29). The religion of the day proceeds on the assumption that God is favorably disposed even unto those who spend most of their time trampling His commandments beneath their feet. That providing they will assume an outwardly devout demeanor, they have but to petition Him and their supplications are acceptable unto Him. Priests and parsons who encourage such a delusion are but throwing dust in the eyes of the people: *"the sacrifice of the wicked is an abomination unto the Lord"* (Prov. 15:8).

The religion of our day deliberately ignores the fact of sin, with its terrible implications and consequences. It leaves out of sight that sin has radically changed the original relationship which existed between God and His creatures. It conceals the truth that man is outlawed by God and is *"far off"* (Eph. 2:11) from Him. It tacitly denies that *"they that are in the flesh cannot please God"* (Rom. 8:8), that He *"hears not sinners"* (John 9:31). Yea it insists that they can please Him with their hypocritical piety and sanctimonious playacting. But the Holy One cannot be deceived by their pretences nor bribed by their offerings. Nor can they so.much as draw nigh unto Him while they despise and reject the One who is the only Way of approach to Him. Make no mistake upon this point, my reader. Until that awful breach which sin has made be healed, you can have no fellowship with God; until He be reconciled to you and you to Him, He will accept nothing at your hands not can you obtain audience with Him. Unless reconciliation is effected you will be *"punished with everlasting destruction from the presence of the Lord"* (2 Thess. 1:9).

The need for reconciliation is unmistakable. A fearful breach exists, brought about by the entrance of sin, and continued by the perpetuation of man to God. Not only had man now forfeited His favor but he had incurred His wrath. God could no longer view him with approbation, but instead regarded him with detestation; while man ceased to be a loyal and loving subject, becoming a rebellious outlaw. And *"what fellowship has righteousness with unrighteousness?*

And what communion has light with darkness?" None. They are opposite, the one antagonistic to the other. That breach between God and man, between righteousness and unrighteousness, will be demonstrated in the distance between Heaven and Hell. Therefore did Christ represent Abraham as saying to Dives in the place of torment,*"Between us and you there is a great gulf fixed, so that they which would pass from here to you cannot; neither can they pass to us"* (Luke 16:26). It is only by God's reconciliation to us and of our reconciliation to God the fearful breach can be healed. How that is effected we hope to show in future articles.

CHAPTER III.

In our last we dwelt chiefly upon the fearful breach which the entrance of sin made between the thrice Holy One and His fallen and rebellious creatures. In this we must point out some of the consequences and evidences of that breach, thereby showing in more detail the urgency of the sinner's case. By his act of disobedience in Eden man invaded God's right of sovereignty, spurning as he did His authority, throwing off the yoke of submission, determining to be his own lord. The outcome of such revolt we are not left to guess at. It is plainly made known in the Scriptures. By his fearful offence man lost the favor and friendship of God and incurred His holy displeasure and righteous indignation. The Creator became the punishing Judge. Our first parents were promptly arraigned and sentence was passed upon the guilty culprits. Man had fallen into sin and the Divine wrath now fell upon him. God drove man out of Paradise and unsheathed the flaming sword (Gen. 3:24), thereby making it manifest that Heaven and earth were at variance. As the result of the fall sin became man's delight and henceforth he was an enemy to all holiness and consequently of the Holy One.

1. Fallen man became separated from God. It is easy to write or read those words, but who is competent to fathom their fearful import! Separated from God, the Fountain and Giver of all blessedness! Cast out of His favor. Severed from communion with Him. Cut off from the enjoyment of Him. Devoid of His life, of His holiness, of His love. Such is the terrible and inevitable consequence of sin. Sin snapped the golden cord which had united man to his Maker. Sin broke the happy relationship which originally existed between man and his rightful Lord. Sin made a breach between its committer and the Holy One. Not only did sin conduct man to a guilty distance from God, but sin necessarily placed God at a holy distance from man. God will not suffer those who are hostile to Him and offensive to His absolute purity to dwell in His presence. Therefore do we read that *"God spared not the angels that sinned, but cast them down to Hell, and delivered them into chains of darkness, to be reserved unto judgment"* (2 Pet. 2:4). They were banished from Heaven, excluded from the company of the Most High, imprisoned in the place of unutterable woe.

God had plainly made known unto our federal head the penalty of his disobedience: *"But you shall not eat of the tree of knowledge of good and evil – for in the day that you eat of it, you shall surely die"* (Gen. 2:17). Thus at the very beginning of human history the Lawgiver announced that *"the wages of sin is death"* – death spiritual, death judicial, death eternal if pardon was not obtained. And death is not annihilation but separation. Physical death is the separation of the soul from the body, expulsion from this earth. So spiritual death is the separation of the soul from God, expulsion from His favor. In that tragic yet hope-inspiring parable of the prodigal son our Lord represented the sinner as being in *"the far country"* a *"great way off"* from the Father's house (Luke 15:13,20), and when he returned in penitence the Father said, *"this My son was dead* (separated from Me) *and is alive again* (restored to Me)*; he was lost and is found."* When Christ as the Substitute and Surety of His people bore their sins in His own body on the Tree (1 Pet. 2:24) He received the wages of sin, crying to God *"why have You forsaken Me!"*

But the death inflicted upon Adam and all whom he represented was also

18

judicial. Fallen man is a malefactor, dead in Law, lying under its sentence, a criminal in chains of guilt, held fast in fetters until the day of execution, unless he obtains a pardon from God. If no pardon is obtained, then he shall be cast into *"the lake which burns with fire and brimstone,"* and that is expressly denominated *"the second death"* (Rev. 21:8), because it is a being *"punished with everlasting destruction from the presence of the Lord"* (2 Thess. 1:9). Man then, every man while unregenerate, is living *"without God in the world"* *"far off"* from Him (Eph. 2:12,13). Being *"dead in trespasses and sins"* he is cut off from God, having no access to Him. He is a castaway from the Divine presence. God will have no commerce with him, nor receive any offering at his hands. He is outside the kingdom of God, and cannot enter it save by the new birth (John 3:5). He is born into the world alienated from the life of God (Eph. 4:18). When the Lord came down upon Sinai Israel was not suffered to draw near Him (Exod. 19). Sin had imposed an effectual barrier.

2. Fallen man became an object of abhorrence to God. Once more we use language the meaning of which no mortal is capable of fully entering into. It is not that we have employed terms which the case does not warrant, for we have but paraphrased the words of Holy Writ. Nor can it be otherwise if God is what Scripture affirms and if man has become what he is represented to be. God is light (1 John 1:5) and man is darkness (Eph. 5:8). God is holy, man totally depraved. God is our rightful Lord and King, man is an insurrectionist, a defiant rebel. God is immaculately pure, man a loathsome leper. If man saw himself as he appears to the Divine eye or even as he is protrayed by the Divine pencil, it would be evident that he must be an object of repugnance unto Him who sits enthroned on high. *"From the sole of the foot even unto the head there is no soundness in it, but wounds and bruises, and putrifying sores. They have not been closed, neither bound up, neither soothed with oil"* (Isa. 1:6). What a repulsive object! Yet that is precisely what you and I (by nature) look like in the eyes of God.

"You hate all workers of iniquity" (Ps. 5:5). In this Psalm God's alienation from and detestation of the wicked is set forth in six steps. First: He has no delight in them. *"You are not a God that has pleasure in wickedness"* (v. 4). Second: they cannot reside in His presence *"neither shall evil dwell with You"* (v.4). Third: they have no status before Him. *"The foolish shall not stand in Your sight"* (v. 5). Fifth: He will pour upon them the fury of His indignation. *"You shall destroy them that speak leasing"* or *"lies"* (v. 6). Sixth: they will for all eternity be abhorred by Him. *"The Lord will abhor the bloody and deceitful man"* (v. 6). None would be shocked at such frightful declarations as these if he had anything like an adequate conception of the exceeding sinfulness of sin and of the infinite holiness of God. Though they are scarce ever heard from any pulpit today, whether we believe them or not, they are the words of Him who cannot lie and throughout eternity their verity will be borne amply witness to.

"You hate all workers of iniquity." Not merely their evil works, but the workers themselves; not some of the most notorious of the workers but all of them. My reader, if you are out of Christ, still unregenerate, whether you are British, American, or Australian, you are an object of God's hatred. Rightly did C. H. Spurgeon point out from these words, "It is not a little dislike, but thorough

hatred which God bears to workers of iniquity. To be hated of God is an awful thing. O let us be very faithful in warning the wicked around us, for it will be a terrible thing for them to fall into the hands of an angry God...How forcible is the word 'abhor' (in the next verse). Does it not show us how powerful and deep-seated is the hatred of the Lord against the workers of iniquity!" It is the very nature of righteousness to hate unrighteousness. Those who are so corrupt and abominable must be loathed by One who is ineffably holy. It is the very perfection of the Divine character to hate the totally depraved.

3. Fallen man came under the condemnation and curse of the Divine Law. *"It is written, Cursed is everyone that continues not in all things which are written in the Book of the Law to do them"* (Gal. 3:10). Those words are a quotation from Deut. 17:26 — a verse which contains the conclusion of the maledictions pronounced upon the disobedient of the context, being really the sum and substance of them all. It is the solemn declaration that those who have despised God's authority and trampled His commandments beneath their feet are exposed to the Divine displeasure and to condign punishment as the expression of that displeasure. The *"curse of the Law"* is that sentence and penalty which is due unto sin. Sin and the curse are inseparable. Wherever the one is, the other must be. Therefore the unrestricted *"every one,"* and that not only for multiplied transgressions but for a single offence. The Divine Law is perfect, and demands perfect and perpetual conformity to it. A single transgression brings down upon its perpetrator the Divine curse, as was evidenced in Eden, and in consequence of our representative participation therein, all of us entered this world under the maledictions of God's Law.

"Cursed is every one." Those solemn words, so little known, so faintly apprehended even by those who are acquainted with them, reveal the fearful situation of every soul out of Christ. They are under sentence of execution. Their position is identical with the convicted murderer in the condemned cell, awaiting the dread summons of vindictive justice. If you are unregenerate, my reader, at this very moment you are under sentence of death: *"condemned already."* Since the curse of the Law falls upon men for a single sin, then what must be the punishment that will be meted out upon those with multiplied transgressions to their account! *"The curse of the Lord is in the house of the wicked"* (Prov. 3:33). That unspeakable malediction rests upon all that he has and all that he does. *"You shall be cursed in the city and you shall be cursed in the field. You shall be cursed in your basket and your store,"* (Deut. 28:17). Nay, God has said *"I will curse your blessings; yea, I have cursed them already"* (Mal. 2:2). To those out of Christ He will yet say.*"Depart from Me you cursed into everlasting fire"* (Matt. 25:41).

4. Fallen man came under the wrath of God. This follows inevitably from what has already been pointed out. Since a rebel against the Divine government is necessarily an object of abhorrence unto his holy Lord, since he has come beneath the curse and condemnation of the Divine Law, justice cries aloud for vengeance. The Maker of heaven and earth is no indifferent Spectator of the conduct of His creatures. He was not of Adam's. The father and head of the race was summoned before His judgment bar, fairly tried, justly condemned, and made to experience the beginnings of God's wrath, for the full measure thereof is reserved for the transgressor in the next life. As the consequence of their sin

and fall in the person of their representative all of Adam's posterity are *"by nature the children of wrath"* (Eph. 2:3). Not only defiled and corrupt, but the objects of God's judicial indignation. *"The children of wrath."* Those words should be to the ungodly reader as the handwriting on Belshazzar's wall (Dan. 5:5,6). They should blanch his countenance, trouble his thoughts, and make his knees smite together.

This fearful expression *"the children of wrath"* is more forceful than many conclude. In the previous verse we read of *"children of disobedience,"* which means more than disobedient children, for such may the regenerate be. It means such as are addicted to disobedience, who make a trade of it. So *"children of wrath"* signifies more than to be liable to wrath. It connotes the objects of God's wrath, wholly devoted thereto, born to it as their portion and heritage – the corruptions of their nature being its fuel. When the angels sinned the wrath of God was visited upon them (2 Pet. 2:4), thereby evidencing that no natural excellence in the creature can exempt it from the judgment of God. Further demonstrations of His wrath were given when the flood was sent to drown the antediluvian world, when fire and brimstone destroyed Sodom and Gomorrah, and when Pharaoh and his hosts were overwhelmed at the Red Sea. And the execution of God's wrath upon you, my unsaved reader, is hourly drawn nearer. Ignorance cannot shield you from it. Outward privileges will not save you from it. Nor will a mere profession of religion. The only way of deliverance is for you to *"flee from the wrath to come"* by betaking yourself to Christ for refuge.

"God is angry with the wicked every day" (Ps. 7:11), on which Spurgeon remarks, "He not only detests sin, but is angry with those who continue to indulge in it. We have no insensible and stolid God to deal with. He can be angry, nay, He is angry today and every day with you, you ungodly and impenitent sinners. The best day that ever dawned on a sinner brings a curse with it. Sinners may have many feast days, but not safe days. From the beginning of the year even to its ending, there is not an hour in which God's oven is not hot and burning in readiness for the wicked, who shall be as stubble." And on the words of the verse which immediately follows – *"If He turn not, He will whet His sword"* – that faithful preacher declared: "What blows are those which will be dealt by that long uplifted arm! God's sword has been sharpening upon the revolving stone of our daily wickedness, and if we will not repent, it will speedily cut us to pieces. Turn or burn is the sinner's alternative."

Fallen man is the subject and slave of Satan, under a more terrible bondage than ever the Hebrews were to Pharaoh, for it is a bondage of the soul. Yet this is justly inflicted. At the beginning our first parents preferred Satan's lie to God's truth, and therefore did He allow Satan to obtain dominion over them. Yet with each of his descendants it is a willing bondage therein. As the Jews desired Barabbas rather then Christ, so we entered this world with a nature that is in harmony with Satan's. Yes, without a single exception, every member of our race is born so depraved that he voluntarily serves and obeys the arch enemy of God. There are but two spiritual kingdoms in this world: that of Christ's (Col. 1:13) and that of Satan's (Matt. 12:26), and every human being is a subject of the one or the other. Those who have not come to Christ and surrendered to His sceptre are ruled by Satan and are fighting under his banner against God. Therefore when Paul was sent forth to preach the Gospel it was in order to open the eyes of men *"to turn them from darkness to light and from the power of Satan unto God"* (Acts 26:18).

The Devil is the sinner's master, as he was the Christian's before Divine grace regenerated him. *"And He has made you alive who were dead in trespasses and sins — in which you once walked according to the course of this world, according to the Prince of the power of the air, the spirit that now works in the children of disobedience"* (Eph. 2:1,2). He not only tempts from without but dominates them from within. As God works in His people *"both to will and to do of His good pleasure"* (Phil 2:13) so the devil operates in the hearts of his subjects to perform his fiendish pleasure. He *"put into the heart"* of Judas to betray Christ (John 13:2). He made Pilate and Herod condemn Him to death, for it was *"their hour and the power of darkness"* (Luke 22:53). He *"filled the heart"* of Ananias to lie to the Holy Spirit (Acts 5:3). Yet each of them acted freely and according to the inclinations of his own evil nature. Satan's subjects render him a voluntary and cordial obedience. *"You are of your father the Devil, and the lusts of your father you will do"* (John 8:44).

6. Fallen man is under the reigning power of sin. This abominable thing which God hates has entered the human constitution like a deadly poison that has completely corrupted our whole being. Sin has full dominion and undisputed sway over the human soul. The mind makes no opposition to it, for it is sin's servant (John 8:34) and not captive. It exerts a determining power on the will. Sin so reigns in the heart of the unregenerate that it directs their affections and controls all the motives and springs of their actions, causing them to walk after their own evil imaginations and devisings. As the air is the native element of the birds, so sin is the natural element of fallen man. *"Abominable and filthy is man, who drinks in iniquity like water"* (Job 15:16). Like a parched traveler in the desert who craves water, seeks after it, and greedily swallows it when found, so is iniquity unto the sinner.

The course of the natural man is described as *"serving divers lusts and pleasures"* (Titus 3:3), as *"bringing forth evil fruits"* (Matt. 7:17), as yielding his members *"servants to uncleanness and to iniquity"* (Rom. 6:19). The service rendered by the unregenerate to sin is a whole-hearted one, voluntary, and cordial. Man is in love with sin, preferring darkness to light, this world to Heaven. His lusts are his idols. Therefore does he persist in sin despite all pleadings, warnings, threatenings, chastisements. While he is unregenerate he does nothing but sin in thought and word and deed. Solemn it is to think that every one is in continual remembrance with God, set in the light of His countenance, recorded in that book which will be opened in the day of judgment. Not one of them is pardoned, or can be, while he is out of Christ. So much guilt lies upon his soul as is sufficient to sink it into the lowest Hell, and will do so unless blotted out by atoning blood.

7. Fallen man hates God. *"The carnal mind is enmity against God, and is not subject to the Law of God"* — and so inveterate is that *"enmity"* it is at once added — *"neither indeed can be"* (Rom. 8:7). We may not believe it, or be conscious of it, but there is the Divinely-revealed fact. God is an Object of aversion unto the natural man. The language of the hearts of sinners unto the

Almighty is, *"Depart from us; we desire not the knowledge of your ways,"* (Job 21:14). They do not hate Him as their Provider and Preserver, but as a Being who is infinitely holy and who therefore hates sin and is *"angry with the wicked every day."* They detest Him as a sovereign Being, who dispenses His favors according to His absolute pleasure. They abominate Him as the Moral Governor of the world, demanding obedience to His Law, and pronouncing cursed all who break it. They abhor Him as the Judge, who shall yet cast all His enemies into the Lake of Fire. Proof of this was furnished when God became incarnate and was manifested unto men. They crucified Him.

"Can two walk together except they be agreed?" (Amos 3:3). Obviously not; then how much less could rebels dwell together with a holy God for all eternity! For that reconciliation must be effected. But how is peace possible? How are alienated sinners to be restored to friendship with God without Him denying His own perfections? Some grand provision must be made whereby the wrath of God is appeased, whereby His Law is magnified, His honor vindicated, His justice satisfied. Some wondrous redemption is imperative if sinners are to be delivered from that dreadful state of enmity, darkness, and slavery into which the Fall conducted them. Some marvel of wisdom and miracle of grace is necessary if those so far off are to be made nigh, if the unholy are to be made holy, if those dead in sin are to be quickened into newness of life. Some unique Mediator is indispensable if the breach between an offended God and offended creatures is to be healed. A Mediator who is capable of conserving the interests and promoting the glory of God, and who also can win the hearts of those in revolt. The needs be for reconciliation is crystal clear; the effectuation of it is the grand subject of the Gospel, the wonder of angels, and will be the theme of the song of the redeemed throughout the unending ages of the future.

CHAPTER IV.

This doctrine of Reconciliation presents to our view that which is both indescribably horrible and also that which is inexpressibly blessed. The dark background of it is formed by the fearful calamity of Eden, when the entrance of sin into the world involved the ruination of our race and its alienation from God. The sin of Adam (and of ours in him) was a revolt against God's authority, a contempt of His government, a declaration of war against Him. Man is a rebel, an outlaw, an enemy of God, cut off from access to Him. This has already been before us in previous articles. Now we turn to contemplate the blessed contrast wherein God determined to deliver a part of Adam's descendants from the effects of the fall, and this in such a way that His absolute sovereignty, His free grace, His inexorable justice, unsearchable wisdom, ineffable holiness, all-mighty power, infinite goodness and rich mercy, might be equally honored. This is actually accomplished in the saving of His elect by Jesus Christ.

The Author of reconciliation is God. Most distinctly, it is God the Father, for there is an order of the Divine Persons in this work, as in all others. *"But to us there is but one God, the Father, of whom are all things, and we by Him"* (1 Cor. 8:5). *"God who created all things by Jesus Christ"* (Eph. 3:9). As that was the order of Their operation in connection with the old creation, so it is with regard to the new creation – the Father has effected reconciliation by the death of His Son (Rom. 5:10). Distinct offices are ascribed to each of the Eternal Three. The Father is the Deviser, the Son transacts the part of Mediator, being the One by whom the work of reconciliation is performed; the Holy Spirit is the Recorder of the Father's plan and of the satisfaction offered by the Son and of the peace He has made, and is also the One who sheds abroad Their love in the hearts of the redeemed.

The order pointed out above is still more observable in connection with our approach to God. It is through Christ and by the Holy Spirit that we have access unto the Father (Eph. 2:18). All the spiritual blessings we have in Christ are expressly attributed unto the Father (Eph. 1:3), by no means the least of which is reconciliation. Our election is ascribed particularly unto the Father (Eph. 1:3,4) and so is our regeneration (James 1:17,18). It is the Father who has made us meet to be partakers of the inheritance of the saints in light, having delivered us from the power of darkness and translated us into the kingdom of His dear Son (Col. 1:13). In accord with this Divine order we find the opening salutation in the Epistles is *"grace unto you and peace from God the Father, and the Lord Jesus Christ."* Therefore the Father is due the same honor and love from us for the sending of His Son, as the Son is for His willingness in being sent. Scripture represents the Father as the One directly wronged by sin, for we are told that Jesus Christ is *"an Advocate with the Father"* (1 John 2:1).

1. His will. When accountable creatures rebel against their Maker and King, they cut themselves off from all right to claim any blessing or benefit at His

hands, for they deserve nothing from Him but wrath and punishment. If they are recovered from the ruin which they have brought upon themselves and are made partakers of Divine salvation, it is solely from the good pleasure of His will, and must be in a way that does not injure any of His perfections; but if they are left to suffer the direful consequences of their apostasy, God is in nowise unjust, for He inflicts no more upon them than they deserve. When a large company of the angels and their chiefs, under Satan's lead, conspiring against the Most High, proudly aspiring to a higher position than had been allotted them, God promptly cast them down from their exalted state, banished them from His presence, and doomed them to suffer everlasting woe (2 Pet. 2:4). He had not a thought of mercy toward those celestial creatures when they revolted against Him.

In view of that unspeakably solemn example, it ought to be unmistakably clear to each of us that God might, without the slightest stain upon His own honor, without any unbecoming severity, have left the whole of Adam's guilty race to suffer eternal destruction, for certainly they had no more claim upon His favor than had the fallen angels. That He did not immediately consign the entire family of fallen mankind to irremediable woe, was due alone to His imperial will. That He was pleased to appoint a remnant of them to obtain salvation and eternal glory, is to be attributed solely to His sovereign and amazing grace. That such a concept is no invention of harsh theologians, but is plainly taught by the Word of God, is clear from His own declarations. *"Having predestinated us unto the adoption of children by Jesus Christ to Himself, according to the good pleasure of His will, to the praise of the glory of His grace"* (Eph. 1:5,6). *"Who has saved us, and called us with a holy calling, not according to our works, but according to His own purpose and grace"* (2 Tim. 1:9).

"Having made known unto us the mystery of His will, according to His good pleasure, which He has purposed in Himself" (Eph. 1:9). The mystery refers to the everlasting covenant in which God arranged and provided for the recovery and salvation of His people who fell in Adam. In proof of which assertion we cite 1 Cor. 2:7: *"But we speak the wisdom of God in a mystery, even the hidden wisdom, which God ordained before the world unto our glory"* amplified in vers. 9,10. Now that which is germane to our present design is, that God *"purposed in Himself"* or resolved to reconcile some of the sons of men to Himself, even though they had become guilty rebels against Him, and this purpose He purposed *"before the world began"* (2 Tim. 1:9). One portion or aspect of that purpose is expressly stated in what immediately follows. *"That in the dispensation of the fulness of times He might gather together in one all things in Christ, both which are in heaven, and which are on earth, even in Him"* (Eph. 1:10). Sin alienates and separates, but the putting away of sin by Christ healed the breach between God and man, between believing Jews and Gentiles, and between them and the holy angels. Now *"The whole family in heaven and in earth"* (Eph. 3:15) is one – see Rev. 5:11,12.

The restoration and reconciliation of His guilty and alienated people is attributed to God's *"good pleasure"* whereof no reason is given save that He purposed it in Himself which means that the idea was suggested by none other and that no external motive influenced Him. There was no necessity put upon Him for this resolution. Without the least dishonor to Himself He might have destroyed the entire apostate race, yea, and have been glorified in their destruction. He who was able out of stones *"to raise up children unto Abraham"* (Matt. 3:9), could have consigned Adam and Eve to eternal woe before they produced any children, and have made a pair from the dust of the ground. There was nothing whatever in the creature that moved God to show mercy unto him. But there is another concept conveyed by this expression, namely, the certainty and powerful efficacy of what He has decided upon. God cannot possibly be disappointed in the accomplishment of His purpose, for none can overthrow it; nor will He ever alter it. *"My counsel shall stand and I will do all My pleasure"* (Isa. 46:10); *"I am the Lord. I change not"* (Mal. 3:6).

Here is sure and solid comfort for the spiritually awakened sinner. The simple fact that God is merciful in His nature is not sufficient. Satan knows that, but such knowledge affords him no peace! But the Divine assurance *"I will show mercy"* (Ex. 33:19) opens a real door of hope. Suppose that Christ had died and there had been no Gospel revelation and proclamation of the Divine purpose of His death. The mere knowledge of His crucifixion avails me nothing unless I am assured that it was the will of God to accept Christ's death in lieu of the death of believing sinners. *"by which will we are sanctified through the offering of the body of Jesus Christ once for all"* (Heb. 10:10). The will of God is not only the foundation of the mystery or plan of redemption, but it is also its blessedness. This is the very pith and preciousness of the Gospel. That it is the revealed will of God to save and accept every sinner who puts his or her trust in the atoning blood of Christ. *"Who gave Himself for our sins, that He might deliver us from (the corruption and doom) of this present evil world, according to the will of God and our Father"* (Gal. 1:4).

2. His love. A few may be surprised that we should distinguish between the will and love of God, but probably a far greater number will wonder why any explanation should be required from us for so doing. Yet John Owen in his *"Arguments against Universal Redemption"* (chap. 8, para. 5) said, "The eternal love of God towards His elect is nothing by His purpose, good pleasure a pure act of His will, whereby He determines to do such and such things for them in His own time and way." And again, in his *"Vindiciae Evangelicae"* (chap. 29), after referring to John 3:16 and other passages: "Now the love of God is an eternal free act of His will, His purpose." Such a cold and bare definition may suit philosophers, and metaphysicians, but it will scarcely appeal to the hearts of the regenerate. When Scripture affirms that Christ is the *"Son of His love"* (Col. 1:13) we are surely to understand something more than that the Son is merely the Object on which the Divine will is set. Rather do we believe, with many others, that the Son is the Darling of the Father's heart. How, too, are we to understand the Savior's representation of the Father in His welcome of the returning prodigal. He *"ran, and fell on his neck, and kissed him"* (Luke 15:20).

While we are far from believing that God's unfathomable love in anywise resembles ours, as an emotion or passion, subject to fluctuation, yet we refuse to regard it as a mere principle. When the voice of the Father audibly declared *"this is My beloved Son in whom I am well pleased,"* He gave expression to the language of deep and warm affection. When the Lord Jesus affirmed *"The only begotten Son which is in the bosom of the Father, He has declared Him"* (John 1:18), we grant that He employed an anthropomorphism (ascribing to God what pertains properly to man), nevertheless we cannot allow that it was a mere figure of speech devoid of real meaning. *"God is love"* (1 John 4:8), and no refinements of the most eminent theologians must be suffered to rob us of the blessedness and preciousness of that fundamental truth. All things issue from the will of God (Eph. 1:11), but Scripture nowhere tells us that all things proceed from God's love. The non-elect are the subjects of His will, but they are not the objects of His love. Thus there is a clear distinction between the two things.

We greatly prefer the statement of Thos. Goodwin. Near the beginning of his massive work on *"Christ the Mediator,"* he shows what was done by God the Father from all eternity in connection with our salvation. First, He points out His eternal purpose and grace, and then inquires *"If you would further know, What should be the reason of this strange affection in our God* (that is, exercised unto those who had rebelled against Him): *why the Scripture gives it. Our God being love, even love itself."* Love is an essential perfection in God's very nature, and as it has pleased Him to exercise the same unto His elect. It is an act of His will, yet not of His will absolutely considered but of *"the good pleasure of His will"* toward them. All the acts of God unto His people in Christ, all the blessings which He has bestowed upon them in Christ, all His thoughts concerning them, all the operations of His grace in them, and the workings of His providence for them, all the manifestations of His kindness and mercy unto them, proceed from His love for them. Love is the fountain from which flows every stream of His goodness unto them.

The wondrous love of God for His people can only be known by its blessed manifestations toward them. As the effects which it produces discovers to us the nature of the cause which produces them, so the love which God bears unto His elect is revealed by His acts unto them and bestowments upon them. God's love for us does not commence when we first respond to His gracious overtures unto us through the Gospel, nor even when He capacitates us to respond by first quickening us into newness of life, for His very calling of us out of darkness into His own marvellous light proceeds from His love for us. Nor did God's love for the Church begin when Christ died for her and put away her sins, for it was because God so loved her that He gave up His beloved Son to die in her room and stead. *"I have loved you with an everlasting love"* (Jer. 31:2) is God's own ringing declaration. Therefore it was in love that He *"predestinated us unto the adoption of children by Jesus Christ unto Himself"* (Eph. 1:4,5), which is the foundation of all our blessings. Nor did our fall in Adam produce the slightest change of God's love unto His elect.

Though our sin in Eden did not quench God's love for His people nor even chill it to the slightest degree, yet that horrible disobedience of theirs raised such formidable obstacles from the holiness of His nature and the righteousness of His government, yea opposed such a barrier against us as appeared to all finite intelligences, an insuperable one to prevent the exercise of God's compassion unto His guilty and corrupted people. In a word, the Law of God with its inexorable demand for satisfaction, seemed to effectually prevent the operation and manifestation of His love toward its transgressors. Consider carefully an example on the human plane. Darius was induced to sign a decree, that if any person asked a petition during the next thirty days from any save himself, he should forfeit his life (Dan. 6). Daniel himself defied that decree, making supplication of his God as before. His watchful enemies promptly reported this to the king and demanded that Daniel should be cast into the den of lions. Darius was displeased with himself *"and set his heart on Daniel to deliver him, and labored till the going down of the sun to deliver him"* (v. 14). But in vain. The honor of his law barred the outflow of his love; justice triumphed over mercy.

Consider still another case. Absalom committed a grievous offence against his father, for he sought to rob him of his sceptre and wrest the kingdom from his hands, and furthermore, murdered another of his sons. His attempt to gain the kingdom failed, and he fled the country, and remained an exile for three years. David mourned for his son every day and *"longed to go forth unto him"* (2 Sam. 13:39), but the honor of his throne clearly prohibited such an action. When Joab perceived *"that the king's heart was toward Absalom"* (14:1) and that he knew not how to make an advance toward him without disgracing his character and government he decided to further his own plans. Accordingly the unscrupulous Joab resorted to guile and employed a woman to speak to David, pleading that Absalom's crime might be pardoned, his attainder reversed, and be released from banishment. Strangely enough she reminded the king that God *"doth devise means whereby His banished be not expelled from Him"*(v. 14). But such a task of restoring his son without sullying his own honor was quite beyond David. The best he could devise was *"Let him turn to his own house; and let him not see my face"* (v. 24).

3. His wisdom. Where the wit of Darius completely failed before the requirements of human law, the wisdom of God gloriously triumphed over the obstacles interposed by the Divine Law. Where the wit of David could contrive nothing better than a wretched compromise, for which he later paid dearly, the omniscience of Deity found a way whereby His banished sons are restored and which redounds unto His everlasting honor. In pursuance of His gracious design to recover and reconcile His elect from their fall and alienation, the love of God set His consummate wisdom to work in contriving the fittest means for accomplishing the same. Therefore it is that we read in connection with God's grand purpose concerning our salvation that He *"works all things after the counsel of His own will"* (Eph. 1:11). "He works all by counsel to effect and bring to pass what His will is pitched upon, and the stronger His will is in a thing, the deeper are His counsels as to it" (Thos. Goodwin).

CHAPTER V

In our last we were only able to barely mention that the wisdom of God was engaged in the salvation of His people. Before we attempt to illustrate this particular aspect let us point out that it was in His character of Judge that the Father then acted. It is most important that this should be recognized, yea, essential if we are to view our subject from the correct angle, for reconciliation was entirely a judicial procedure. In Heb. 12:23 God the Father is expressly spoken of as *"the Judge of all,"* which is an offical title. He it was who passed sentence upon sinning Adam and all whom he represented as a federal head. None but *"the Judge of all,"* could have *"made Christ to be sin"* for His people, or them to be *"the righteousness of God in Him"* (2 Cor. 5:21). *"It is God that justifies"* (Rom. 8:33). That is, it is the Father as the Judge who actually and formally pronounces righteous in His sight the sinner who believes on Christ. It is on this two-fold ground that the apostle there argues the irreversibility of our justification: that the sentence of justification is pronounced by the Supreme Judge, and that, on the basis of the full satisfaction which has been made to Him by Christ.

We closed our last by calling attention to the fact that the determination of the Father to recover His lapsed people is described as the purpose of Him who works all things after the counsel of His own will which signifies there was an exercise of His infinite understanding in devising how that resolve should be made good to His own glory. To speak after the manner of men, the Father consulted with Himself, called His omniscience into play, and drew up a plan in which His *"manifold wisdom"* (Eph. 3:10) is exemplified. That many sided plan is termed the mystery because it has to do with the deep things of God (1 Cor. 2:7,10). "There is variety in the mystery and mystery in every part of the variety. It was not one single act, but a variety of counsels met in it: a conjunction of excellent ends and means" (Charnock). What those excellent ends and means were we shall now try to set forth, yet knowing full well that our utmost efforts can convey only a most inadequate and fragmentary idea of what will be our wonderment and admiration for all eternity. God's consummate and manifold wisdom is seen.

1. In Love's triumph over the Law. We begin here because it the better links up with the closing paragraph of our last and the opening one of this. Continuing that line of thought, be it said, the solution to the problems raised by sin and the harmonization of Love and Law is termed a *"mystery"* because it transcends human reason and can only be known by Divine revelation. It is called *"the hidden wisdom"* of God because it remained an impenetrable secret until He was pleased to disclose it. No discovery of it was made in creation. Though *"the heavens declare the glory of God and the firmament shows His handiwork"* yet they gave no indication it is His will to show mercy unto rebels: rather does the universe exhibit an inexorable reign of law. If a devoted mother gives her child medicine from the wrong bottle, the result would be the same as if an enemy poured poison down its throat. Break one of Nature's laws, even in ignorance, and no matter how deep our regret, there is no escaping the penalty. Divine Love has triumphed over the Law not by trampling upon it, but by fully meeting its demands and rendering it honorable. Divine wisdom contrived a way in which

there was no compromise between Love and Law, but each was given fullest expression.

The way in which God has dealt with what to human wit appears insoluable, both manifests His perfect wisdom and greatly redounds to His glory. He has dealt with the problem raised by sin by taking it into the court of His Law and settling it on a righteous basis. The needs-be for that is evident. Sin is far too great an evil for man to meddle with and every attempt he assays in that direction only makes bad matters worse — as appears in both the social and international spheres. Still more is this the case when man attempts to treat with God. His very efforts to remove sin do but aggravate it, and any attempt to approach God in spite of it only serves to increase his guilt. None but God is capable of dealing with sin, either as a crime or as pollution, as that which is a dishonor to Him or as it is a barrier to our access to Him. Moreover as sin is too great an evil for us to deal with, so righteousness is too high for the fallen creature to reach unto, yea too high for holy creatures to bring down to us. Only God Himself can bring near His righteousness (Isa. 46:13).

Yes, God has dealt with the momentous issue raised by sin by taking it into the court of His Law. For fallen man to have taken it there would have inevitably meant the losing of his case, for he is a transgressor of the Divine statute and a moral bankrupt utterly unable to make any reparation for his offence. But His consummate wisdom enabled the Judge of all to deal with it in such a manner that the honor of His Law has been maintained unimpeached, and yet the case has been settled on a basis equally favorable to God and the sinner! Settled in such a way that the wondrous love of God is free to flow forth unto His elect, children of disobedience though they be in themselves, without ignoring or condoning their disobedience, and so that His love remains a holy love. It is on that judicial settlement that an all sufficient and final answer has been furnished to man's anguished and age-long questions, *"How then can man be justified before God? Or how can he be clean that is born of a woman?"* (Job 25:4). *"Wherewith shall I come before the Lord?"* (Micah 6:6).

2. In exercising two Contrary principles in Redemption. This is an achievement worthy of Omniscience. God is love, nevertheless, He is *"light"* (1 John 1:5) as well. Not only is He full of kindness and benevolence, but He is immaculately pure and holy. God is abundant in mercy, but He is also just and *"will by no means clear the guilty."* Here then are two of the Divine perfections moving in opposite directions. How can such contraries be reconciled? Love goes out unto the prodigal, but Light cannot look upon iniquity (Hab. 1:13). Mercy would fain spare the offender, but justice demands his punishment. Grace is ready to bestow a gratuitous salvation, but righteousness insists that the defaulter cannot be released til he has *"paid the uttermost farthing"* (Matt. 5:26). Shall then the tenderness of the Father yield to the severity of the Judge? Or shall the rights of the Judge give place to the desires of the Father? Each must be satisfied. But how? Admire and adore that wondrous wisdom which devised a means whereby *"Mercy and Truth have met together, Righteousness and Peace have kissed each other"* (Ps. 85:10).

It is said God loves the sinner, but hates his sin. Yet that provides no solution to the problem. For the question still returns, Will God sink His love to the sinner in His hatred of his sin or allow His love for the sinner to override His hatred for sin? God has sworn *"The soul that sins it shall die"* (Ezek. 18:4). But He has also sworn *"I have no pleasure in the death of the wicked, but that the wicked turn from his way and live"* (Ezek. 33:11). The oath of justice and the oath of pity appear irreconcilable. Must then one yield to the other? No, both must stand. But how? In redemption God has manifested two opposite perfections at the same time, and in one action, in which there is shown supreme hatred of sin and superlative love of the sinner. Justice and mercy are alike maintained its ground without compromise, yea, has issued from the conflict honorable and glorious. Divine wisdom contrived a plan whereby God has punished transgression without scourging the transgressors, and has repaired the ruin of the sinner without condoning his sin.

3. In appointing a suitable Mediator. Clearly this was the first step necessary in order to a solution of the intricate problems to which we have alluded. The fall of man placed him at an immeasureable distance from God — *"your iniquities have separated between you and your God"* (Isa. 55:2). Not only so but the fall produced an infinite moral difference, man becoming polluted and a hater of God, God Himself ineffably holy and at legal enmity with man. Such a breach appeared unbridgeable, for on the one hand it became not the glory of His nature nor the honor of His government for God to make any direct advance towards rebellious subjects; and on the other hand, man had no desire to be restored to His image of favor, and even if he had, was barred from any access to Him. Thus all intercourse between God and men was at an end, an impasse was created, an utterly hopeless situation seemed to exist. *"Our God is a consuming fire"* and who was there that could interpose himself between Him and us? But Divine wisdom provided a means and remedy, decreeing there should be a Mediator who would bridge the distance and heal the difference between them, affecting a mutual reconciliation.

But where was such an one to be found? One capable of laying his hand upon both (Job 9:33). He must be entirely clear of any participation in the offence. He must, on account of his personal excellence, stand high in the esteem of the injured One. He must be a person of exalted dignity if the weight of his mediation was to bear any proportion to the magnitude of the crime and the value of the favor he would confer. He must be able to fully maintain the interests and subserve the honor of God. He must also possess a tender compassion towards the wretched offenders or he would not cordially interest himself on their behalf. And to give greater fitness to such a procedure it would be eminently proper that he should be intimately related to each of the parties. But where was one with so many and so necessary qualifications to be found? There was no creature worthy of so high office and so honorable an undertaking, no, not *"in heaven, nor in earth, neither under the earth"* (Rev. 5:3). None but Omniscience had ever thought of appointing God's own beloved and co-equal Son to take upon Him our nature.

4. In the union of such diverse natures in the person of Christ. It was necessary that the Mediator should be a Divine person in order that He might be independent and not the mere creature of either party; in order that He might reveal the Father (John 1:18; 14:9), in order to render unto the Law an obedience He did not owe for Himself (as all creatures do) and be one of infinite value. And in order that He might be capacitated to administer the realms of providence and

grace, which are committed to Him as Mediatorial Prince (Matt. 28:18; John 17:2). None other than God can forgive sins, impart eternal life, restore the fallen creature to true liberty, or bestow the Holy Spirit. Yet it was equally necessary that the Mediator should be Man. In order that He might truly represent men as *"the last Adam,"* in order that He might be *"made under the law"* to obey it, in order that He could suffer its death-penalty, and in order that, in His glorified humanity, He might be Head of the Church. He was to be *"The Apostle and High Priest"* (Heb. 3:1): God's Apostle unto us, our *"High Priest"* with God, for He must both pacify God's wrath and remove our enmity.

But how furnish the Son for His office? How become partaker of human nature without contracting its corruption? How unite Godhood and manhood, the Infinite with the finite, Immortality with mortality, Almightiness with weakness? How produce such a union that the two natures were perfectly wedded in one Person and yet preserve their distinctness, conjoined yet not confounded? So that the Diety was not changed into flesh nor flesh transformed into God? Before the Word's becoming flesh, must we not exclaim *"O the depth of the riches both of the wisdom and knowledge of God"* (Rom. 11:33)! By that unique and wondrous union Christ was fitted to be *"the Mediator of a better covenant"* (Heb. 8:6). There was nothing that belonged to Deity which He did not possess, and nothing that pertained to humanity but He was clothed with (Heb. 2:17). He had the nature of Him that was offended by sin, and of him that offended. "As sin was our invention (Eccl. 7:29) so Christ alone is God's and therefore is He called *"The Wisdom of God"* (1 Cor. 1:34), which is not spoken of Him essentially as Second Person, but as Mediator, because in Him God's wisdom to the utmost is made manifest" (Thos. Goodwin).

5. In constituting Christ the federal Head of His people. "When God in wisdom had found a suitable Person, yet since thus must be His only Son, here was a greater difficulty to be overcome: how to give Him for us" (Thos. Goodwin). To satisfy both the requirements of His justice and the abundance of His mercy, God determined that a full satisfaction should be made unto His Law, and such a satisfaction that it was thereby more honored than if it had never been broken, or the whole race damned. In order thereto, He appointed that Christ should serve as the Surety and Substitute of His people. He must stand as their Representative and both fulfil all righteousness for them and endure the curse in their stead, so that they might be legally reckoned to have obeyed and suffered in Him. By transferring their guilt to the Surety, God both punishes sin and pardons the sinner. In the same stupendous Sacrifice God has upheld the claims of His Law and lavished His kindness on His people. "The depths of God's love are seen here, as of His wisdom before, in not sparing His own Son, but exposing Him to all the rigors of justice, which would not make the least abatement" (Thos. Goodwin).

Christ then was made the *"Surety of a better covenant"* (Heb. 7:22). There could be no thought of reconciliation between a holy God and polluted rebels until sin had been put away and everlasting righteousness brought in, and as our Surety the Lord Jesus accomplished both. But O my reader, marvel at and stand in awe before what that involved. It involved that He who was in the form of God should take upon Him the form of a Servant. That the Lord of angels should be laid in a manger. That the Maker of the universe should not have anywhere to lay His head. That He should be constantly engaged in doing good and injuring none, yet be cast out by the world and deserted by His own followers. That the Lord of glory should be condemned as a malefactor, His own holy face fouled by the vile spittle of men and His back scourged by them. That the King of kings should be nailed hand and foot to a convict's gibbet. That the Beloved of the Father should be smitten and forsaken for Him. Such contrasts transcend the wit of man and could never have been invented by him. Must we not exclaim *"O Lord, how great are Your works! Your thoughts are very deep"* (Ps. 92:5).

6. In overruling sin to our gain. What a marvel of Divine wisdom is this: that God has not only removed the reproach which the entrance of sin brought upon His government, but that He made sin to be the foil for the greatest and grandest display of His perfections, and that He has not only devised a plan whereby His people are completely recovered from all the direful consequences and effects of the fall, but that they obtain a vastly superior inheritance than was the portion of unfallen Adam. God would have His people not only saved from Hell, but also brought into Heaven, yet in such a way as should be to the most honor of Himself and of His Son. The apostle speaks of *"the salvation which is in Christ with eternal glory"* (2 Tim. 2:10). Not only salvation, but a glorious one: one that is to the glory of Him who contrived it, of Him who purchased it, of Him who applies it, and of them who enjoy it. What a truly amazing thing is this that shame should be the path to glory, that fallen sinners are enriched by the Redeemer's poverty, that those grovelling in the mire of sin should be advanced to the highest dignities by Christ's making Himself *"of no reputation."*

What honor it brings to God's wisdom not only to restore fallen men, but to make the fall issue in their superior excellence. If they had only been restored to their forfeited estate and the enjoyment of that happiness which they had lost, it had been a remarkable triumph of grace, but to make them *"joint-heirs with Christ"* (Rom. 8:17) and partakers of His glory (John 17:24) leaves us lost in amazement. It is a mystery of nature that the corruption of one thing is made to minister to the generation of another (as the bones of animals fertilize vegetation), but it is a grander mystery of grace that our fall in Adam should occasion a nobler restitution. Innocence was not our last end. A superior felicity awaits us on High. Human nature is raised to a far higher degree of honor than had man retained his innocency, for through redemption and regeneration the elect are vitally united to the God-man Mediator and made members of His Body. The devil's empire is overthrown by the very same nature as he overthrew (Gen. 3:15; Rom. 16:20).

7. In winning rebels unto Himself. Having contemplated something of the wisdom and love of the Father, the willingness and work of the Son, here we are to behold (more distinctively) the power and grace of the Holy Spirit. When He first draws near to the elect in their unregenerate state He finds them in a most deplorable condition. Their understandings are darkened by sin, their hearts are filled with enmity toward God, their wills are steeled against Him. Not only have they no regard for His glory, but they are without any desire for His so-great salvation, yea positively and strongly averse to it. Here too are obstacles which need removing, obstacles so formidable that nothing short of omniscience and omnipotence could overcome the same. How shall captives be delivered who are thoroughly satisfied with their prison? How shall slaves be freed who are in love

with their bonds? Particularly, how shall that be effected while treating them as rational and responsible beings, without offering violence to their wills and reducing them to mere machines?

Some may regard the above as a very exaggerated statement of the case, supposing that a complete solution is found by presenting the Gospel to them. But Scripture teaches, and experience and observation verifies it, that the natural man has no eyes capable of beholding the beauty of the Gospel, and that his heart is so desperately wicked he will not receive the Saviour that it offers him. How then are such creatures to be saved from themselves? How shall those who detest holiness be brought to desire it? The dead in sins made to walk in newness of life? That such a miracle is performed we know, but how it is wrought we know not. Christ Himself declares it is a mystery as inscrutable to man as the workings of the wind (John 3:8). All we know is that life, light, love and supernaturally communicated, by which the unwilling are made willing. Not by compelling them to do what they abhor, but by sweetly overcoming their aversion. *"With lovingkindness have I drawn you"* (Jer. 31:3).

8. In making our holiness and happiness conserve each other. This is yet another of the marvels of God's wisdom: that He has contrived that the same Gospel which secures our everlasting felicity shall also promote our present purity. The sanctity of God is not comprised by His clemency to sinners, for the Redeemer is Himself both the principle and pattern of holiness unto all who are saved by Him. Moreover, the same grace to send His Son to die for us gives the Holy Spirit to renew us according to the Divine image and thereby make us meet for communion with Him. What a wonder of Divine wisdom to so highly exalt those who are so utterly unworthy in themselves and yet at the same time effectually humble that they cry *"Not unto us, O Lord, not unto us, but unto Your name give glory, for Your mercy and for Your truth's sake"* (Ps. 115:1). God's lovingkindness unto His people neither loosens the bonds of duty nor breaks that relation in which they stand to Him as their sovereign Lord and Govenor. The Gospel does not permit its beneficaries to return hatred for love nor contempt for benefit, but lays them under deeper obligations of gratitude to obedience. Those chosen to salvation are also *"predestinated to be conformed unto the image of God's Son."* The law of faith requires us to submit to Christ's sceptre as well as depend upon His sacrifice.

CHAPTER VI.

ITS ARRANGEMENT.

In our last we dwelt upon God's decision to redeem and reconcile fallen rebels: His love originating, His will determining, and His wisdom planning the outworking of the same. In illustrating how the Divine wisdom found a solution to all the formidable problems which stood in the way, we unavoidedly anticipated somewhat the ground which we hoped to cover in future articles. That Divine decision and scheme was *"eternally purposed in Christ Jesus our Lord"* (Eph. 3:11), for God's purpose to reconcile and His provision for the same are inseparable. That purpose respected not simply the exercise of mercy unto His lapsed people, but also the exercise of it in such a way that His Law was honored. Yet it must not be supposed that God was under any moral necessity of saving His people, or that redemption was an expedient to deliver the Divine character from reproach on account of the strictness of the Law in condemning all transgressors – no atonement was provided for the fallen angels! Rather has redemption vindicated the Law, and that in such a way that no transgressor is exempted from suffering its curse, either in himself or in a Substitute.

Reconciliation has been procured by the incarnate Son, the Lord Jesus Christ, for He is the grand and all-sufficient Provision of God for the accomplishing of His purpose. But it was effected by the Lord Jesus in fulfilment of a Covenant agreement. Unless that be clearly perceived we are without the principal key to the understanding of this stupendous undertaking. There was a time when Christians generally were well instructed in Covenant truth, but alas, a generation has grown up the great majority of which have heard nothing or next to nothing on it. It will therefore be necessary for us to proceed slowly in connection with this fundamental aspect of our subject and enter into considerable detail, for we do not ask the reader to receive ought from our pen until clearly convinced it is in full accord with and has the definite backing of God's Word. A few of our readers are more or less familiar with what we shall advance, yet it will do them no harm to have brought before them again the foundation on which faith should rest and to ponder the proofs which we now bring forward.

The great majority of our readers know that *"it is the blood* (and that alone, plussed by nothing from us) *that makes an atonement for the soul"* (Lev. 17:11), but we wonder how many of them have pondered and grasped the purport of that blessed and remarkable statement *"The God of peace that brought again from the dead our Lord Jesus, that great Shepherd of the sheep, through the blood of everlasting covenant"*(Heb. 13:20). That implies, first, that there was a covenant-agreement between God and our Lord Jesus; second, that it was a covenant made with Him as the Head of His people – *"that great Shepherd of the sheep;"* third, that Christ performed the condition of the covenant; fourth, that it was as the propitiated and reconciled One that God here acted; fifth, that it was in fulfilment of covenant purpose that He raised Christ; sixth, that Christ's blood was the meritorious ground on which He (and all the saints in Him) was delivered from the prison of the grave; seventh, that hereby the Church has Divine assurance of its complete redemption and salvation. We cannot dwell upon these points but would request a careful weighing of them as introductory to what follows.

Three things are necessary in order to a *"covenant."* the parties, the terms, the agreement. A *"covenant"* is a solemn pact or contract in which there are certain *"articles"* or conditions to be performed, in return for which performance an agreed award is promised and assured. It is a mutual agreement in which one party guarantees a stipulated return for the other's fulfilment of the work he had pledged himself to undertake. It is an agreement entered into voluntarily by both parties (see Matt. 26:15). The two parties in *"the everlasting covenant"* were the Father and the Son – the Holy Spirit concurring therein, being the Witness, and agreeing to co-operate in the same. In Scripture the Father is represented as taking the initiative in this matter, proposing to His Son the terms of the covenant. The Father proposed a federal transaction in which the Son should take upon Him the Mediatorial office and serve as the Head of His people, thereby assuming and discharging their liabilities and bringing in an everlasting righteousness for them. The Son is represented as freely and gladly consenting to it.

It needs to be pointed out and emphatically insisted upon that the Son was not so circumstanced antecedently to His susception of the Mediatorial office that He could not have avoided the humiliation and sufferings which He endured. We shall explain later the precise meaning of His words *"My Father is greater than I"* (John 14:28), *"neither came I of Myself, but He sent Me"* (John 8:42), *"this commandment* (to lay down His life) *have I received of My Father"* (John 10:18); sufficient now to point out they have no reference whatever to His condition and position prior to the Covenant, for He then enjoyed absolute equality with the Father in every way. The Son might have resigned the whole human race to the dire consequences of their apostasy and have remained Himself everlastingly blessed and glorious. It was by His own voluntary consent that He entered into covenant engagement with the Father. In that free consent lay the excellency of it. It was His willing obedience and personal merits which gave infinite value to His oblation. Behind that willingness lay His love for the Father and His love for the Church.

On the other hand it is equally true that though the Son had pitied, yea to loved the elect (foreviewed as fallen) that He was willing to become their Surety and Substitute, yet He could not have redeemed them without the Father's acceptance of His sacrifice. The Father too must consent to such an undertaking. Thus, there must be a mutual agreement between Them. The relation which Christ assumed to His people and the work He did for them presupposed the Father's willingness to it. Before passing on it must also be pointed out that in consenting to become Mediator and Servant, and as such in subjection to the Father, the Son did not surrender any of His perfections not relinquish any of His Divine rights, but He agreed to assume an inferior office and for a season to be subordinate to the Father's will. This was for the glory of the whole Godhead and the salvation of His people. After He became incarnate He was still in possession of His essential glory, though He was pleased to veil it in large measure from men and make Himself of *"no reputation"* in the world.

Before adducing proof-texts of the covenant made between the Father and the Son, let us call attention to a number of passages which clearly imply it and which otherwise are not fully intelligible. Take Christ's very first recorded utterance after He became incarnate: *"Do you not know that I must be about My Father's business"* (Luke 2:49). Did not that intimate He had entered this world with a clearly defined and Divinely designed task before Him? *"I came down from heaven not to do Mine own will, but the will of Him that sent Me"* (John 6:38) is even more explicit. Such subordination of one Divine person to another argues a mutual agreement between Them, and that, for some unique end. *"Say you of Him whom the Father has sanctified and sent into the World; You blaspheme, because I said, I am the Son of God?"* (John 10:36). Observe carefully the order of the two verbs: Christ was *"sanctified"* by the Father – that is, set apart and consecrated to His mediatorial office -- before He was *"sent"* into the world! *"Other sheep I have ... them also I must bring"* (John 10:16) – why *"must"* unless He was under definite engagement to do so?

That Christ went to the cross in fulfilment of a covenant-agreement may be gathered from His own words: *"truly the Son of man goes as it was determined"* (Luke 22:22), with which should be linked *"Of a truth against Your holy child Jesus, whom You have anointed, both Herod and Pontius Pilate with the Gentiles and the people of Israel, were gathered together, for to do whatsoever Your hand and Your counsel determined before to be done"* (Acts 4:27,28). When you stand before the cross and gaze by faith upon its august Sufferer recognize that He was there fulfilling the compact into which He entered with the Father before the world was. His blood shedding was necessary – *"ought not Christ to have suffered these things!"* (Luke 24:26). He asked – because of the relation He sustained to His people as their Surety. He was pledged to secure their salvation in such a way as glorified God and magnified His Law, for that had been Divinely *"determined"* and mutually agreed upon in the everlasting Covenant. Had not Christ died there had been no atonement, no reconciliation to God; equally true is it that had there been no covenant, Christ had never died!

Every passage where Christ owns the Father as His God witnesses to the same truth. When Jehovah established His covenant with Abraham He promised *"I will...be a God unto You and to your seed"* (Gen. 17:8), and therefore when He *"remembered His covenant with Abraham, with Isaac and with Jacob"* (Ex. 2:25) and revealed Himself to Moses at the burning bush preparatory to delivering His people from Egypt, He declared Himself to be *"The Lord God of your fathers: the God of Abraham, the God of Isaac, and the God of Jacob: this is My name forever and this is My memorial to all generations"* (Ex. 3:15). This is My covenant title and the guarantee of My covenant faithfulness. So too the grand promise of the new covenant is *"I...will be their God"* (Jer. 31:33 and Heb. 8:10). If then the Father had entered into covenant with His Son we should expect to find Him owning Him as His God during the days of His flesh. And this is excatly what we do find. *"My God, My God, why have You forsaken Me"* was not only a cry of agony, but an acknowledgement of covenant relationship. *"I ascend to My Father and your Father, and to My God and your God"* (John 20:17). So also after His ascension. He declared, *"Him that overcomes will I make a pillar in the Temple of My God...and I will write upon Him the Name of My God, and the name of the city of My God"* (Rev. 3:12).

Turning to the Epistles we find many passages which presuppose the Father's covenant with Christ before creation on behalf of His people. *"Who has saved us...according to His own purpose and grace which was given us in Christ Jesus before the world began"* (2 Tim. 1:9). Even at that time, if time it may be called, there was a federal relationship subsisting between Christ and the Church, though it was not made fully manifest until He became incarnate. That subsisting relationship formed the basis of the whole economy of Divine grace toward them after the fall, as it was the ground on which God pardoned the O.T. saints and bestowed spiritual blessings upon them. *"In hope of eternal life which God, that cannot lie, promised before the world was"* (Titus 1:2). Does not that *"promised"* imply an agreement that God made promise to Christ as the Covenant Head and to His people in Him? Christ was faithful to Him that appointed Him (Heb. 3:2). As *"obedience"* implies a precept, so *"faithfulness"* connotes a trust, and a trust wherein one has engaged himself to perform that trust according to directions given him.

Passing now from indirect allusions to what is more specific, we begin with Ps. 89:3. *"I have made a covenant with My chosen, I have sworn unto David My Servant."* The immediate allusion is to the historical David, but the spiritual reference is to David's Son and Lord. This is clear from many considerations. First, the striking and lofty manner in which this Psalm opens intimates that its leading theme must be one of great weight and value. *"I will sing of the mercies of the Lord forever, with my mouth will I make known Your faithfulness to all generations. For I have said, Mercy shall be built up forever, Your faithfulness shall You establish in the very heavens"* (vers. 1,2). Such language denotes that no ordinary or common *"mercies"* are in view, but those which when apprehended fill the hearts of the redeemed with holy songs and cause them to magnify the fidelity of Jehovah as nothing else does. Thus, such an introduction should prepare us to expect Divine revelation of extreme importance and blessedness.

Second, *"I have made a covenant with My Chosen"* (same word as My Elect in Isa. 42:1). I have sworn unto David (which means Beloved) My Servant. In the following passages it may be seen that Christ is expressly referred to as *"David"* by the prophets (Jer. 30:9; Ezek. 34:23; 37:24; Hos. 3:5) and let it be duly borne in mind that all those predictions were made long after the historical David had passed away from this scene. *"You spake in vision to Your Holy One and said: I have laid help upon One that is mighty, I have exalted One chosen out of the people* (Deut. 18:15), *I have found David My Servant, with My holy oil have I anointed Him"* (vers. 19,20). Who can doubt that a greater than the son of Jesse is here before us? But more: God goes on to say *"I will make Him My Firstborn higher than the kings of the earth...My covenant shall stand fast with Him"* (vers. 27,28) — does not that establish beyond a doubt the identity of the One with whom Jehovah made the covenant! Such declarations pertain to no mere human being.

Third, the covenant promises here made establish the same fact. *"His seed will I make to endure forever and His throne as the days of heaven"* (v. 29) — the throne of the historical David perished over two thousand years ago! That this promise was to be fulfilled in Christ is clear from Luke 1:31-33, where it was said to Mary. You *"shall call His name Jesus. He shall be great and shall be called the Son of the Highest; and the Lord God shall give unto Him the throne of His father David, and He shall reign over the house of Jacob forever and of His kingdom there shall be no end."* Another proof that it is not the typical David who is viewed in this Psalm appears in *"If His children forsake My Law...then will I visit their transgression with the rod"* (vers. 30-32). Had it been the successor of Saul who was the subject of this Psalm it had said *"If he shall break My Law...I will visit his transgression with the rod"* — as he was sorely chastised for so grievously wronging Uriah. No, it is Christ and His spiritual children who are referred to, and it is because of God's covenant with Him that He casts then not off. (See vers. 33-36).

Fourth, in Acts 13:34 Paul proved the resurrection of Christ thus: *"As concerning that He raised Him from the dead to return no more to corruption, He said on this wise: I will give you the sure mercies of David."* But in what did that quotation from Isa. 55:3 provide proof? By the resurrection of Christ the *"sure mercies of David"* are confirmed unto His children. If they are in possession of them, then Christ must have risen! That word of Paul's looks back beyond Isa. 55 to Ps. 89, which, as we have seen, begins thus: *"I will sing of the mercies of the Lord forever."* The principal mercies are *"I have made a covenant with My chosen...Your seed will I establish forever, and build up Your throne for all generations"* (vers. 3,4). Here then are *"the sure mercies of David:"* that God has covenanted to raise up Christ and set Him at His own right hand from where, on His mediatorial throne, He communicates those mercies to His seed. All doubt on this point is removed by Peter's avowal that through David God had sworn that *"Of the fruit of his loins...He would raise up Christ to sit on His throne"* (Acts 2:30 and see v. 33).

On Ps. 89:3,4 the immortal Toplady said, "Do you suppose that this was spoken to David in his own person only? No, indeed; but to David as the type, figure, and forerunner of Jesus Christ. *'I have sworn unto David My Servant'* unto the Messiah, who was typified by David, unto My co-equal Son, who stipulated to take upon Himself *'the form of a servant.' 'Your seed'* all those that I have given unto you in the decree of election; all those whom you shall live and die to redeem. Those *'will I establish forever,'* so as to render their salvation irreversible and inadmissable. *'And build up Your Throne:'* Your mediatorial throne, as King of saints and covenant Head of the elect. *'To all generations:'* there shall always be a succession of favored sinners to be called and sanctified, in consequence of Your federal obedience unto death, and every period of time shall recompense Your covenant sufferings with an increasing revenue of converted souls, until as many as were ordained to eternal life shall be gathered in" (Author of that precious hymn *"Rock of Ages."*).

CHAPTER VII

A solemn covenant was entered into between the Father and the Son before ever the world was. A compact was made in which the Father assigned the Son to be the Head and Saviour of His elect, and in which the Son consented to act as the Surety and Sponsor of His people. There was a mutual agreement between Them, of which the Holy Spirit was both the Witness and Recorder. It was in there that the Son was appointed unto the Mediatorial office, when He was *"set up"* (or anointed, as the Heb. signifies), when He was *"brought forth"* from the eternal decree (Prov. 8:23,24) and given a covenant subsistence as the God-man. It was then that Christ as a lamb without blemish and without spot *"verily was foreordained before the foundation of the world"* (1 Pet. 1:18,19). It was then that every thing was arranged between the Father and the Son, concerning the redemption of the Church. It is this which throws such a flood of light upon many passages in the N.T. which otherwise are shrouded in mystery.

As the One more especially offended (1 John 2:1) the Father is represented as taking the initiative in this matter: *"I have made a covenant with My Chosen"* (Ps. 89:3), yet the very fact that it was a *"covenant"* necessarily implied the willing concurrence of the Son in it. Before the covenant was settled there was a conference between Them. As there was a conferring together of the Divine Persons concerning our creation (Gen. 1:26), so there was a consultation together over our reconciliation, as to how peace could be righteously made between God and His enemies and as to how their enmity against Him might be slain; and thus we are told *"the counsel of peace shall be between Them both"* (Zech. 6:13). The terms which the Father proposed unto the Son may be gathered from the office He assumed and the work He performed, for the relation into which He entered and the task He discharged were but the actual fulfilling of the conditions of the covenant. The Son's acceptance of those terms, His willingness in entering office and discharging its duties, is clearly revealed in both Testaments.

This covenant was made by the Father with Christ on behalf of His people: *"Your seed will I establish forever"* follows immediately after Ps. 89:3. So again *"My covenant shall stand fast with Him: His seed also will I make to endure forever"* (vers. 28,29). In the next verses His seed are termed *"His children"* and should they be unruly God says *"I will visit their transgression with the rod, nevertheless My lovingkindness will I not take from Him"* — showing their covenant oneness with Him. The elect were committed to Christ as a charge or trust so that He is held accountable for their eternal felicity: *"Of them which You gave Me have I lost none"* (John 18:9). Since the covenant was made with Christ as the Head of the elect it was virtually made with them in Him, they having a representative concurrence therein.

The terms of the covenant may be summed up thus. First, it was required that Christ should take upon Him the form of a Servant, be made in the likeness of men, and act as the Surety of His people. Second, it was required of Him that He should render a full and perfect obedience to the Law and thereby provide the meritorious means of their justification. Third, it was required of Him that He should make full satisfaction for their sins, by serving as their Substitute and having visited upon Him the entire curse of the Law. In consideration of His acceptance of those terms the Father promised Him adequate supports; and on fulfilment of the task prescribed, specified rewards were promised Him. Let us briefly amplify these points. Little needs to be said on the first, for it should be clear to the reader that in order for the Son to render obedience to the Law He must become a subject of it and be under its authority. Equally evident is it that to be the Substitute of His people and suffer the penalty of their sins. He must become partaker of their nature — yet without sharing its defilment.

It was required from our Surety that He should comply in every respect with the precepts of the Divine Law. Such obedience was required of man originally under the Adamic covenant, and since the nature of God and His relation to the creature changes not, that requirement holds good forever. If then a Surety engages to discharge all the obligations of God's elect then He must necessarily meet that requirement on their behalf, which is only another way of saying that He would thereby provide or bring in an everlasting righteousness for them. "There was no possibility that man could obtain happiness unless this obedience was performed by him, or by another whom the Law should admit to act in his name. *'If you will enter into life, keep the commandments'* (Matt. 19:17) is the answer which the Law returns to the sinner who asks what he shall do to inherit eternal life. It is evident the same obedience was required from our Saviour when acting as our federal Head" (J. Dick).

The Father required from our Surety full satisfaction for the sins of His people. Since they had broken the Divine Law its penalty must be inflicted, either on them or on One who was prepared to suffer in their room. But before the penalty could be inflicted the guilt of the transgressors must be transferred to Him. That is to say, their sins must be judicially imputed to Him. To that arrangement the Holy One willingly consented, so that He who *"knew no sin"* was legally *"made sin"* for His people. God laid on Him the iniquities of them all, and therefore the sword of Divine justice smote Him and exacted satisfaction. Without the shedding of blood there was no remission of sins. The blotting out of transgressions, procuring for us the favor of God, the purchase of the heavenly inheritance, required the death of Christ.

The Son's free acceptance of those terms is revealed in Ps. 40. All the best of the commentators from Calvin to Spurgeon have expounded this Psalm throughout of Christ as the Head of His Church. Its opening verses contain His personal thanksgiving for deliverance from death and the grave, but in His new song He makes mention of *"our God"* (v. 3) — His people sharing His glorious triumph. In v. 5 Christ owns Jehovah as *"My God"* and speaks of His thoughts to *"Us-ward,"* that is, to the elect as one with Himself. But it is in vers. 6-10 we have that which is most germane to our present subject — a passage quoted in Heb. 10, and which looks back to the far distant past. The force of *"sacrifice and offering You did not desire"* (v. 6) is given us in *"it is not possible that the blood of bulls, and goats should take away sins"* (Heb. 10:4). *"My ears have You digged"* speaks in the type of Ex. 21:5,6 and tells of our Lord's readiness to serve and His love to His Father and His children. *"A body have You prepared Me"* (Heb. 10:5) announces the Son's coming into this world equipped for His arduous undertaking.

"Then said I:" when alternatives had been discussed and it was agreed that animal sacrifices were altogether inadequate for satisfying Divine justice. *"Lo, I come"* willingly of My own volition — from the ivory palaces to the abodes of misery. Those words signified His cheerful acceptance of the terms of the cove-

nant. *"In the volume of the book it is written of Me:"* thus it was recorded at the very beginning of the Divine decrees – of which the Scriptures are a faithful transcript – that I should make My advent to earth. Thus it was registered by the Holy Spirit who witnessed My solemn engagement with the Father so to do. Thus it was formally and officialy inscribed that in the fullness of time I should become incarnate and accomplish a purpose which lay beyond the capacity of all the holy angels. *"I delight to do You will, O My God"* tells us first of the object for which He came – to make good the Father's counsels; second, His freeness and joy in it; third, the character in which He acted – as covenant Head: *"My God."*

"I delight to do Your will, O My God." Here consists the very essence of obedience: the soul's cheerful and loving devotion to God. Christ's obedience, which is the righteousness of His people, was pre-eminent in this quality. Not withstanding unparalleled sorrows and measureless griefs our Lord found delight on His work. *"Who for the joy that was set before Him endured the cross, despising the shame"* (Heb. 12:2). *"Yea, Your Law is within My heart"* He declared. No mere outward and formal subjection to the Divine will was His. That Law which is *"holy, just and good"* (Rom. 7:12) was enshrined in His affections. *"O how love I Your Law"* (Ps. 119:97) He averred. The Law did not have to be written on His heart, as it has on ours (Heb. 8:10), for it was one with the holiness of His nature. Then what a horrible crime for any to speak disparagingly of or want to be delivered from that Law which Christ loved!

The two things – the Father's proposing the terms of the covenant and the Son's free acceptance of them – are brought together in a striking yet rarely considered passage. *"And their Noble* (the Hebrew is in the singular number) *shall be of themselves and their Governor shall proceed from the midst of them, and I will cause Him to draw near, and He shall approach Me: for Who is this that engaged His heart to approach Me, says the Lord"* (Jer. 30:21). That is one of the great Messianic prophecies, and it is closely parallel with Ps. 89:19,20,27. In it we see the Father taking the initiative, and equally so the Son's cheerful compliance. The Son is to become incarnate, for He was to *'proceed from the midst of"* the people of Israel. He was to be their *"Governor,"* and in order thereto is seen *"approaching"* the Father, or voluntarily presenting Himself to serve in that capacity. His free consent and heartiness so to act appears in His *"that engaged His heart to approach Me."*

We cannot now enter into the connections of the above verse, but if the reader compares v. 9 of the same chapter and ponders what follows, he will find confirmation of our interpretation. There the Father announced, *"They shall serve the Lord their God and David their King, whom I will raise up* (not from the grave, but exalt to office, as in Deut. 18:15; Luke 1:69 etc.) *unto them."* That can be meant of none other than Christ, the antitypical David, for *"serve"* includes rendering Divine homage (Matt. 4:10), and worship will never be performed to the resurrected son of Jesse. Now it is the antitypical David, the Father's *"Beloved,"* who is the King and Govenor of the spiritual Israel and to whom Divine honors are paid. And He is the One who before earth's foundation was laid *"engaged His heart,"* or as the Heb. signifies *"became a Surety in His heart"* (for so the word is rendered in Gen. 44:32, Prov. 6:1 etc.,) and that is the ground of the covenant which follows: *"and you shall be My people and I will be your God"* (v. 22).

Before looking at some of the assurances made by the Father of adequate assistance to His incarnate Son in the discharge of His covenant engagements, we must consider closely the office in which He served. In previous articles we pointed out the needs be for a Mediator if God and His people were to be reconciled in a way that honored His Law, as we also intimated His consummate wisdom in such an arrangement, and showed the perfect fitness of Christ for such an office. As the Mediator He was to serve as our Surety and also fulfill the functions of Prophet, Priest and King. As the Mediator He was *"set up"* or *"anointed"* from the beginning (Prov. 8:23): that is, was given a covenant subsistence as such before God, in which He acted all through the O.T. era. The prophets (equally with the apostles) were His ministers, and therefore the Spirit who spoke in them is termed *"the Spirit of Christ"* (1 Pet. 1:11). In Zech. 1:11,12 and 3:2 we find Him interceding:and in anticipation of the incarnation He appeared as *"Man"* (Josh 5:13,14; Dan. 12:6,7).

Christ is Mediator in respect of His person as well as office. Only thus could He be the Representative of God unto us, the Image of the invisible God, the One in whom He is seen (John 14:9), the light of whose glory shines in His face (2 Cor. 4:6). It must be ever remembered that it was a Divine person who became flesh, and it is equally necessary to insist that the whole of His mediatory work is inseparably founded on the exercise of both of His natures. It is quite unwarrantable to predict certain things of His Divine nature and others of His human, for though not confounded there is perfect oneness between them. It was the God-man who was tempted, suffered and died — *"the Lord's death"* (1 Cor. 11:26). This is indeed a subject beyond human comprehension, nevertheless, thought *"great is the mystery of godliness"* yet it is *"without controversy"* (1 Tim. 3:16) unto all those who bow to the all-sufficient authority of Divine revelation and receive the same as *"little children."*

As the Mediator Christ became the Father's *"Servant"* (Isa. 42:1; Phil. 2:7). Yet in so doing He ceased not to be a Divine person, but rather the God-man in whom *"dwells all the fullness of the Godhead bodily"* (Col. 2:9). As our Surety Christ became subordinate to the Father's will, nevertheless He still retained all His Divine perfections and prerogatives. When the Holy Spirit announced that unto a Child should be born and a Son given, He was careful to declare that such an One was none other than *"the mighty God"* (Isa. 9:6). When the Father brought His Firstbegotten into the world He gave orders *"Let all the angels of God worship Him"* (Heb. 1:6). Yet as our Surety and the Father's Servant He was sent into the world, received commandment from His Father and became obedient unto death. Retaining as He did His Divine perfections He could rightly say *"I and My Father are one"* (John 10:30), co-equal and co-glorious; yet as the Servant *"My Father is greater than I"* (John 4:28) — not essentially so but officially, not by nature but by virtue of the place which He had taken. This distinction throws a flood of light upon many passages.

To be Himself *"the true God"* (John 5:20) and yet subject to God — owning Him as *"My God;"* to be the Law-Giver and yet *"under the Law"* (Gal. 4:4), to be one with the Father and yet inferior to Him, to be *"The Lord of glory"* (1 Cor. 2:8) and yet *"made both Lord and Christ"* (Acts 2:36), are, according to all human reason and logic, inconsistent properties: nevertheless Scripture itself expressly predicates these very things of one and the same Person – yet looked at in different relationships! In the days of His flesh Christ was *"over all, God blessed forever"* (Rom. 9:6), yet as our Surety *"the Head of Christ is God"* (1 Cor. 11:3). While walking this earth as the Man of sorrows the disciples beheld His glory *"as of the Only-begotten of the Father"* (John 1:4), yet as our Substitute He was *"crucified through weakness"* (2 Cor. 3:4). As God manifest in flesh He both laid down His life and took it again (John 10:18), but as our Shepherd God *"brought again from the dead our Lord Jesus"* (Heb. 3:20). There is perfect harmony amid wondrous variety.

Christ's entrance into covenant engagement was entirely voluntary on His part: there existed no prior obligation, nor was there any authority by which He could be compelled to it. As the Father's *"Fellow"* He was subject to no law and acknowledged no superior, supreme dominion was Him, and He *"thought it not robbery to be equal with God"* (Phil. 2:6). But having freely entered into the covenant and agreed to fulfill its terms, the Son became officially subordinate to the Father, and as our Surety He *"sent Him into the world"* (John 13:7), and as our Surety he was *"anointed"* with the Holy Spirit and with power (Acts 10:38), was *"delivered up for us all"* (Rom. 8:32), was raised from the dead (Acts 2:24), was *"given all power"* (Matt. 28:18), was elevated to the right hand of the Majesty on high (Heb. 1:3), was exalted *"to be a Prince and a Saviour, for to give repentance to Israel and forgiveness of sins"* (Acts 5:31), and was *"ordained of God to be the Judge of quick and dead"* (Acts 10:42). Thus, the very passage over which *"Unitarians"* have stumbled and broken their necks speak of Christ not in His essential Person but in His mediatorial office: the former giving value to the latter, the latter endearing the former to our hearts.

CHAPTER VIII

Upon the Son's cheerful acceptance of the terms proposed to Him concerning the federal undertaking He was to engage in, the Father in turn bound Himself to do certain things for and unto the Son. This it was which constituted the very essence of that compact which was made by Them, for a covenant is an agreement between two parties who come under mutual engagements. Something is to be done by one party, in consequence of which the other party binds himself to do another thing in return. As there must be two parties to a covenant, so there must be two parts in a covenant – a condition and a promise. It is the performing of the condition or terms of the covenant – the work or service specified – which gives the first party the right to the promised reward. Having already shown what Christ consented to do, we turn now to consider what the Father promised to bestow. First, He agreed to make all needful preparations for the incarnation of His Son. Second, to give Him all requisite assistance in the performing of His work. Third, to bestow upon Him a meet reward.

The promise to make all needful preparation for the incarnation of His Son comprehended the whole of the Father's providences or governance of this world from the creation of man until Christ began His public ministry: *"My Father works until this time, and* (now) *I work"* (John 5:17). The Father's *"work"* included the ordering of human history, and particularly His dealings with Abraham and his descendants and the separation of Israel from the rest of the nations, for it was from Israel that Christ, according to the flesh, would issue. The Father's *"work"* included the giving of a written revelation, in which the covenant was made known and the advent of His Son promised, so that an expectation of His appearing was created and a foundation was laid for His mission. The Father's *"work"* also involved the *"preparation of a body"* for His Son, which was accomplished by the miracle of the virgin birth. When *"the fullness of time was come – when all the necessary preparations were completed – God sent forth His Son, made of a woman"* (Gal. 4:4).

The Father promised to give His Son all requisite help for the performing of His work. First, in order for the discharge of His mediatorial office there was that which fitted Him to it. *"There shall come forth a Rod out of the stem of Jesse and a Branch shall grow of of his roots. And the Spirit of the Lord shall rest upon Him: the spirit of wisdom and understanding and spirit of counsel and might, the spirit of knowledge and of the fear of the Lord"* (Isa. 11:1,2). Upon which the Puritan Charnock said, "All the gifts of the Spirit should reside in Him as in a proper habitation, perpetually. The human nature being a creature could not beautify and enrich itself with needful gifts. This promise of the Spirit was therefore necessary. His humanity could not else have performed the work it was designed for. So that the habitual holiness residing in the humanity of Christ was a fruit of this eternal covenant. Though the Divine nature of Christ, by virtue of its union, might sanctify the human nature, yet the Spirit was promised Him because it is His proper office to confer those gifts which are necessary for any undertaking in the world; and the personal operations of the Trinity do not interfere. It might also be because every person in the Trinity should plainly have a distinct hand in our redemption."

The Father, then, furnished and equipped Christ for His arduous work by a plentiful effusion of the graces and gifts of the Holy Spirit. Thus He declared *"Behold My Servant whom I uphold, My Elect in whom My soul delights: I have put My Spirit upon Him"* (Isa. 42:1,2). Those promises were fulfilled at His baptism, when the Spirit descended upon Him (Matt. 3:16), for it was then that *"God anointed Jesus of Nazareth with the Holy Spirit and with power"* (Acts 10:38). This was freely owned by the Saviour Himself, for in the synagogue He read *"The Spirit of the Lord is upon Me, because He has anointed Me to preach the Gospel to the poor, He has sent Me to heal the brokenhearted, to preach deliverance to the captive, and recovering of sight to the blind, to set at liberty them that are bruised"* and then declared *"This day is this Scripture fulfilled in your ears"* (Luke 4:18,21). So too we find Him acknowledging *"I cast out demons by the Spirit of God"* (Matt. 12:27).

Second, the Father promised to invest His Son with a threefold office. In order to the saving of His people it was most requisite that whatever Christ did He should act by the authority of the Father, by a commission under the broad seal of Heaven. Accordingly He said *"I will raise them up a Prophet from among their bretheren"* (Deut. 18:15,18 and see Acts 3:22). Christ did not run without being sent. It was God who *"anointed Him to preach."* Again, *"Christ glorified not Himself to be made an High Priest* (He did not intrude Himself into that office), *but He that said unto Him, You are My Son"* (Heb. 5:5); Christ was *"made a High Priest forever after the order of Melchizedek"* (Heb. 6:20). So also God the Father invested Him with the royal office: *"yet have I set My King upon My holy hill of Zion"* (Ps. 2:6). *"I will raise unto David a righteous Branch and a King shall reign and prosper"* (Jer. 23:5), for the *"the Father loves the Son and has given all things into His hand"* (John 3:35); and therefore has He made Him *"higher than the kings of the earth"* (Ps. 89:27).

Third, the Father promised Christ strength, support and protection to execute the great work of redemption. His undertaking would be attended with such difficulties that creature power, though unimpaired by sin, would have been quite inadequate for it. It was to be performed in human nature, and that had failed in a much easier task, even when possessed of untainted innocence. Therefore did the Father assure Him of help and succor, to carry Him through all the obstacles and dangers, trials and opposition He would meet with. *"Behold My Servant whom I uphold...I the Lord have called You in righteousness and will hold Your hand and keep You, and give You for a covenant of the people, for a light to the Gentiles"* (Isa. 42:1,6). "The work of redemption was so high and so hard that it would have broken the hearts and the backs of all the glorious angels and mighty men on earth had they entered on it; therefore the Father engaged Himself to stand close to Jesus Christ and mightily assist and strengthen Him in all His mediatorial administrations" (Thos. Brooks, Puritan).

Christ is said to be *"The Son of man whom You made strong for Yourself"* (Ps. 80:17), for He had sworn *"My arm also shall strengthen Him"* (Ps. 89:21). It is blessed to see how that the Redeemer, in the days of His flesh, acknowledged these promises. *"I was cast upon You from the womb, You are My God from My mother's belly"* (Ps. 22:10). *"Listen O isles unto Me, and hearken your people from afar: The Lord has called Me from the womb, from the bowels of My Mother* (see Matt. 1:21,22) *has He made mention of My name. And He has made My mouth like a sharp sword, in the shadow of His hand has He hid Me"*

(Isa. 49:1,2). *"The Lord God has given Me the tongue of the learned...the Lord God will help Me...and I know that I shall not be ashamed"* (Isa. 59:4-7). In unshaken confidence, when His enemies were conspiring against Him and His friends were on the point of forsaking Him, He declared *"yet I am not alone, because the Father is with Me"* (John 16:32).

Those promises of the Father were the support of His soul in the hour of His supreme crisis. His heart laid hold of them, acted faith on them, and received comfort and strength therefrom. *"Preserve Me, O God, for in You do I put My trust"* (Ps. 16:1), was His petition and plea. *"I gave My back to the smiters and My cheeks to those that plucked off the hair. I hid not My face from shame and spitting, for the Lord God will help Me therefore shall I not be confounded, and therefore I set My face like a flint, and I know that I shall not be ashamed"* (Isa. 50:6,7). When He was denounced by the Jews and condemned by Pilate, He consoled Himself with the assurance *"He is near that justifies Me"* (Isa. 50:8). *"I have set the Lord always before Me: because He is at My right hand I shall not be moved. Therefore My heart is glad and My glory rejoices; My flesh also shall rest in hope, for You will not leave My soul in Sheol, neither will You suffer Your holy One to see corruption. You will show Me the path of life"* (Ps. 16:8-11). In the prospect of death, He rejoiced in the sure knowledge of resurrection.

Fourth, the Father promised Him a glorious reward. First, a glory for Himself personally, as the God-man Mediator. As He was to endure the cross, so He was also to receive the crown. The enduring of the cross was a covenant engagement on His part, and the bestowing of the crown was a covenant engagement on the Father's part. That was plainly borne witness to by His prophets, for the Spirit in them *"testified beforehand the sufferings of Christ and the glory which should follow."* (1 Pet. 1:11). That glory consisted in His being fully invested with His priestly and royal offices. As it was with the type, so with the Antitype. David was anointed incipiently and privately before he slew Goliath (1 Sam. 16:13), but formally and publicly after his victories (2 Sam. 5:13). The antitypical David was indeed *"anointed with the Holy Spirit"* at the Jordan, but not until after He had triumphed over sin, Satan and the grave, did God anoint Him *"with the oil of gladness above His fellows"* (Heb. 1:9) and publicly make Him to be *"both Lord and Christ"* (Acts 2:36).

"The solemn inauguration into all His offices was after His making reconciliation: making an end of sin, bringing in everlasting righteousness, and thereby shutting up all prophecy and vision, because all the prophecies tended to Him and were accomplished in Him; and then as manifesting Himself the most holy, He was to be anointed — that is, fully invested in all the offices of Prophet, Priest and King (Dan. 9:24). The compact ran thus: Do this, suffer death for the vindication of the honor of My Law, and You shall be a Priest and King forever. He could not, therefore, be solemnly installed till He had performed the condition on His part (for the promise was made to Him considered as Mediator or God-man); then it was that He was advanced, for the ground of His exaltation is pitched wholly upon His sufferings. Therefore God has given Him a glory as a just debt due to the price paid, the sufferings undergone, and the obedience yielded to the mediatory Law" (S. Charnock). Therefore it is that the general assembly of Heaven say with a loud voice *"Worthy is the Lamb that was slain to receive power, and riches, and wisdom, and strength, and honor, and glory, and blessing"* (Rev. 5:12).

Subsidiary to that glorious investiture was the Father's promise to raise Christ from the dead. *"He asked life of You, and You gave it Him, even length of days forever and ever"* (Ps. 21:5). Beautifully does that link up with Ps. 102:23-27 — quoted by the apostle in Heb. 1:12 as the words of the Father to the Son. In Ps. 102:23,24 we hear the incarnate Son saying, *"He shortened My days: I said, O My God, take Me not away in the midst of My days,"* to which the Father made answer, *"Your years are throughout all generations...Your years shall have no end"* (v. 27). So again, He received assurance *"He shall prolong His days!"* (Isa. 53:10). The Father made promise that the One who had been bruised by Him and whose soul He had made *"an offering for sin"* should have a glorious deliverance and should reign in life. It was in fulfilment of such promises as these that *"The God of peace (the reconciled One) brought again from the dead our Lord Jesus, that great Shepherd of the sheep, through the blood of the everlasting covenant"* (Heb. 13:20).

In like manner subsidiary to Christ's glorious investiture of His full priestly and kingly offices was His ascension, for though He was born King and acted as Priest at the cross when He *"offered Himself to God"* and *"made intercession for the transgressors,"* yet not until He had completely performed His part of the covenant could He enter into His rightful reward. Accordingly we find promise of ascension made unto Him. It was clearly implied in *"I will make Him My Firstborn, higher than the kings of the earth"* (Ps. 89:27). It was revealed in *"Who shall ascend into the Hill of the Lord? Who shall stand in His Holy Place?"* answered by *"Lift up your heads O you gates and be lifted up you everlasting doors, and the King of glory shall come in"* (Ps. 24:3,7). It was plainly announced in *"You have ascended on high, You have led captivity captive"* (Ps. 68:18). It was such promises as these the Saviour had in mind when He said *"Ought not Christ to have suffered and to enter into His glory"* (Luke 24:26).

"Behold, My Servant shall deal prudently. He shall be exalted and extolled, and by very high" (Isa. 52:13). The 53rd of Isaiah — that wondrous chapter in which we have so solemnly, so strikingly, and so evangelically depicted, the vicarious sufferings of Christ — closes with that blessed promise of the Father: *"Therefore will I divide Him a portion with the great and He shall divide the spoil with the strong, because He has poured out His soul unto death"* (v. 12). The similitude used there is taken from the honoring of military conquerors who, having in fight defeated and routed their enemies, gained a great victory and in consequence are suitably rewarded by their princes, being exalted by them and given a share of the spoils or fruits of war. It was as though God the Father said: This My incarnate and successful Son shall receive such honor, glory, renown and riches after His toils and conflicts as are meet for His triumphs. He shall have a glorious recompense for all His humiliation and sufferings at the hands of men, for His opposition from Satan, and for His enduring of My wrath. For nothing less is due Him. The fulfilment of Isa. 53:12 is seen in Eph. 4:8, Col. 2:15, etc.

"The obedience of Christ bears to these blessings not only the relation of antecedent to consequent, but of merit to reward, so that His obedience is the cause: and the condition being fulfilled by virtue of obedience, He has a right to the reward" (H. Witsius — the Dutch Puritan). That is the precise force of the

"Wherefore" in the above verse, as it is also in *"You love righteousness and hate wickedness, therefore God, Your God, has anointed You with the oil of gladness above Your fellows"* (Ps. 45:7).It was not only that justice required it, but the covenant fidelity of the Father was involved therein. Therefore His assurance *"My faithfulness and My mercy shall be with Him, and in My name shall His horn be exalted"* (Ps. 89:24). Thus also the N.T., Christ *"became obedient unto death, even the death of the cross, wherefore God also has highly exalted Him and given Him a name which is above every name"* (Phil. 2:8,9). It was Christ's meriting the reward for Himself which was the ground of His meriting life and glory for us.

"Therefore let all the house of Israel know assuredly that God has made that same Jesus, whom you have crucified, both Lord and Christ" (Acts 2:36). That was the whole burden or theme of Peter's pentecostal sermon, the grand truth proclaimed therein and enforced by Scripture: that He whom the Jews had vilified God had glorified. Having faithfully fulfilled the terms of the everlasting covenant, the Saviour was elevated to dominion and empire over the world. God's exaltation of Him in His human nature to His own right hand (v. 33) was a full confirmation and demonstration of what He had acquired by His death. He made Him *"both Lord and Christ,"* seating *"Messiah the Prince"* (Dan. 9:25) upon the throne of the universe. This is an economical Lordship, a dispensation committed to Him as God-man by the Father — just as He has *"given Him authority to execute judgment also"* (John 5:27). The One whom His enemies crowned with thorns God has *"crowned with glory and honor"* (Heb. 2:9). He must be received by us as *"Lord"* before we can have Him for our *"Christ."* He must have the throne of our hearts if we are to receive His benefits.

It was promised Christ that *"He should have dominion from sea to sea and from river unto the ends of the earth . . . yea all kings shall fall down before Him, all nations shall serve Him. For He shall deliver the needy when he cries, the poor also, and him that has no helper"* (Ps. 72:8,11,12). All of this in consequence of, *"The Lord* (the Father) *said unto My Lord, Sit You at My right hand, until I make Your enemies Your footstool . . . The Lord has sworn and will not repent, You are a Priest forever, after the order of Melchizedek"* (Ps. 110:1,4); that is, a royal Priest — *"He shall be a Priest upon His throne"* (Zech. 6:13). A regal inheritance was assured Him. Not only has He acquired the mundane inheritance forfeited by the first Adam, but as the risen Redeemer declared, *"all power is given unto Me in heaven and in earth"* (Matt. 28:18), for the Father *"has appointed* (Him) *Heir of all things,"* so that now He is *"upholding all things by the word of His power"* (Heb. 1:2,3), wielding the sceptre or universal dominion. The *"government"* is upon *"His shoulder"* (Isa. 9:6).

It was promised that a blessed harvest should crown His undertaking, that He should reap the fruit of His sufferings. *"The pleasure of the Lord shall prosper in His hand"* (Isa. 53:10). What that signifies is intimated in such passages as the following: *"I will preserve You and give You for a covenant of the people to establish the earth, to cause to inherit the desolate heritages, that You may say to the prisioners, Go forth"* (Isa. 49:8,9). *"Behold You shall call a nation that You know not and nations that know not You shall turn unto You, because of the Lord Your God, and the Holy One of Israel, for He has glorified You"* (Isa. 55:5). The Gentiles shall come to Your light and kings to the brightness of Your rising (Isa. 6U:3). To the One who came forth from Bethlehem it was promised

"He shall be great unto the ends of the earth" (Micah 5:2,4). How fully these promises have yet been fulfilled or how much longer human history must yet continue we do not profess to know, but even now *"angels and authorities and powers"* are *"subject unto Him"* (1 Pet. 3:22).

CHAPTER IX

Consider now Christ's relation to the covenant. 1. He is the very substance of it. *"I will give Him for a covenant of the people"* (Isa. 49:8): as He is our *"propitiation"* (1 John 2:1) and *"peace"* (Eph. 2:14) so He is our covenant. 2. He is the Witness of the covenant (Isa. 55:3,4) for He saw, heard and testified it all, and therefore is He termed *"the faithful and true Witness"* (Rev. 3:14). 3. He is *"the Prince of the covenant"* (Dan. 11:22), called *"Messiah The Prince"* (Dan. 9:25), because He is given the royal right to administer it. 4. He is *"the Messenger of the Covenant"* (Dan. 9:25), because He is given the royal right to administer it. 4. He is *"the Messenger of the covenant"* (Mal. 3:1), acting as God's *"Apostle"* to us (Heb. 3:1) and our Representative before God. 5. He is the *"Surety of the covenant"* – *"testament"* is the same Greek word (Heb. 7:26) – because He engaged Himself to discharge the obligations of His people, its coventees. 6. He is *"the Mediator of the covenant"* (Heb. 8:6) because He stands between and serves both parties – God and His people. 7. He is the Testator of the covenant (Heb. 9:16,17) because He has sealed it with His blood.

Consider its various and descriptive designations. 1. It is an *"everlasting covenant"* (Heb. 13:20) because it was entered into before all worlds and because its blessings shall be administered and enjoyed in perpetuity. 2. It is a *"covenant of salt"* (Num. 18:19; 2 Chron. 13:5) because it is incorruptible, inviolable, perpetual; because its provisions season us and makes all our services savory to God. 3. It is a *"covenant of peace"* (Isa. 54:10) for therein Christ engaged to pacify the Divine Judge, remove the enmity of His people, and effect a mutual reconciliation. 4. It is a *"new covenant"* (Jer. 31:31) for it secures for His people a new standing before God, makes them new creatures in Christ and puts a new song in their mouths. 5. It is a *"covenant of life"* (Mal. 2:5) for by its terms life is promised, restored and given more abundantly 6. It is a *"holy covenant"* (Luke 1:72) manifesting the ineffable purity of God in all its arrangements. 7. It is a covenant *"of promise"* (Eph. 2:12) both to Christ and His seed.

In view of what has just been pointed out well may we adopt the language of O. Winslow and say, "This covenant must be rich in its provisions of mercy, seeing it is made by Jehovah Himself, the Fountain of all holiness, goodness, mercy and truth, whose very essence is 'Love.' It must be glorious, because the second Person in the blessed Trinity became its Surety. It must be stable, because it is eternal. It must meet all the circumstances of a necessitous Church, because it is 'ordered in all things.' It must be sure, seeing its administration is in the hands of an infinitely glorious Mediator, who died to secure it, rose again to confirm it, and ever lives to dispense its blessings as the circumstances of the saints require." To which might be added, it must be inviolable, since the eternal God is its Author, and the precious blood of Christ has sealed it. And therefore it should be *"all my salvation and all my desire"* (2 Sam. 23:5), for what more could I ask or wish!

Returning now to the covenant promises which the Father made unto the Mediator. In addition to those considered in our last, Christ was assured of a *"seed." "When You shall make His soul an offering for sin, He shall see His seed"* (Isa. 53:10). In the previous verses we are shown what was required from Christ in the discharge of His covenant engagements; here we have revealed the reward which the Father bestowed upon Him because of His fidelity. In the last three verses of this wonderful chapter we also behold the prophet replying to the Jews, who regarded the cross as a *"stumblingblock,"* being scandalized at the idea of their Messiah suffering such an ignominious death. But it is here pointed out that Christ's crucifixion is not to be accounted an infamy to Him because it was the very means, ordained by God, whereby He propagated unto Himself a spiritual seed. He had Himself pointed out, *"except a corn of wheat fall into the ground and die, it abides alone; but if it die, it brings forth much fruit"* (John 12:24).

Observe well that in Isa. 53:10 it was promised Him *"He shall see His seed"* which, coming immediately after *"when You shall make His soul an offering for sin,"* clearly implied His resurrection; accordingly this is more explicitly stated in what at once follows: *"He shall prolong His days."* The figure is used again in the next verse. *"He shall see of the travail of His soul and be satisfied." "A woman when she is in travail has sorrow because her hour is come. But as soon as she is delivered of the child, she remembers no more her travail, for joy that a man is born into the world"* (John 16:21), considering her sufferings to be more than recompensed by the happy issue of them. So the Redeemer deems Himself richly rewarded for all His pains by the children which are His as the result of His dying travail. He is *"satisfied"* and *"rejoices"* (Luke 15:7) as each one of them is brought forth.

"This seed" which was promised Christ occupies a prominent place in the great Covenant Psalm — the 89th. There we hear the Father saying, *"I have made a covenant with My Chosen, I have sworn unto David My Servant, Your seed will I establish forever"* (vers. 3,4). And again, *"I will make Him My Firstborn, higher than the kings of the earth. My mercy will I keep for Him for evermore and My covenant shall stand fast with Him. His seed will I make to endure forever"* (vers. 27-29). In the verses that follow His *"seed"* are termed *"His children,"* and assurance is given that though they be wayward and the rod be visited upon their transgressions, yet God's covenant faithfulness shall be seen in their preservation (vers. 31-36). In the Cross Psalm it was declared *"A seed shall serve Him, it shall be accounted to the Lord for a generation"* (22:30). It was to be a perpetual seed. *"His name shall be childed as long as the sun"* (Ps. 72:17).

Christ then was assured by the Father from the beginning of the success of His undertaking and promised a seed which should bear His image, serve Him, and show forth His praises. *"I will bring Your seed from the east and gather You from the west. I will say to the north to give up, and to the south keep not back; bring My sons from far and My daughters from the ends of the earth"* (Isa. 43:5,6). Though they are born into this world in a state of unregeneracy, God promised they should be born again and savingly drawn to embrace Christ as their Lord and Saviour. *"Your people* (said the Father to the Mediator — see ver. 1) *shall be willing in the day of Your power, in the beauties of holiness from the womb of the morning You have the dew of Your youth"* (Ps. 110:3). Yet again, Christ is represented as saying *"Behold I and the children whom the Lord has given Me"* (quoted by the apostle of Christ in Heb. 2:13) are for signs and for wonders in Israel, for the Lord of hosts which dwells in mount Zion (Isa. 8:18).

As there are two parts of the covenant so the elect were given to Christ in a twofold manner. As He was to fulfill the terms of the covenant they were entrusted to Him as a charge, but in fulfilment of it the Father promised to

Christ to bestow them upon Him as a reward. The elect are to be regarded, first, as those who were beloved of the Father before time began. They are designated *"God's own elect"* (Greek of Luke 18:9), which signifies both His delight with and singular propriety in them. He chose them before all others: He preferred them above all others, and set His heart upon them. As such the Father gave them to Christ as God-man Mediator — *"set up"* in the Divine councils and therefore having a real subsistence — as a choice expression of His love for Him. Second, they are to be regarded as God foreviewed them under their defection in Adam, and as such God gave them as a charge to Christ to be raised up from all the ruins of the fall, and also as a reward for His work on their behalf. The twofoldness of Truth needs ever to be borne in mind.

Viewed as fallen the elect were given to Christ as a charge for whose salvation He was held responsible. They were committed to Him as *"prisoners"* (Isa. 49:9), whose lawful discharge He must obtain. They were committed to Him as desperate patients, whom He must bind up and heal (Isa. 61:1). They were committed to Him as straying and lost sheep (Isa. 53:6), whom He must seek out and bring into the fold (John 10:16). God placed His elect in the hands of the Mediator and made them His care. How graciously and tenderly He discharged His trust appears in that touching word *"He shall feed His flock like a Shepherd, He shall gather the lambs with His arm and carry them in His bosom, and shall gently lead those that are with young"* (Isa. 40:10,11). It appears again in that wonderful word *"And when He has found it, He lays it on His shoulders rejoicing"* (Luke 15:5). Finally, it was evidenced at the moment of His arrest. *"If therefore you seek Me, let those go their way, that the saying might be fulfilled which He spoke, Of them which You gave Me have I lost none"* (John 18:8,9).

On the fulfilment of His covenant engagement that people were given to Christ as His reward, as the fruit of His travail, as the trophies of His glorious victory over sin, Satan and death, as His crown of rejoicing in the day when all the inhabitants of the universe shall be assembled together, as His beloved and glorious Bride when the marriage of the Lamb is come. In contemplation of this God made certain promises to the Surety concerning them. He promised to bestow upon them the gift of eternal life. *"Paul a servant of God and an apostle of Jesus Christ, according to the faith of God's elect and the acknowledging of the Truth which is after godliness, in hope of eternal life which God, that cannot lie, promised before the world began"* (Titus 1:1,2). As the elect then had no actual existence, that promise must have been made in their name to the Surety. That particular promise virtually included all the benefits which Christ procured for His people, for as *"eternal death"* contains the essence of all evils, so *"eternal life"* contains the essence of all blessings.

"The Lord commanded the blessing, even life for evermore" (Ps. 133:3). *"This is the promise that He has promised us, even eternal life"* (1 John 2:25) — how perfect is the harmony between the Two Testaments! If we break up that promise into its component parts we may say that, first, God promised to regenerate His people or bestow upon them a spiritual nature which delights in His Law: *"I will put My laws into their minds, and write them upon their hearts"* (Heb. 8:10). Second, He promised to justify them, the negative part of which is to remit their transgressions. *"For I will be merciful to their righteousness and their sins and iniquities will I remember no more"* (Heb. 8:12). Third,

He promised to sanctify them. *"I will sprinkle clean water upon you and you shall be clean. From all your filthiness and from all your idols will I cleanse you"* (Ezek. 36:25). Fourth, He promised to preserve them. *"I will not turn away from them to do them good, but I will put My fear in their hearts that they shall not depart from Me"* (Jer. 32:40). Fifth, He promised to glorify them. *"They shall obtain joy and gladness and sorrow and sighing shall flee away"* (Isa. 35:10).

Finally, God made promise of the Holy Spirit to Christ. What we are now to contemplate is admittedly one of the deep things of God and therefore requires to be handled with prayerful concern and godly caution. But if on the one hand we are certain to err should we deviate one iota from the Scriptures, on the other hand it is to the glory of God and His Christ and to the needful instruction of our souls that faith humbly receives all that is revealed to us in Holy Writ. Now Scripture teaches not only that the Spirit of the Lord rested upon Christ (Isa. 11:1,2) during the days of His earthly ministry, that God put His Spirit upon Him to furnish Him for His great work (Isa. 42:10), that He was anointed with the Spirit in order to preach the Gospel (Isa. 61:1) and work miracles (Acts 10:38); Matt. 12:28), but the oracles of Truth make it very clear after Christ received the Spirit in another manner and for a different purpose after His ascension to heaven, namely, that to the God-man Mediator has been given the administration of the Spirit's activities and operations; and this both in the sphere of grace Churchward, and in the spere of providence worldward.

In John 7:39 we read that *"the Holy Spirit was not yet* (given) *because Jesus was not yet glorified,"* but He was both promised to Christ (Ps. 45:7) and by Christ. Let us seek to attentively consider some of His statements concerning the Holy Spirit's relation upon Himself. *"But the Comforter, the Holy Spirit, whom the Father will send in My name"* (John 14:26), the force of which is intimated in *"whatsoever you shall ask the Father in My name He will give it you"* (John 16:23). Again, *"But when the Comforter is come, whom I will send unto you from the Father"* (John 15:26) – which is parallel with Christ's being *"sent"* by Him (John 3:17). And again, *"It is expedient for you that I go away, for if I go not away the Comforter will not come unto you; but if I depart, I will send Him unto you"* (John 16:7). Such repetition argues both the importance of this truth and our slowness to receive it.

To the writer three things are clear concerning the above passages. First, each was spoken by the God-man Mediator, for they were the utterances of the Word made flesh. Second, from John 8:39 and 16:7 it is apparent that the advent of the Spirit was dependent upon the ascension of Christ, Third, from His repeated *"whom I will send unto you"* we learn that in this present era the activities of the Spirit are regulated by the will of the Lord Christ. That the Spirit is at the economical disposal of the Redeemer was evidenced after His resurrection and before His ascension, for to the apostles He said, *"Peace be unto you. As My Father has sent Me, even so send I you,"* and then we are told *"when He had said this He breathed on them and said unto them, Receive the Holy Spirit"* (John 20:22; Gen. 2:7). And as He was on the point of leaving them the Saviour said *"Behold, I send the promise of My Father upon you"* (Luke 24:49), which was duly accomplished ten days later.

In Acts 2, when Peter explained the supernatural phenomena of the day of

Pentecost he said, *"This Jesus has God raised up, of which we all are witnesses. Therefore being by the right hand of God exalted, and having received of the Father the promise of the Holy Spirit, He has shed forth this which you now see and hear"* (vers. 32,33) — the glorified Saviour has poured forth this effusion of the Spirit's gifts. On which the Puritan Thos. Goodwin, after quoting Ps. 45:7 and explaining it by Acts 2:36 and said on ver. 33 "which receiving is not to be only understood of His bare and single receiving the promise of the Holy Spirit for us, by having power given Him to shed Him down upon them, as God has promised, though this is a true meaning of it; but further, that He had received Him first as poured forth on Himself, and so shed Him forth on them, according to that rule that whatever God does unto us by Christ, He first does it unto Christ" (Vol. 4, pg. 121). It was the Saviour's outpouring of the Spirit's gifts which demonstrated He had been *"made both Lord and Christ"* (ver. 36).

From the passages quoted above it seems plain that upon the completion of His covenant work the Father bestowed the Spirit on Christ to administer from His mediatorial throne. In full accord with that we hear the Lord Jesus saying from heaven, *"These things says He that has the seven Spirits of God"* (Rev. 3:1), that is, has to administer the Holy Spirit in the plenitude of His power and the diversity of His manifestations — compare the seven-branched candlestick in Ex. 25:30,31 and the sevenfold gift of the Holy Spirit to Christ in the days of His flesh (Isa. 11:1,2). On the words *"He that has the seven Spirits of God"* (Rev. 3:1) Thos. Scott says, "that is, the Divine Saviour, through whom the Holy Spirit, in the variety and abundance of His precious gifts and graces was communicated to all the churches." So again, in Rev. 5:6 we read *"I beheld and in the midst... stood a Lamb as it had been slain, having seven horns and seven eyes, which are the seven Spirits of God sent forth into all the earth"* (Compare Matt. 28:18). Here it is Christ exercising His governmental power and administering the Spirit toward the world — as in 3:1 it was toward the Church. Thus, if on the one hand none other ever suffered such ignominy as did the Mediator, on the other hand none other ever has received or ever will such marks of honor as He has.

CHAPTER X.

ITS EFFECTUATION.

To refresh your memories we will here epitomise what has been presented in previous chapters. First, we pointed out the distinctions which require to be recognized if confusion is to be avoided. (1) That in connection with reconciliation God acts both as a loving Father and as an inflexible Judge. (2) That His elect are viewed both in the purpose of His grace and under the condemnation of His Law. (3) That they are viewed by Him both in Christ as their covenant-Head and as the depraved descendents of fallen Adam: in the one case as *"His dear children,"* and in the other as being *"by nature the children of wrath"* (4) That though there is no change in God yet there is in His attitude unto and His dealings with them. (5) That God's purpose concerning His elect in eternity and the actual accomplishment of that purpose in a time-state must not be confused. Failure to observe these distinctions has caused many to err in their preaching and writing on this important subject.

Next, we demonstrated the need for reconciliation. Therein we dwelt upon the fearful breach which the entrance of sin made between God and man, the creature casting off all allegiance to his Maker, revolting from his rightful Lord, despising His authority, trampling under foot His commandments. We showed that while the original offence was committed by Adam, yet he was acting as the federal head of his race, and therefore that the guilt and consequences of his transgression are justly imputed to all his descendants. Moreover, they take sides with him by perpetuating his evil course. The life of the unregenerate is one unbroken course of rebellion against God. The consequences of that breach are that fallen man is separated from God, he is an object of abhorrence to God, he is under the wrath of God, he is in bondage to Satan and so under the reigning power of sin that he hates God. Obviously such an one is in urgent need of being restored to His favor and having his vile enmity removed.

Then we saw that the Author of reconciliation is God, and more particularly, God the Father. In the development of which we pointed out that the recovery of His fallen elect proceeds from the good pleasure of His will or *"the eternal purpose which He purposed in Himself."* That gracious design was suggested by none other, and no external motive influenced Him. No necessity was put upon Him to form such a resolution: it was simply His own sovereign design – *"I will show mercy"* Yet it was His own nature which prompted His decision: it originated in the everlasting love which God bore to His elect – a love so great that even their awful sins could not quench nor produce any change in it. Nevertheless, since the Divine holiness was infinitely antagonised by sin, Divine justice required that full satisfaction should be made for the dishonor it had wrought. Nought but Divine wisdom could find a way in which Love and Law were perfectly harmonized and solve the problem of how mercy and justice might alike maintain its ground without the slightest compromise, yea, issue from the conflict honorable and glorious.

Under the last division of our subject we turned our attention to the Divine arrangement for the accomplishment of reconciliation, namely, *"The Everlasting Covenant,"* in which is displayed the Divine perfections in their blessed unity. In that covenant God gave His elect to Christ as a trust or charge, holding Him responsible for their everlasting felicity. In that covenant all the details of the wondrous plan of redemption were drawn up and settled. In that covenant the Father made known unto the Son the terms which He must fulfil and the task He must perform in order to the saving of *"that which was lost;"* while the Son voluntarily concurred therein and gladly consented to carry out its stipulations. In that covenant we have revealed the office which Christ was to assume and the nature of the work He was to do, namely, to serve as the Substitute and Surety of His people in the full discharge of all their obligations unto the Divine Law. In that covenant the Father gave assurance of rendering adequate assistance to the Mediator in the performing of His engagement and the guarantee of the glorious reward upon the successful completion thereof.

We are now to see how the eternal purpose of God was effected, how the mutual engagements of the everlasting covenant were fulfilled. *"When the fullness of time was come, God sent forth His Son, made of a woman, made under the Law, to redeem them that were under the Law, that we might receive the adoption (or "status") of sons"* (Gal. 4:4,5). The *"fullness of time"* means more than that the ordained hour had arrived: it signifies when all the preliminary operations of Divine providence had been completed, when the stage was thoroughly prepared for this unparalleled event, when the world's need had been fully demonstrated. The advent of God's Son to this earth was no isolated event, but the climax of a lengthy preparation. That He was now *"made of a woman"* was the fulfilment of the Divine announcement in Gen. 3:14 and Isa. 7:14. That He was *"made under the Law"* which His people had broken is what supplies the key to that which is otherwise an inexplicable mystery, in fact, throws a flood of light upon the experiences through which He passed from Bethlehem to Calvary.

The very circumstances of Christ's birth at once made unmistakeably manifest that God had sent forth none other than His own Son and clearly intimated the unique mission upon which the Beloved of the Father had then entered. Nothing less than a supernatural birth befitted so august a Person, and such was accomplished by the miraculous conception of His virgin mother, by means of which a *"holy"* humanity became His (Luke 1:35) — a real human spirit, and soul and body, yet without the slightest taint of our corruption. The amazing event of the Incarnation and the Divine dignity of the One who had become flesh was signalized by the appearing again of *"the Shekinah"* (which had left Israel in the days of Ezekiel — 10:4,18; 11:23), for *"the glory of the Lord* (namely, the Shekinah) *shone round about"* the shepherds on Bethlehem's plains, so that they were *"sore afraid;"* and an angel announced to them that the One just born was none other than *"Christ the Lord;"* while suddenly there was with the angel a multitude of the *"heavenly host"* praising God and saying *"glory to God in the highest, and on earth, peace, good will toward men"* (Luke 2:9-14).

But, if what we have just alluded to were clear proofs that God had indeed *"sent forth His Son, made of a woman,"* there were other attendant circumstances which no less plainly intimated (to an anointed eye) that His Son was also *"made under the Law,"* and that, as the Surety of His people, as the One who had entered their Law-place, He must receive what is due them. This has not been sufficiently recognized. In that same second of Luke we read that Mary *"brought forth her firstborn son, and wrapped Him in swaddling clothes and laid Him in a manger, because there was no room for them in the inn"* (v. 7). The force of that is better perceived if it be linked with *"so He drove out the man"* (Gen. 3:24) from Eden, for he had become an outcast from his Maker. Do we not behold then in His exclusion from the inn and birth in a cattle shed a definite shadowing forth of the fact that Christ had vicariously entered the place of His outcast people! In the circumcising of Him on the eight day (v. 21) there was an evident prefigurement that He had been made *"in the likeness of sinful flesh"* (Rom. 8:3). That was unspeakeably solemn, but amazingly wonderful.

A little later it was made evident that the One cradled in the manger was more than human. The wise men saw *"His star in the east"* and came to Jerusalem enquiring *"Where is He that is born King of the Jews?"* That extraordinary star *"went before them until it came and stood over where the young Child was."* Entering the house where He abode, they *"fell down and worshipped Him"* (Matt. 2:11), presenting gifts of gold, frankincense, and myrrh – thus were Divine honors paid Him. Yet immediately after a determined effort was made by Herod to slay Him, as though to show us from the beginning that His life was forfeit and that a death by violence awaited Him! But His hour had not then arrived and Joseph was warned to flee with Him. His sojourn in Egypt was not without significance, for it intimated that as the Surety of His people He had taken His place alongside of them in the typical house of bondage. With what awe and astonishment should we contemplate these things!

What we sought to point out unmistakeably opens up to us the deeper meaning of much that is recorded in the Gospels, supplying the key to the strange mingling of the lights and shadows in the earthly career of our Lord. That key lies in the distinction which must ever be drawn between the adorable Person and the awful place which He took, between the Son of God incarnate and the office He was discharging. Though His essential glory was veiled by flesh, yet that glory frequently broke forth in splendor. Or to put it in another way: God had suffered His Beloved to *"make Himself of no reputation"* in this world, yet He was so jealous of His honor that again and again He afforded proof that the despised One was Immanuel. Thus if Christ – to the amazement of His forerunner – submitted to the ordinance of baptism, yet at that very time the heavens were *"opened unto Him,"* and the Spirit descended like as a dove upon Him and the voice of the Father was heard saying *"This is My beloved Son in whom I am well pleased."*

Yes, the key to the deeper meaning of much in the Gospels is found in keeping before us the distinction between the Person and the place He took. He was the Holy One, but He took the place of His sinful people. As the Holy One ineffable joy, unclouded blessedness, the love and homage of all creatures was His legitimate due. Treading the path of obedience, the smile of God and the ordering of His providences accordingly was what He was justly entitled to. Wisdom's ways are *"ways of pleasantness, and all her paths are peace,"* and Christ ever trod Wisdom's ways without any deviation – why then did He encounter so much unpleasantness and opposition? *"When a man's ways please the Lord, He makes even his enemies to be at peace with him"* (Prov. 16:7), and Christ always pleased Him (John 8:29); yet the Father was far from making His enemies at peace with Him. Why? Ignore the office which Christ had taken (and was discharging from Bethlehem onwards!) and we are left without any possible solution.

"The foxes have holes, and birds of the air have nests; but the Son of man has no where to lay His head" (Matt. 8:20). The real force of that pathetic statement can best be perceived by grasping the meaning of the particular title which the Saviour here employed. It has its roots in the following O.T. passages: *"The stars are not pure in His sight. How much less man that is a worm, and the son of man which is a worm!"* (Job 25:5,6); *"What is man that You are mindful of him, and the son of man that You visit him"* (Ps. 8:4; and cf. 146:3), from which it will be seen that it is a term of abasement and ignominy, expressive of lowly condition. In its application to Christ it connotes not only His true humanity, but also the humiliation and shame into which He descended. It is descriptive of His person, but more especially of His office; in other words, it points to Him as *"the Second Man,"* the *"last Adam,"* and as such, entering our lot, sharing our misery, serving as our Surety. Christ appropriated this title unto Himself as marking His condescending grace and as displaying the condition which He had taken to Himself.

A certain scribe had offered to follow Jesus wherever He went, and *"the Son of man has no where to lay His head"* was His response. It was not only a word bidding him count the cost, but an announcement that His path led to the place where none could accompany Him. It was more than a declaration that He who was rich for our sakes became poor in order to reinstate us: it was an intimation that He had voluntarily subjected Himself to the consequences of sin, that He would therefore be treated as a sinner both by God and by men, that He had entered the place of His disinherited people (driven out: Gen. 3:24) and therefore that He had no claim to ought in this world. *"The Son of man came not to be ministered unto, but to minister, and to give His life a ransom for many"* (Matt. 20:28). Thus it is clear that this *"Son of man"* title contemplates Christ as the humbled One. Confirmatory of this it is the fact that He is never referred to by it after His resurrection, though as *"the Son of man"* He appropriately receives His reward (Dan. 7:13, Matt. 26:64, John 5:27).

Justice demands that each one shall receive his due. Now the Lord Jesus was *"holy, harmless, undefiled, separate from sinners:"* then to what was He lawfully entitled at the hands of a righteous God? Does not the Judge of all the earth do right! then how shall He order His governmental dealings toward the One who eminently honored and glorified Him? Must He not show Himself strong on His behalf? Must He not shower upon Him the ceaseless tokens of His favor? Must He not turn the hearts of all men unto Him in loving homage? Certainly – but for one thing! Though personally holy, yet officially the guilt of His people rested upon Him. In view of Ps. 37:25 how can we possibly account for the righteous One Himself being forsaken by God in the hour of His acutest extremity? Only one answer is possible, and that is furnished by what we have sought to set before the reader.

> "Bearing the shame and scoffing rude
> In my place condemned He stood."

Blessed be God if the reader can, by sovereign grace, respond with us

> "Sealed my pardon with His blood,
> Hallelujah, what a Saviour!"

If we shut our eyes to the solemn fact that the Son of God entered this world charged with the guilt of His people, then are we confronted with the supreme anomaly, the most flagrant injustice of all history. For on the one hand, we have the Personification of all virtue and moral excellency; and on the other, God suffering Him to be traduced as One possessed of a *"demon"* (John 10:20). On the one hand we have the supreme Benefactor of mankind ever going about and doing good, and yet God so ordering His lot that He *"had no where to lay His head."* On the one hand we have Him preaching glad tidings to the poor and binding up the broken hearted, and on the other hand God allowing Him to be so dealt with by those whom He befriended that He cried *"reproach has broken My heart"* (Ps. 69:20). On the one hand we have Him manifested as Love incarnate, yet on the other, God permitting His enemies to vent their bitterest hatred upon Him. In the case of all others we discern the principle of sowing and reaping, of the connection between conduct and the consequences which it righteously entails; but in the case of our Lord there was not, so far as He personally acted and was treated. Yet bring into account the relation which He sustained to His guilty people and the anomaly and seeming injustice vanishes.

Perhaps some readers are inclined to say: I can see why it was necessary for Christ as our Substitute to endure the wrath of God, but I am rather at a loss to understand why He should have to suffer such cruel treatment at the hands of men; true, their vile conduct against the Lord of glory demonstated as nothing else has the fearful depravity of human nature, but why did the Father, under His righteous government of the world, permit His Son to be so unjustly dealt with by Jews and Gentiles alike? Though it was ordained that He should be crucified and slain by wicked hands (Acts 2:23), yet wherein lay the necessity for Him to be so mistreated by His own creatures? and that not only during *"the Passion week"* but throughout the whole course of His ministry? In the light of what we have sought to point out, there should surely be no difficulty at this point: it is only a matter of giving a wider application to that basic and illuminating principle.

As the Surety of His people Christ entered this world charged with all their guilt, and therefore He had to suffer not only for their sins against God but also against their fellows. We have broken both tables of the Law, and therefore the Redeemer must endure the penalty of both. See then in the treatment meted out to Him by men, what we deserve because of our woeful failure to love our neighbor as ourselves. As our Substitute a life of reproach among men was His due. Therefore *"He came unto His own and His own received Him not,"* but instead, despised and rejected Him. Therefore was He, throughout His course, *"a Man of sorrows and acquainted with grief"* subjected to contempt, constantly persecuted by His enemies. The very next verse in Isa. 53 explains why He was the Man of sorrows: *"surely He has borne our griefs and carried our sorrows."* Therefore was the sin-Bearer deserted by all His apostles (Matt. 26:56) as well as forsaken by God.

It is indeed in the closing scenes of *"the days of His flesh"* that we may perceive most clearly Christ occupying the place of His people and receiving both from man and God that which was due unto us. As we view Him before Caiaphas and Herod we must not be occupied only with the human side of things, but look higher and see Divine justice directing all. The Romans were renowned for their respect of law, their equity of dealings, and their mild treatment of those they conquered. Then how shall we account for the conduct of Pilate and his soldiers? and especially, why did God require His Son to be mocked with a trial that appears worse than a farce. Because though personally innocent, He was officially guilty.

CHAPTER XI.

ITS EFFECTUATION

That which is here to engage our attention is the work performed by the Mediator in order to heal the breach between a righteous God and His sinful people and thus effect a mutual reconciliation. This will bring before us the most wonderful, awe-inspiring and glorious events in all the ways and works of God. It will conduct us to ground which is ineffably holy, and on which it becomes to tread with the utmost reverence and circumspection. The work of Christ is absolutely unique, being without precedent or parallel. Nothing whatever can be known about it save that which is revealed on it in Holy Writ. Neither philosophy, science, nor metaphysics can afford us the slightest assistance in the understanding of it. Carnal reasoning concerning it is utterly worthless and highly presumptuous. The great mystery of godliness is made known unto faith. Yet the utmost diligence and earnest prayer for the Holy Spirit's aid are called for in our searching of the Scriptures and in carefully weighing all they make known on the Death Divine, that faith may lack no part of the foundation on which it is to rest and none of the materials on which it is to feed.

In our last we sought to present more or less a general survey of the ground we hope to cover under this particular aspect of our subject. Now we must proceed to more detail. This will require us to examine closely what the Incarnate Son did in order to *"make peace"* between an offended God and His lawbreaking people, which was the relation.Christ bore to them, the character in which He acted in that stupendous undertaking, and what was the office He discharged. It is all important at the outset to recognize that the Person we are to be occupied with was none other than Jehovah's *"Fellow"* (Zech. 13:7), co-essential and co-equal with the Father and the Spirit. Though God the Son took upon Him human nature and became the Son of man, yet in so doing He did not'cease to be a Divine Person. It was the theanthropic (Divine-human) constitution of His person which qualified Him for His mediation, for as the God-man nothing could be too difficult for Him to effect or too great for Him to accomplish. The dignity of His person gave infinite value to His work.

The wrong done by sin unto God was so incalculably enormous and His hatred of the same is so great that only a perfect and infinitely meritorious satisfaction could appease Him, and obviously such a satisfaction could be rendered by none but a person of infinite dignity and worth. Our sins are committed against the infinite Majesty of Heaven and therefore are they infinitely culpable, and unless an atonement of infinite value is made for us, our sins must entail infinite suffering – therefore the punishment of the wicked is necessarily eternal. Sin, so far as it could do so, struck at the very throne of God. It was an act of high treason, a disowning of His authority, an attempt on the part of the creature to overthrow the Divine government. Sin has made such a breach in the order of things appointed by God that no mere creature could possibly repair it – least of all man, for he is the culprit, guilty and defiled. If then the breach is to be healed, God must *"lay help upon One that is mighty"* (Ps. 89:19).

Writing on "The heinousness of human guilt" Jas. Hervey said, "Ten thousand volumes, written on purpose to display the aggravations of my various acts of disobedience, could not so effectually convince me of their inconceivable enormity as the consideration of that all-glorious Person, who, to make an atonement for them, spilt the last drop of His blood. I have sinned, may every child of Adam say; and what shall I do unto you, O You Observer of men? Shall I give my firstborn for my transgression, the fruit of my body for the sin of my soul? Vain commutation, and such as would be rejected by the blessed God with the utmost abhorrence. Will all the potentates, that sway the sceptre in a thousand kingdoms, devote their royal and honored lives to rescue an obnoxious creature, from the stroke of vengeance? Alas, it must cost more, incomparably more, to expiate the malignity of sin and save a guilty wreth from Hell. Will all the principalities of Heaven be content to assume my nature and resign themselves to death for my pardon? Even this would be too mean a satisfaction for inexorable Justice, too scanty a reparation of God's injured honor.

"So flagrant is human guilt that nothing but a victim of infinite dignity could constitute an adequate propitiation. He who said 'Let there be light, and there was light,' let there be a firmament, and immediately the blue curtains floated in the sky; He must take flesh, He must feel the fierce torments of crucifixion and pour out His soul in agonies, if ever such transgressors are pardoned." There could be no satisfaction for the sinner without atonement, for God has declared He "will by no means clear the guilty" (Ex. 34:7). Equally evident is it that no atonement can be made by the violator of God's Law, for he can neither provide reparation for past offences — being a moral bankrupt, devoid of any merit; nor render perfect obedience in the present — being a depraved creature. God's Law requires righteousness of character before it will receive righteousness of conduct, and therefore a fallen creature is utterly disqualified to render acceptable obedience. The Law will not compound with our sinfulness by modifying its holy requirements. "Pay that which you owe" is its unchanging demand.

After what has been pointed out it should be quite clear that first, in order to save His people from their sins the incarnate Son of God must serve as their Substitute, acting in their stead and rendering satisfaction to the Law for them. By substitution is meant the transference of obligation from those who incurred it to One who willingly shouldered the same in their stead. The substitutionary death of Christ means far more than that He died for the benefit of all who savingly believe in Him. It signifies that He entered their Law-place and received what was due them and that through His sacrificial death He so expiated their sins that nothing can be laid to their charge, that they stand "unblameable and unreproveable" in God's sight (Col. 1:22). "He was wounded for our transgressions, He was bruised for our iniquities; the chastisement of our peace was upon Him, and with His stripes we are healed" (Isa. 53:4). "For Christ also has suffered for sins, the Just for the unjust, that He might bring us to God" (1 Pet. 3:18).

Though there is no parallel to the greatest transaction in all history, though there is no analogy to the relations sustained to God and to His people in any of the relations of mere creatures to one another, yet God has graciously adapted a series of types, historical and ceremonial, to the illustration of His grand plan of redemption and to adumbrate various aspects of the office and work of Christ, and in them the wisdom of God is signally displayed. Of the first person to whom the Holy Spirit ascribes faith it is recorded that, "Abel offered unto God *a more excellent sacrifice than Cain, by which he obtained witness that he was righteous"* (Heb. 11:4). Cain brought of the fruit of the ground (the product of his own toil) an offering unto the Lord, but unto it He *"had not respect."* But Abel brought *"of the firstborn of his flock and the fat of it"* — showing it had been slain. Realizing that death was his due, but that God graciously accepted a substitute in his place, he put a bleeding lamb between his sinful self and the Holy God.

The same elementary yet fundamental truth was taught the Hebrews on that most memorable night in their history. Jehovah had declared, *"about midnight will I go out into the midst of Egypt, and all the firstborn in the land of Egypt shall die"* (Ex. 11:4,5). Sufficient attention had not been paid to the words *"all, in."* There were to be no exceptions: the firstborn sons of Israel equally with the Egyptians were to be slain. But though no exception was made, a difference was drawn: a substitute was provided for the former, though not for the latter. The Israelites were bidden to take a male lamb, without blemish, to slay it, and sprinkle its blood on the posts of their doors, and the Lord promised, *"when I see the blood, I will pass over you"* (Ex. 12). The angel of death entered not their houses, for judgment had already been executed there, the Lamb being slain as the substitute. In the light of that we are to understand *"Christ our Passover is sacrified for us.'* (1 Cor. 5:7).

But it was in the wilderness, after the Levitical priesthood was appointed and the tabernacle had been erected, that the Lord taught His people more fully the grand truth of pardon and cleansing, acceptance and blessing, through a substitute. A wide field of study is here opened to us, but we can only now briefly mention its outstanding lessons. First, in the unblemished animal required for sacrifice, God showed His people the perfections of the substitute in the room of their imperfections. Second, in their being required to bring such an offering, the claims of God were enforced. Third, in the words *"he shall put his hand upon the head of the burnt offering, and it shall be accepted for him to make atonement for him"* (Lev. 1:4) there was an identifying of the offerer with his offering. Fourth, on the great day of atonement, Aaron was required to *"lay both his hands upon the head of the live goat, and confess over him all the iniquities of the children of Israel and all their transgressions in all their sins, putting them upon the head of the goat"* (Lev. 16:21), thereby a transfer of guilt being signified.

Fifth, an Israelite was not only required to furnish the offering, but *"he will kill the bull before the Lord"* (Lev. 1:5) was the order: in this way he acknowledged that death was his own due and proof was furnished of God's displeasure against sin. Sixth, *"and there came fire out from before the Lord and consumed upon the altar the burnt offering and the fat: which when all the people saw, they shouted, and fell on their faces"* (Lev. 9:24 and compare 1 Kings 18:38; 2 Chron. 7:1). In that fire we see the holy wrath of the Judge consuming the victim in the sinner's room. Seventh, *"And a man that is clean will gather up the ashes of the heifer, and lay them up without the camp in a clean place, and it will be kept for the congregation of the children of Israel for a water of separation. It is a purification for sin"* (Num. 19:9). "In the ashes we have the proof that the wrath had spent itself, that the penalty was paid, that the work was done. *'It is finished'* was the voice of the ashes" (H. Bonar). Thus was God's mercy expressed in a righteous way.

The main thing to grasp in connection with the sacrifices to which we have all too briefly alluded is, that they were not eucharistic but expiatory - not tokens of thanksgiving, but vicarious oblations. The animal or bird was put in the place of the one who brought it and is termed an *"offering unto the Lord for his sin"* and it would *"make an atonement for him concerning his sin"* (Lev. 5:6). It was then, a subsititutionary sacrifice, slain in the stead of the offerer, to signify what he deserved and by which he was personally saved from undergoing the penalty. It was literally and specifically a life for a life, a life devoted to God in sacrifice. *"For the life of the flesh is in the blood, and I have given it to you upon the altar to make an atonement* (a propitiation or appeasement) *for your souls. It is the blood that makes an atonement for the soul"* (Lev. 17:11). Therefore did God enjoin upon His people *"No soul of you will eat blood"* (v. 5), it was to be held sacred by them.

Should it be asked, Why did God appoint the slaying of animals, the bringing of so many costly offerings to His altar, which were so frequently repeated? The answer is simple and conclusive, though it may be stated in a variety of ways. It was to signify that, in the purpose of God, the antitypical Lamb was slain from the foundation of the world. It was to inform His people that they must look outside themselves for salvation. It was thus to keep before them a continual reminder of His righteousness and what sin called for at His hands. It was to educate men for *"the good things to come"* by shadowing forth the great sacrifice. It was to furnish the N. T. saints with an infallible dictionary, for if we would understand the language which Christ and His apostles used in connection with the Sacrifice of Calvary we must needs define the terms employed by the grand Antitype by the meaning they obviously bear in the types – as 1 Cor. 5–7 is to be interpreted in the light of Ex. 12.

It is the light of the Levitical offerings we should read *"the Gospel of Isa. 53"* and regard the N. T. references to the atoning sacrifice of our Saviour. Who can fail to see that the words *"The Lord has laid on Him the iniquities of us all"* (Isa. 53:6) look back to *"Aaron shall lay both his hands on the head of the live goat and confess over him all the iniquities of the children of Israel...and the goat shall bear upon him all their iniquities unto a land not inhabited"* (Lev. 16:21,22), and that *"who His own self bear our sins in His own body on the tree"* (1 Pet. 2:24) is an echo of the same language. When we read that *"Christ died for our sins according to the Scriptures"* (1 Cor. 15:3) are we not to regard the reference as being both the types and the prophecies of the O.T. When we are told that *"while we were yet sinners, Christ died for us"* (Rom. 5:8) can it signify anything else than, that as a sacrificial offering was slain in the stead of the offerer, so Christ endured the penalty which our sins call for!

It needs to be insisted upon that the death of Christ was something more than an unparalleled act of benevolence, enduring crucifixion for the good of others. It was a penal death, in which He vicariously endured the penalty of the Law in the stead of others. The suffering of martyrs for the good of their cause, of patriots for their country, of philanthrophists for mankind, are not *"vicarious"* for they are not substitutionary. Vicarious suffering is suffering endured in the place of others. Christ's sufferings were vicarious in precisely the same way that the death of animals in the O. T. sacrifices was in lieu of the death of the transgressors offering them. While in many passages of the N. T. the Holy Spirit has used the Greek *"huper"* which is rendered *"for"* yet in Mark 10:45 He has employed the decisive *"anti."* He gave his life a ransom for (*"anti"* – in the stead of), many. In Matt. 2:22 *"anti"* is rightly rendered *"in the room of."* Compare Matt. 5:38, Luke 11:11, Rom. 12:17 where *"anti"* is rendered *"For."*

But does not the substitutionary sufferings of Christ·raise a difficulty even in the minds of the reverent. Let us face it squarely and state it frankly. Was it altogether just that an innocent person should suffer in the stead of the guilty? At the back of many minds there lurks the suspicion that, though it was amazing grace and surpassing love which gave the Lord of glory to die for poor sinners, yet was it not, strictly speaking, a breach of equity? Was it right that One who perfectly honored God and illustriously magnified His Law by a flawless and perpetual obedience, should have to suffer its penalty and endure its awful curse? To answer, It had to be. There was no other way of saving ßs, supplies no direct answer to the question. It is merely arguing on the jesuitical basis that *"the end justifies the means."* Far better to remain silent in token of our ignorance than thus to sully the character of God. But such a suspicion is groundless and such ignorance causeless as we hope to yet show.

To say that sin must be punished that the penalty of the broken law could not be revoked, is but to repeat what Scripture clearly affirms. But to draw the conclusion that therefore an innocent Substitute had to be penalized in the Stead of the guilty is to impeach the Divine justice. Every regenerated person must feel that it had been infinitely better for the whole of Adam's race to have suffered eternally in Hell, rather than that God should act unrighteously in delivering His people from there. Such a thing could not be, for God *"cannot deny Himself"* that is act contrary to His own perfections. *"The Lord is righteous in all His ways and holy in all His works"* (Psa. 145:17), and most certainly the greatest and grandest of His works, that which supremely manifested and promoted His glory, is no exception to that rule. He has declared Himself to be *"a just God and a Saviour"* (Isa. 45:21) and never was His justice more gloriously displayed than at the Cross.

Of old the question was asked, "Who ever perished being innocent?" (Job 4:7) and surely we may unhesitatingly reply, No one ever did under the righteous government of God. He who *"will by no means clear the guilty"* (Ex. 34:7) will by no means afflict the innocent. Startling as it must sound, it was not the innocent whom the sword of Divine justice smote at Calvary. And this brings us to say, second, in order to be our Saviour Christ had to act as the Substitute of His people, and in order to be their Substitute He first assumed the office of Surety. As their Surety, as their legal Representative, Christ took upon Him their legal obligations - as the husband assumes the debts of the woman he marries. The guilt of His people's sins were charged to Christ's account, and therefore justice legally and righteously exacted payment from him. Though personally innocent, Christ was officially guilty when He suffered *"the Just for the unjust."* Much remains yet to be said but here we must stop.

CHAPTER XII.

In our last we showed, first, that in order to satisfy the requirements of Divine justice the incarnate Son was *"made under the Law"* and that the work He did and the sufferings He endured in order to heal the break between an offended God and His offending people was performed and undergone by Him while acting as their Substitute. Then, second, in the concluding paragraphs we briefly pointed out that in order to be the Substitute of His people Christ had taken upon Him the office of Suretyship. It is of great importance that we should be quite clear upon the latter, for much harm has been done by novices who have grievously misrepresented the Atonement by their crude and carnal conceptions, and the cause of Truth has been much injured by their unwarrantable attempts to illustrate the central fact of the Gospel from supposed analogies in human relations. It cannot be insisted upon too emphatically that the plan of redemption, the office sustained by Christ, and the satisfaction which He rendered to the claims of Justice against us, have no parallel in the relations of men to one another.

But how often has a popular preacher pictured a criminal, in whose character was no relieving feature, condemned to death for his aggravated crimes. While lying in the condemned cell, or perhaps as he stands upon the scaffold itself, the reigning monarch is supposed to send his or her own son and heir to die in the villain's stead, and then turn him loose on society. Such a monstrous supposition has frequently been offered as an illustration of the amazing fact that *"God so loved the world that He gave His only begotten Son, that whosoever believes in Him should not perish, but have everlasting life."* Not only is that imaginary illustration a gross misrepresentation of the Truth, but it is utterly revolting to serious minds and those who love righteousness. It is, too, a horrible degrading of the Gospel and a denial of the uniqueness of the Atonement. The Atonement carries us far above the sphere of the highest relations of created beings into the august counsels of the eternal and incomprehensible God, and it is nothing but a species of impiety for us to bring our petty line to measure counsels in which the *"manifold wisdom"* of Omniscience is contained.

Here as everywhere in connection with the things of God, spiritual things must be compared *"with spiritual things"* (1 Cor. 2:13) and not with carnal. One part of the Truth must be interpreted by – not drawing upon our imagination, but – by another part of the Truth. It is only in the light of the Word itself – our hearts being opened to receive the same – that we can see light. It is only as *"we speak, not in the words which man's wisdom teaches but which the Holy Spirit teaches"* that we can accurately express the grand mysteries of our Faith. Now the term *"Surety"* is one of the words the Holy Spirit has used of Christ Himself to enable us to understand the better the relation He sustained toward those on whose behalf He transacted and the special office He discharged for their sakes. Now a *"surety"* is one who is legally obligated to answer for another. A *"surety"* is one who undertakes for another or for others and who thereby makes himself responsible to render what is due from them or to suffer what is due to them.

"I have done judgment and justice. Leave me not to my oppressors. Be Surety for your servant for good. Let not the proud oppress me." (Psa. 119:121, 122) In like manner we find the godly Hezekiah praying, *"O Lord, I am oppressed. Be*

Surety for me." Is. 38:14 — the Hebrew rendered *"undertake for me"* is the same as translated *"be Surety for me"* in Ps. 119:122. Thus, in each instance believers made a request that the Lord would not barely bestow some favor on or confer some privilege on them, but do so under the particular character of a *"Surety."* By addressing themselves unto their Deliverer under that character it is clear they had knowledge that He had agreed to act in this office for His people. Since the O.T. saints, equally with the N.T. ones, were to benefit from the mediatorial work of the incarnate Son, they were not left in ignorance of the grand truth that He was appointed by the Father, and by His own consent, to serve as the Surety of His people.

On Ps. 119:122, John Gill pointed out, "What David prays to God to be for him, that Christ is for all His people. He drew near to God, struck hands with Him, gave His word and bond to pay the debts of His people. He put Himself in their law-place and stead and became responsible to Law and Justice for them. He engaged Himself to make satisfaction for their sins and bring in everlasting right-eousness for their justification, and to preserve and keep them and bring them safe to eternal glory and happiness, and thus was being a *'Surety for good'* for them." It is worthy of special notice that this particular verse wherein the Lord is besought to act as *"Surety"* is the only one in the 176 of this Psalm wherein the Word of God is not mentioned under the name of *"Law" "Command-ments," "statutes," "judgments"* etc., thereby intimating that Christ as the Surety of His people met all their obligations and thereby fulfilled the Law in their stead.

In the O.T. is found a most striking and blessed type of N.T. teaching on this subject, and, as we might expect, it is found in connection with its initial occur-rence. It is an almost if not an entirely unvarying rule that the first mention of anything in Scripture more or less defines its meaning and scope — from the way in which it is employed and the connections in which it is found — and forecasts it's subsequent significance. Such is the case here. When seeking to persuade Jacob to allow his beloved Benjamin to accompany his brethren on their journey into Egypt, Judah said, *"Send the lad with me. . . I will be surety for him, of my hand shall you require him. If I bring him not unto you, then let me bear the blame forever."* (Gen. 43:8,9). That was no idle boast on the part of Jacob's son, as the sequel shows, for he remained true to his promise, though God intervened and spared him from actually fulfilling his trust.

The reader will remember how that Joseph's cup was found in Benjamin's sack while they were returning home with the sorely-needed grain and how the whole company went back to Egypt and were brought before its governor. Joseph said, *"The man in whose hand the cup is found, he shall be my servant, and as for you, get you up in peace unto your father."* Whereupon Judah interposed and after explaining the situation in a most touching way, declared, *"Thy servant became surety for the lad to my father saying, if I bring him not unto you, then I shall bear the blame of my father forever. Now therefore, I pray you, let your servant abide instead of the lad a bondman to my lord, and let the lad go up with his brethren."* (Gen. 44:17,18,32,33). Equally beautiful is the sequel and equally striking in completing the type: *"Then Joseph could not refrain him-self. . . he kissed all his brethren and wept upon them, and after that his brethren talked with him* " (Gen. 45:1,15).

It seems strange that no writer – of the many we are acquainted with – has made any attempt to *"develop"* this blessed evangelical picture and bring out the wondrous details of the type. First, observe the occasion of this incident. It was a matter of life and death, when Jacob and his household were faced with the prospect of starvation, that this proposal was made (Gen. 43:1-8). In like manner, unless Christ has interposed as the Surety of His people they had received the wages of sin. Second, it was not Reuben, Jacob's firstborn, but Judah who offered to act as *"bondman"* for Benjamin. Surely it is not without Divine design that in the only chapter in the N.T. where Christ is specifically designated *"Surety"* we are therein reminded that *"our Lord sprang out of Judah "* (Heb. 7:14,22). Third, it is to be particularly noted that this office was not compulsorily thrust upon Judah, but that he freely and voluntarily assumed it, as did the antitypical Surety.

Fourth, let it also be duly observed that it was not for one unrelated to him but for his own brother that Judah proposed to serve – with which should be linked *"he that is surety for a stranger shall smart for it "* (Prov. 11:15). Fifth, it was in order to satisfy his father that Judah proposed to act. This at once refutes the error of the Socinians on Heb. 7:22. Christ was not God's Surety unto us, rather did He serve as the Surety of His people to satisfy the justice of His Father. This is made very clear in the type: *"your servant became surety for the lad unto my father."* Sixth, the nature of suretyship is here clearly defined, namely, serving as a bondman in the room of another, discharging his obligations, *"let your servant abide instead of the lad a bondman to my lord "* (Gen. 44:33). Seventh, the result of this typical suretyship was that reconciliation was effected between Joseph and his estranged brethren. So the antitypical Surety secured reconciliation between an estranged God and his alienated people.

How very much better, then, is it to take our illustrations of any aspect of Divine Truth from the Word itself, rather than draw upon our imagination or stoop to human history for incidents which supply no analogy! They must indeed be devoid of spiritual vision who fail to see in what has been brought out above a truly remarkable foreshadowment of the Suretyship of Christ. If any regard as 'far fetched' the seven details to which we have called attention, they are to be pitied. It is true that at the last moment God intervened on Judah's behalf, as He did on Isaac's when his father had bound him to the altar and took a knife to slay him – God accepting the will for the deed. Yet just as surely as Abraham *"received Isaac in a figure"* from the dead (Heb. 11:19), so did Judah in a *"figure"* and literally so in intention, serve as surety for Benjamin. That God interposed both in Abraham's and Judah's case, exempting them from finalizing their intentions, only serves to emphasize the contrast that He *"spared not His own Son "* (Rom. 8:32).

That which is most relevant to our present subject is the result obtained by Judah's suretyship, namely, healing the breach which had for so long obtained between Joseph and his brethren – the type turning from Judah's relation to his father and the bringing in of Joseph and its effect upon him, being parallel to the type in Gen. 22 turning from Isaac, the willing victim on the altar, to the *"ram"* caught in the thicket and being slain in his stead. For many years Joseph had been separated from his brethren and they alienated in spirit from him. When they came into his presence the first time, he *"made himself strange"* to them and *"spake roughly to them"* (Gen. 42:7) – as God did to us through His Law prior to our conversion. Though the heart of Joseph yearned toward them, he made not himself known to them. It was not until Judah stepped forward as the surety of Benjamin that everything was changed. *"Then Joseph could not refrain himself"* (45:1) and reconciliation was at once effected!

Now it is in the light of all that has been before us above that we are to interpret that blessed declaration *"By so much* (as the Melchizedek priesthood excelled the Levitical) *was Jesus made a Surety of a better testament"* or *"covenant"* (Heb. 7:22) – the contrast being not between an inferior *"surety"* and Christ, but the more excellent covenant. Christ is the Surety provided by the Everlasting Covenant, which was administered under the O.T. era (the *"old covenant"*) beneath shadows and figures, but now (in this N.T. era) under the *"new covenant"* His Suretyship is fully revealed in its actual and historical fulfilment. The typical case of Judah exhibits every essential feature of the Suretyship of Christ and the more clearly it is fixed in our minds the better shall we be able to understand the Antitype. As the Surety of His people Christ undertook to yield that obedience to the Law which they owed and to make reparation to Divine justice for their sins – to discharge their whole debt both of obedience and suffering.

"God did not mince the matter and say, Son, if you will take flesh and die by the hands of wicked men, I will pardon all you die for, for your sake, and you will have an easy task of it. It shall be only enduring the corporeal pains of death, which thousands have undergone in a more terrible manner. But God says this, *'If you will be their Saviour, you must be their Surety. You must pay all the debt of doing the Law and suffering for the breach of the Law. You must bear all their sins. You must suffer all their direful pains of body and soul, all the terrors and horrors due to them for sin from the wrath of God. I will make their sins fall on you with all the weight which would press all the elect into the vengenance of Hell-fire forever,'* Those are the terms. Hard enough indeed, but if sinners be saved by My free grace in giving you for them, My righteousness and holiness must be satisfied and glorified. Do you have such a love to My glory and to their poor souls as to undergo all that for them? Yes, said our blessed Lord. I am content, Lo, I come to do your will, O God." (S. Crisp 1691).

Third, we have seen that in order to be our Saviour Christ had to be our Substitute. We have shown that to legally act as our Substitute He had to take upon Him the office of Surety. We now push our inquiry still further back, and ask, What was it that justified the Holy One serving as our Surety and the government of a righteous God taking vengeance upon Him for our sins? Not until we obtain the Scriptural answer to this question do we arrive at bed-rock and find a sure foundation for faith to rest upon – such a foundation as none of the sophistical reasonings of the carnal mind can shake, and against which the objections of scepticism are shattered into nothing, like the spray of the sea as its proud waves spend themselves upon the granite cliff. Nor do we have far to seek if we attend closely to Heb. 7:22 federal relationship or covenant oneness is what makes manifest the righteousness of the Great Transaction. There is reciprocal identification between the covenant-Head and the Covenantees. Christ transacted for His people because He was one with them.

That Christ acted as the covenant-Head or federal Representative of His people is clear from 1 Cor. 15:45 and 47, where He is designated *"The last Adam"* and *"the second Man,"* the one expression explaining the other. Christ was not *"the second man"* in order of time and number, for such was Cain, but He was in the sense that He sustained the same relation to His people as the first man did to the whole of his posterity. As the margin of Hos. 6:7 shows, God made a *"covenant"* with the first Adam, in which he acted and transacted for all his natural seed as their legal head and representative, and therein was *"the figure of Him that was to come"* (Rom. 5:14), for Christ acted and transacted for all His spiritual seed as their legal Head and Representative. Thus in that sense there have been but two men who have sustained this special relation to others before the Divine Law: that each served as a public person, and that thereby a foundation was laid for the judicial consequences of the acts of each to be righteously charged to the account of all for whom each stood.

It has been well said that "The Atonement is founded upon the unity of Christ and His people, with whom He took part in flesh and blood " (Jas. Haldane). It is indeed true that all mankind are partakers of flesh and blood, but Christ *"took part"* only with the children whom God had given Him. This is brought out very clearly in the language of Heb. 2. *"For both He that sanctifies and they who are sanctified are all of one, for which cause He is not ashamed to call them brethren "* (v. 11). And again, *"Behold I and the children which God has given Me. For as much as the children are partakers of flesh He also Himself likewise took part of the same. . . He took on Him the seed of Abraham"* — not of Adam *"Therefore: in all things it behoved Him to be made like unto His brethren "* (vers. 13,14,15,17). It was that unity between the Sanctifier and the sanctified which laid the foundation for Christ to *"make reconciliation"* (or rather) *"propitiation for the sins of the people "* (ver. 17).

Under human governments there may be expedients by which the innocent are penalized in order that the guilty may escape, but such a device and arrangement is impossible under the righteous government of God. "Such is the perfection of the Divine government that under it no innocent person every suffered and no guilty person ever escaped" (Jas. Haldane 1847). It was not that a stranger, unrelated to the elect, had imposed upon Him their obligations, but that the Head of the body of which they are members — and the unity of the head and the members of our physical body (when any member suffers it is registered in the brain, and when the head is severed all the members at once die) is no closer than of Christ and His people (see Eph. 5:32). Just as every member of the human race has been made responsible for the original offence of the first Adam, so Christ is made responsible for the offences of His people and suffered accordingly. Furthermore, they themselves (legally considered) suffered in Him and with Him.

"Were it not for the unity of Christ and His people, justice, instead of being magnified, would have been violated in His substitution. However great the dignity of the sufferer, however deep his voluntary humiliation, it would have been no atonement for us. In order to purge our sins, in order to ransom His Church, Christ must so entirely unite Himself with His people, that their sins should become His sins, that His sufferings should be their sufferings, and His death their death" (*"The Atonement"* by Jas. Haldane). And this is indeed what took place.

Christ not only bore our sins in His own body on the tree, but each believer can say, *"I am crucified with Christ"* (Gal. 2:20). Christ not only suffered for us, but we suffered in Him, for we were legally one with Him. He was substituted for us, because He was and is one with us and we are one with Him.

CHAPTER XIII

In seeking to show what Christ did in order to effect reconciliation between God and His people two methods of presentation were open to us – each warranted by the analogy of Scripture. To begin with the work of Christ as it is usually apprehended by us, working back to its ordination by God; or to start with the Divine appointment and trace out the progressive accomplishment of the same on the plane of human history. In the last three articles we followed the former plan. Now, to aid the reader still further, we will reverse the process. Under our fifth main division we saw how that a Covenant was entered into between the Father and the Son, in which everything necessary for the redemption of His elect was mutually agreed upon and settled; here we are to contemplate what was actually done in fulfilment of that covenant engagement.

First, having agreed to become the Mediator or Daysman between God and His people, the Beloved of the Father became incarnate. Oneness of nature was indispensable, for there must be a conjunction effected between the Redeemer and the redeemed if He was to be identified with those on whose behalf He acted. Accordingly, *"He took not on Him the nature of angels, but He took on Him the seed of Abraham"* (Heb. 2:16) that He might have a right of property in us as Man as well as God. In Gal. 4:4,5 we are told that the Son became incarnate *"to redeem them that were under the Law."* By the law of Israel the right of redemption belonged to him that was next of blood (Lev. 25:25; Ruth 2:20). It was by being made like His brethren that Christ acquired the human and legal title to pay the ransom-price for His Church.

The obedience of man to the Divine Law is that to which *"life"* is promised (Matt. 19:17; Rom. 7:10). An angel's obeying in our stead would not have been the establishment of the original law, nor could life for men be claimed as the reward of angelic obedience. By man came death, and consequently, by man must come the resurrection from the dead (1 Cor. 15:21,22). It was essential that the Son of God should become incarnate and be in full possession of our humanity that He might obey the Law and bring in everlasting righteousness for His people. It was His becoming flesh which laid the foundation for the imputation of our liabilities unto Christ and His merits, obedience, and sufferings unto us.

Second, in becoming incarnate the Son of God *"took upon Him* (voluntary action!) *the form of a servant"* (Phil. 2:7) – God's Servant, but on our behalf. That service consisted of His entering into the office of Surety. "Suretyship is a relation constituted by covenant engagement, by which parties become legally one so that they can be dealt with as such in law" (J. Armour). Or to state it in other words, a surety is one who gives security for another that he will perform something which the other is bound to do, so that in case of the failure of the first party he will perform it for him. It was His natural union with His people that made possible and proper Christ's federal oneness with them. Thus, Christ as *"the Surety of the covenant"* came under obligation to perform the condition of the covenant in lieu of and behalf of His elect.

It must be carefully borne in mind that the Covenant was made with the covenantees (the saints) in the person of their Head. Thus when Christ came forth as the Surety of the covenant He appeared as the Representative of His people, assuming their liabilities and discharging their responsibilities, making satisfaction for their sins and bringing in an everlasting righteousness, and that in such a way that the Law was *"magnified and made honorable"* (Isa. 42:21) and that He (and His people in Him) became entitled to the award of the Law. We shall devote a disproportionate space to this essential point.

Third, in becoming our Surety Christ engaged to do all that was necessary in order to restore His people unto the favor of God and to secure for them the right of everlasting felicity. The first of those engagements or terms was His meeting the original and righteous demands which God made of them and in Adam under the Covenant of Works, namely, to render in their place perfect and perpetual obedience to the Divine Law. The second of those terms was that He should endure the penalty of the Law which they had broken, and this He did when He was *"made a curse"* for them and suffered the wrath of God on their behalf. From the first Adam the law demanded nothing but full conformity to its precept, but from the last Adam it necessarily demanded not only holy obedience but also penal suffering, that He might atone for our sins and blot out our iniquities.

It has been rightly pointed out that "In the original institute the whole substance of moral obedience was summed up in the single precept, relative to the fruit forbidden. As the Law is a unity, and he who offends in one point is guilty of all; so when the spirit of obedience is tested in a single point only, and confined to that point, a failure here, brings upon man the guilt of the whole – he is liable to the whole penalty. Now this was the sum total of the Law, as a covenant given to Adam, that he should obey, and as the reward of obedience should receive life. This glorious reward was held up as the motive prompting to choice on the side of law and right. The law was ordained unto life (Rom. 7:10). This is its object, and to this it was adapted. But it failed in the hands of the first Adam, and the last Adam comes in to make it good, to establish its principle and secure its object." (G. Junkin, on *"Justification."*)

When Christ appeared as the Surety of His people it was with the affirmation *"Lo, I come, to do Your will, O God"* (Heb. 10:7). Note well the word to *"do"* God's will (before He suffered His wrath for our sins) – to *"do"* what the first Adam failed to perform. The fundamental nature of God's government must needs have been changed had He granted to men *"life"* on any other terms than what He had presented under the Covenant of Works, and to which man agreed. The Gospel contains no substitute for the Law, but reveals that remedial scheme by which is confirmed and made good the principles of righteousness originally laid down by God to Adam. *"Do we then make void the Law through faith* (in the gospel)? *God forbid. Yea,* (is the triumphant answer) *we establish the Law"* (Rom. 3:31).

The unchanging terms of the Covenant of Works is *"This do* (obey the Law) *and you shall live"* (Luke 10:28). And since I have broken the Law and am incapable of keeping it, then *"life"* – the reward of the Law – could never be mine unless the Surety had *"this"* done on my behalf. Therefore was He *"made under the Law"* for His appointed and agreed-upon task was not only to *"make an end of sins"* but also to *"bring in everlasting righteousness"* (Dan. 9:24), that is, a justifying righteousness for the whole election of grace. The Lord Jesus freely consented to pay His people's debts, both in making satisfaction to the Law which they had broken and in rendering perfect obedience in their stead. That *"righteousness"* Christ was working out for us from the moment of His birth until upon the cross He cried *"It is finished."*

In executing the great work of our redemption and reconciliation the incarnate Son paid homage to the Divine Law. He was not only *"made under"* it, but as He declared *"Your Law is within My heart"* (Ps. 40:8) - enshrined in His affections, and His whole life was one of complete subjection to it. Christ as the Sin-bearer and Sin-expiator only gives one side of His work. The other is His holy obedience – the two together furnishing us a complete view of the satisfaction which He rendered to God. Christ's obedience was equally the work of the One for the many, the Head for His body, and equally essential as His death. His first recorded utterance *"Do you not wish that I must be about My Father's business!"* (Luke 2:49) shows clearly that He had entered this world on a special errand, that He was engaged in a specific work unto the Father, that He owed obedience to Him – as the *"must"* plainly intimates.

His first utterance on emerging from His private life struck the same note. When presenting Himself for baptism John demurred, for to comply made Christ appear to be a sinner, for it was *"the baptism of repentance for the remission of sins"* (Luke 3:3). But it was not as a private person Christ presented Himself, but as *"the Lamb of God which takes* (or *"bears"*), *away the sin of the world"* (John 1:29-31). To His forerunner's objection the Saviour replied, *"Suffer it to be so now, for thus it becomes us to fulfil all righteousness"* (Matt. 3:15). The *"now"* is emphatic in the Greek. Now that I have *"made Myself of no reputation,"* now that I am discharging My suretyship. It *"became"* Him to fulfil His engagement. As the One obeying for the many (*"us!"*) it was requisite that He *"fulfil the righteousness"* – submit to God's positive, institutions or ordinances as well as the moral Law.

In His first public address Christ declared *"Think not that I am come to destroy the Law or the Prophets. I am not come to destroy, but to fulfil"* (Matt. 5:17). Those words supply us with a clear-cut definition of His mission and the character of the work in which He was engaged. In what way did He *"fulfil"* the Prophets? Why, by doing those things which they had foretold – such as preaching good tidings (Isa. 61:1) and healing the sick (Isa. 35:4-6) – and by suffering the indignities and pains which they had announced. In precisely the same way He *"fulfilled"* the Law, namely, by rendering the obedience which its precepts required, and by enduring the punishment which its penalty demanded. The grand end of the incarnation was that Christ should provide for His people a righteousness which excelled that of the scribes and pharisees (Matt. 5:20).

"To satisfy both the requirements of His justice and the abundance of His mercy, God determined that a full satisfaction should be made unto His Law, and such a satisfaction that it was in that way more honored than if it had never been broken, or the whole race damned. In order to do this He appointed that Christ should serve as the Substitute and Surety of His people. He must stand as their Representative and fulfil all righteousness for them and endure the curse in their stead, so that they might be legally reckoned to have obeyed and suffered in Him" (Thos. Goodwin, Puritan). Accordingly we find Christ saying *"My meat is to do the will of Him that sent Me and to finish His work"* (John 4:34). The single principle that guided His holy life was obedience to God. In this way He not only left us an example to follow, but was working out for us a righteousness to be imputed to our account and by which we are justified and entitled to the reward of the Law. Calvary was not the beginning but the end of His life of perfect obedience – as the *"unto death"* of Phil. 2:8 testifies.

Fourth, God transferred the sins of His people and placed them upon their Surety the moment He assumed the office. *"The Lord has laid on Him the iniquities of us all"* (Isa. 53:6). Not experimentally, but legally; not the corruption of them, but the guilt; not that He was defiled by them, but that He became subject to their penalty. The sins of His people were charged to the account of the Holy One. So truly was this the case that He acknowledged the actuality of it crying, *"For innumerable evils have compassed Me about. My iniquities have taken hold upon Me"* (Ps. 40:12); and again, *"O God, You know My foolishness, and My sins are not hid from You"* (Ps. 69:5). That was the language of the Surety, as the context clearly shows.

Fifth, because Christ entered this world charged with the guilt of His people, Divine justice dealt with Him accordingly – as was shown under the first article on Christ effectuating reconciliation as our 'Substitute. Because Christ had shouldered the awful burden of His people's sins, He must be paid sin's wages. Because the Just had so united Himself to the unjust, He must suffer *"the due reward of their iniquities."* He must, accordingly, be wounded for our transgressions and bruised for our iniquities. The chastisement of our peace must be upon Him, if by our His stripes we are to be healed (Isa. 53:4,5). It was fore-announced *"He shall bear their iniquities"* (v. 11) and iniquities and guilt are inseparable, and since guilt signifies liability to punishment, Christ must be penalized in our stead. O that this article may be so blest to some reader that he may, for the first time, be able to truly say:

"Upon a life I did not live, upon a death I did not die – Another's life, Another's death, I rest my soul eternally."

Sixth, because Christ was *"made sin"* for His people (2 Cor. 5:21) He was *"made a curse"* for them (Gal. 3:13) – that curse consisted of the avenging wrath of God. The Sinbearer was *"numbered with the transgressors"* (Isa. 53:12). The august dignity of Christ's person did not avail to any abatement of the Divine curse. God *"spared not His own Son"* (Rom. 8:32). So far from sparing Him, the Judge of all the earth, the moral Governor of this world, the Administrator of law cried, *"Awake O sword, against My Shepherd, and against the Man that is My Fellow, says the Lord of hosts. Smite the Shepherd"* (Zech. 13:7). Though He had done no violence, neither was any deceit in His mouth, yet it *"pleased Jehovah to bruise Him. He has put Him to grief"* (Isa. 53:9,10). The wages of sin is death, and as physical death consists of the severance of the soul from the body so spiritual death is the separation of the soul from God, and on the cross Christ was forsaken by God.

We must therefore look higher than the *"band of men and officers"* as the servants of the chief priests and pharisees sent to apprehend Christ in the Garden, and see in them the agents of Divine justice, though they knew not what they did. We must needs direct our eyes above the Roman soldiers as they *"plaited a crown of thorns and placed it on Christ's head"* and see in them the executives of the Divine Law, branding our Surety with the marks of the curse (see Gen. 3:17,18). We are required to exercise the vision of faith and behold in

Caiaphas, Herod and Pilate doing *"whatsoever God's hand and counsel determined before to be done"* (Acts 4:28) in order that the terms of the Everlasting Covenant should be carried out, the requirements of righteousness satisfied, the holy wrath of God appeased, and the sins of His people forever removed from before Him, *"as far as the east is from the west."*

Seventh, because Christ rendered full satisfaction to Divine justice, He redeemed His people unto Himself, and they are not only absolved from all guilt but are reconciled to God. Not only are they no longer under the frown of the Divine Judge, but His smile rests upon them. Not only are they freed from His displeasure, but they are restored to His favor. Not only do they stand *"unblameable and unreproveable in God's sight,"* but they have an inalienable title to everlasting felicity. There cannot be a substitution without a dual imputation. If the debt of the debtor is charged to the surety, then upon his discharge of the same the payment of the surety must be credited to the debtor. Accordingly we are told, *"For He has made Him* (legally) *to be sin for us who knew no sin, that we might be made* (legally) *the righteousness of God in Him"* (2 Cor. 5:21) – there is the counter-imputation. Christ's righteousness is reckoned to the account of His people.

"As by one man's disobedience many were made sinners (legally constituted so, and then as the consequence, experimentally became such) *so by the obedience of One shall many be made* (legally constituted so, and then as the consequence, experimentally become such) *righteous"* (Rom. 5:19). Christ took our place that we might take His. Christ removed our sins that we might be clothed with His merits. Because Christ kept the Law for us, we are entitled to *"reign in life"* (Rom. 5:17). *"The Forerunner is for us entered into Heaven"* (Heb. 6:20). Observe well how Christ demanded this as His legal right. *"Father, I will that they also whom You have given Me, be with Me where I am"* (John 17:24). I have fully discharged their obligations, I have wrought out for them an everlasting righteousness, now give them that which, for My sake, they are justly entitled to.

"The moment the believing sinner accepts Christ as his Substitute, he finds himself not only cleared from his guilt, but rewarded – he gets all heaven because of the glory and merits of Christ. The Atonement we preach is one of absolute exchange. It is that Christ took our place literally, in order that we might take His place literally – that God regarded and treated Christ as the sinner, and that He regards and treats the believing sinner as Christ. From the moment we believe, God looks upon us as if we were Christ. He takes it as if Christ's atonement had been our atonement, and as if Christ's life had been our life; and He beholds, accepts, blesses, and rewards on the ground that all Christ was and did is ours" (G. S. Bishop *"Doctrines of Grace"*). What a glorious Gospel! Then proclaim it freely and boldly ministers of Christ.

From all that has been pointed out it should, we think, be more or less clear to the simplest reader that the breach between God and His sinning people has been righteously healed. That is to say, reconciliation has been effected in a way both gracious and legal. To have brought this suit into the court of Divine Law had availed nothing unless provision had been made for so ordering its process and judgment that the sinner might be honorably accepted and that God might be both *"just and the Justifier of him which believes in Jesus"* (Rom. 3:26). The Law must be on the sinner's side. His absolver and not his condemner, his justifier and not his accuser. That provision has been made by means of the Surety-Substitute, by the transference of total indebtedness from those who incurred it to One to incurred it not and fully discharged the same.

It is by the principle and on the ground of Suretyship and Substitution that God's justice is displayed in all His transactions with the believing sinner. It is this which is the climateric in the good news proclaimed by the heralds of Christ. The grand Evangel not only exhibits the knowledge-surpassing love of God, but as the apostle declares *"therein is the righteousness of God revealed."* Grace indeed reigns, but it does so *"through righteousness"* (Rom. 1:17; 5:21). "Christ bears the sins of many because in His covenanted identification with those *'many'* their sins are sinlessly and truly His. And unto the many sons and daughters of the covenant, the Father imputes the righteousness of the Son, because, in their covenant oneness with the Son, His righteousness is undeservedly but truly their own righteousness. And all throughout *'the judgment of God is according to truth'* and equity" (H. Martin, on *"The Atonement"*). Thus we behold once more that, at the cross, Mercy and Truth met together, Righteousness and Peace have kissed each other (Ps. 85:10). It is not a peace at any price, a peace wherein justice is sacrificed and the law is flouted, but a righteous peace, one that glorifies all the Divine perfections. Such is the wondrous and blessed message of the Gospel.

CHAPTER XIV.

ITS MEANING

It may seem strange to some that we have deferred until now a consideration of the meaning of *"reconciliation,"* and to the critical reader it must appear as a real defect. Ordinarily a writer should define the terms which he uses at the beginning of his treatise, but in this case we wish to do very much more than furnish a mere definition of the word itself. Under the present division of our subject we desire to consider·more closely and definitely the thing itself. We have dwelt upon the need of reconciliation, its Author, its arrangement, and its effectuation, now we must describe more particularly what reconciliation actually is, as it concerns both God and His people. The previous chapters have been paving the way for this, and in measure furnishing materials for the same, and after what has already been presented the reader should be able to follow more easily our present discussion than if we had introduced it at an earlier stage, as it also relieves the writer from taking anything for granted. It is on the foundations already laid we now propose to build.

It is also because that what we are to be engaged with concerns the more controversial aspect of our theme, that we sought to first make clear and establish from Scripture what must be regarded as the essential elements which into the equation. In seeking to ascertain more precisely the nature and character of reconciliation we must carefully distinguish between cause and effect, between the means and end. Many are confused at this point, supposing that *"atonement"* and *"reconciliation"* are one and the same – the sound of the English word *"at-one-ment"* leading· them to miss its true sense. Unfortunately this confusion is fostered by the only verse in the Authorized Version of the N.T. where it occurs: *"by whom* (namely, Jesus Christ) *we have received the atonement"* (Rom 5:11) – unhappily few avail themselves of the marginal alternative (generally the better rendition) where it is rightly given as *"reconciliation."* To speak of our *"receiving"* the Atonement does not make sense, for it was God and not ourselves who required an atonement or satisfaction, but it is correct to say that believers "receive" the reconciliation which Christ effected for them.

To *"atone"* is to placate or appease, to make reparation for injury or amends for wrong done another. *"Atonement"* simply signifies that a satisfaction has been made, that the demands of the Divine Law have been met, that justice has been honored, that God has been propitiated. The literal force of the Heb. *"kaphar"* (generally rendered atonement in the O.T.) is a *"covering,"* and thus its appropriateness for this usage is clear – the sacrificial blood covered what was an affront to the offended eye of God by means of an adequate compensation. The term is applied to the *"mercy-seat"* which was the lid or cover of the ark of the covenant – and therefore a Divinely-appointed symbol closely connected with the presentation of sacrifices on the day of expiation. Thus there can be no objection to rendering *"Christ Jesus: whom God has set forth a mercy-seat through faith in His blood"* (Rom. 3:25) so long as its purport be explained and the *"blood"* be duly emphasized.

The principal idea, then, expressed by the word *"kaphar"* – *"atonement"* is that of averting vengeance by means of a placating offering. It is rendered *"appease"* in Gen. 32:20. When Jacob was about to make the dreaded meeting with Esau, he sent his servants with droves of animals before him, saying, *"I will appease ("kaphar") him with this present that goes before me!"* In Num. 16:31 it is written, *"He shall take no satisfaction (no "kaphar") for the life of a murderer which is guilty of death. But he shall surely be put to death,"* which again helps us to ascertain the force of this most-important Heb. word, the word *"satisfaction"* meaning, of course, a legal compensation — none such being allowed in case of murder. Vengeance must take its course. *"Moses said unto Aaron, Take a censer and put fire in it from off the altar and put on incense, and go quickly unto the congregation and make an atonement for them, for there is wrath gone out from the Lord, the plague is begun"* (Num. 16:46) — here we see that *"atonement"* was plainly the means for propitiating Jehovah, for turning away His vengeance.

Now such was the Atonement made unto God by the Lord Jesus Christ. His sacrifice was offered for the satisfying of Divine justice, for the averting of Divine wrath from His people. God sent His Son to be *"the propitiation for our sins"* (1 John 4:10). The judicial displeasure of God was turned away from His Church by means of the substitutionary interposition of the Lamb, who was slain in their stead. The righteous vengeance of God was appeased by the Surety, pouring out His soul unto death. Certain effects or results followed from that. The sins of God's elect were blotted out, they were redeemed from the curse of the Law, God was reconciled to them. The Atonement was the cause, the means, the root; reconciliation was the effect, the end, the fruit. Thus the two things are clearly distinguished and should never be confounded. The very fact that the N.T. employs two entirely different words (*"hilasmos"* 1 John 2:2; 4:10 and *"katallage"* Rom. 5:11) shows plainly they are not the same — the latter resulting from the former.

It is a pity that the honorable translators of the A.V. did not always preserve that important distinction. Another verse which has served to cloud the judgment of English readers is Heb. 2:17, where we are told the Son became incarnate that *"He might be merciful and faithful High Priest in things pertaining to God, to make reconciliation for the sins of the people,"* which is correctly rendered (as Owen and others of the Puritans long ago insisted that it should be) in the R.V. that is, *"make propitiation for the sins of the people."* Because Christ made propitiation for their sins, the wrath of God was turned away from them and reconciliation was the outcome: *"having made peace through the blood of His cross"* (Col. 1:20) sums it up, and shows both the end and the means by which it was accomplished. That our English word *"at-one"* signifies to reconcilie and not to *"propitiate"* is evident from Acts 7:26 — *"Moses would have set them at one again"* that is, restore them to amity — the Greek word being rendered *"peace"* elsewhere.

But at this point we need to be careful in guarding against a misconception and the drawing of a wrong conclusion. While the atonement of Christ was an appeasement, it must not be regarded as an inducement. That is, as a price which the Redeemer had to pay in order to incline God to love His people. Yet it is right here that the enemies of the Gospel have made their main attack upon that aspect of it which we are now considering. They have accused those who maintain the Scriptural doctrine of propitiation in order to reconciliation as denying the Divine benevolence, as arguing that Christ shed His precious blood in order to induce God to love sinners, that those who insist God required an appeasing sacrifice before He would be gracious unto transgressors, are guilty of grievously misrepresenting the Divine character. But Socinians are the ones who wretchedly pervert the teachings of sound theologians when they charge them with portraying the cross of Christ as the means of changing God from a merciless Tyrant into a benevolent Being.

Socinians grievously wrest the Truth when they argue that those who proclaim the propitiatory character of Christ's death teach that His death wrought a change in God, that He produced a different feeling within Him with regard to sinners. So far from that, the very men who have most faithfully and fearlessly magnified the ineffable holiness of God in its antagonism against sin and His inexorable justice in punishing it, have been the ones who also made it crystal clear that love to sinners, a determination to save His people from the curse of the Law, existed eternally in the Divine mind, that it was the love of God for His Church, His compassion for its members, which moved Him to devise and execute the plan of salvation and to send His beloved to save them by making an atonement for their sins. Christ the Atoner was provided and given by the Father for His people! It was at His own tremendous cost – by not sparing His Son, but delivering Him up for them all – that the Father supplied that very compensation which His holiness and justice demanded.

We must not for a moment suppose that the atonement was in order to change the good-will of the Father toward those on whose behalf it was offered. No, He gave His elect – the objects of His everlasting and unchanging love – to the Son, and He gave the Son of His love to and for them. All that we owe unto Christ we owe unto God who gave Him. *"Thanks be unto God for His unspeakable Gift."* Nevertheless, the atonement was essentially necessary in order that God's love might flow to them in an honorable channel; that, so far from the glory of God being tarnished by their salvation, so far from His evidencing the slightest complicity in their sin, every Divine attribute might be placed in a more conspicuous view. So that in clothing His Church with the everlasting righteousness of His Son and adorning them with all the beauties of holiness, unto the enjoyment of an exceeding, even eternal weight of glory, God might appear *"glorious in holiness, fearful in praises, doing wonders"* (Exod. 15:11) – let it be noted that verse is taken from Israel's song of redemption (v. 13) after the destruction of their enemies at the Red Sea.

Nowhere does the love of God shine so illustriously as at the Cross. To die for a friend is the highest instance of love among mankind – an instance but rarely found. But God commends His love to men in that while they were sinners, Christ died for them – died for those who were *"alienated and enemies in their mind by wicked works"* (Col. 1:21). This is the most amazing feature of it. It may then be reasonably inferred that God loves whatever is lovely; but it may with equal certainty be inferred that whatever is unamiable displeases Him. Human reason, then, could never have discovered a way in which sinners should be the proper objects of Divine love. But the Scriptures reveal how God's wisdom found a way by which He has made the loathsome objects worthy of His love! In the atoning death of Christ all their pollutions are washed away, and in His perfect righteousness they stand graced before God with all the merits of their Surety – more worthy than the highest of the holy angels.

So far from teaching that the atonement of Christ was the procuring cause of God's love unto His people, we emphatically insist that God's love for them was the moving cause of giving Christ to suffer and die for them, that their sins might be atoned for. It is not that there was insufficient love in God to save sinners without the death of His Son, but that He determined to save them in such a way as gloriously exhibited His righteousness too. The love of God wrought in a way of holiness and justice. He did not choose to receive sinners into His favor without giving public expression to His detestation of their iniquities, but, as the entire universe will yet learn, cried, *"Awake O sword against My Shepherd and against the Man that is My Fellow says the Lord of hosts, smite the Shepherd"* (Zech. 13:7), so that *"He might be just and the Justifier of him that believes in Jesus"* (Rom. 3:26). God's love triumphed at the cross, yet not at the expense of Law! Let the reader judge, then, whether the Socinian or the Calvinist furnishes the most Scriptural and blessed exhibition of the Divine character and government.

The main objection made by those who formally reject the Atonement is, that it is inconsistent with the love of God. God needed nothing, they say, but His own goodness to incline Him to show mercy unto sinners, or if He did, it could not be of grace, since a price was paid to obtain it. But in the light of what has been pointed out above it should be quite evident that such an objection is utterly pointless, confusing the moving cause of mercy unto sinners with the manner of showing it. The sacrifice of Christ was not the cause but the effect of God's love. The love of God was amply sufficient to have pardoned the vilest sinner without any atonement, had God deemed it consistent with the holiness of his character and the righteousness of His government. David was not wanting in love for his son Absalom, for *"his soul longed to go forth unto him,"* but he felt for his own honor as the head of the family and the nation, which, had he admitted him immediately to his presence, would have been compromised and the crime of murder connived at. Therefore, for a time he kept him at a distance, and when introduced, it must be by a mediator.

As Winslow so sublimely expressed it: "It is a self-evident truth that, as God only knows, so He only can reveal His love. It is a hidden love, veiled deep within the recesses of His infinitude, yea, it seems to comprise His very essence, for *'God is love.'* Not merely loving and lovely, but love itself, essential love. Who, then, can reveal it but Himself? *'In this was manifested the love of God toward us, because that God sent His only-begotten Son into the world that we might live through Him. Herein is love, not that we loved God, but that He loved us and sent His Son to be the propitiation for our sins'* (1 John 4:9,10). But behold God's love! See how He has inscribed this glorious perfection of His nature in letters of blood drawn from the heart of Jesus. His love was so great that nothing short of the death of His beloved Son could give an adequate expression of its immensity.

'God so loved the world that He gave His only begotten Son, that whosoever

believes in Him should not perish, but have everlasting life' (John 3:16). Here was the great miracle of love. Here was its most stupendous acknowledgment — here its most brilliant victory — and here its most costly and precious offering. *'Herein is love:'* as though the apostle would say *'and nowhere but here.'* That God should punish the (intrinsically) Innocent for the guilty — that He should exact His co-equal Son to cancel the guilt of rebels — that He should lay an infinite weight of wrath on His soul, in order to lay an infinite value of love on ours — that He should sacrifice His life of priceless value for ours, worthless, forfeited and doomed — that the Lord of glory should become the Man of sorrows — the Lord of life should die and the Heir of all things be as *'He that serves.'* O the depths of love unfathomable! O the height of love unsearchable! O the length and breadth of love unmeasureable! O the love of God which passes knowledge!"

"Great is the mystery of godliness" is the Spirit's own express declaration. Therefore the finite mind, especially in its present condition (impaired by sin and clouded by prejudice) must expect to encounter features that are beyond its comprehension. Nevertheless, it is both our privilege and duty to receive all that Holy Writ reveals on it and beg God for a spiritual understanding of the same, and refuse to reject any aspect of the Truth, because, we no doubt, are unable to perceive its harmony with some other aspect. The Scriptures plainly teach that the Atonement of Christ was an appeasement of the wrath of God against His people, yet they are equally clear in making known that the Atonement was not made as an inducement of the love of God unto His people. The Saviour did not shed His blood in order to procure God's love for His Church, rather, was God's gift of the Redeemer the supreme expression of His love for it. The Atonement appeased the wrath of God in His official character as the Judge of all; the love of God is His good-will unto the elect as the covenant God and Father of our Lord Jesus Christ.

CHAPTER XV.

In our last chapter we pointed out the needs-be for and the importance of making a clear distinction between the Atonement and reconciliation, that the sacrifice of Christ was the cause and the means of which reconciliation was the effect and end. Some theologians, and good ones too, have demurred against terming the offering of Christ a *"means,"* insisting that it was the procuring cause of our salvation. The fact is, it was both a means and a cause according as we view it in different relations. It was the meritorious cause of re-instating us in the favor of God and of procuring for us the Holy Spirit; the means by which God's mercy is exercised in a way of justice. *"Being justified freely by His grace through the redemption that is in Christ Jesus"* (Rom. 3:24). It may be regarded as a mean or medium in respect of the originating cause: thus grace is presented as the source from which it sprang, the redemptive work of Christ the channel by which it flows. In Heb. 9:15 Christ's death is expressly termed the *"means."*

Some may be inclined to chafe at the *"distinctions"* we frequently call attention to, considering we are too prone to confuse the minds of the simple by introducing *"theological niceties."* But did not the apostle pray that the Philippian saints might be moved by God to *"try things that differ."* We rather fear that such disrelish of these distinctions is a sign of mental slovenliness and spiritual slothfulness. Is it of no significance, or of no importance to us, to take notice of the fact that while the Scriptures speak of *"the wrath of the Lamb"* and of the *"wrath of God"* being upon both the nonelect and elect in a state of nature, they never once make reference to *"the wrath of the Father!"* If any of our readers sneer or shrug their shoulders at that as a mere *"splitting of hairs,"* we are very sorry for them. God's Word is made up of words, and it behooves us to weigh every one of them attentively. If we do not, we shall obtain little more than a blurred impression rather than a clearcut view of the Truth.

The work of Christ was indeed one and indivisible, nevertheless, it is capable of and requires to be viewed from various angles. For that reason, among others, the typical altar was not round but *"foursquare"* (Ex. 27:1). The nature of Christ's work was fourfold in its character: being a federal work – as the Representative of His people, a vicarious work – as their Surety and Substitute, a penal work – as He took their Law-place, a sacrificial work – offering Himself unto God on their behalf. The work of Christ accomplished four chief things. It propitiated God Himself, it expiated the sins of His people, it reinstated them in the Divine favor, and it estated them an everlasting inheritance of glory. There is also a fourfold consequence of Christ's work so far as His people are concerned. The guilt of their transgressions is cancelled so that they receive remission of sins; they are delivered from all bondage – redeemed, they are made legally and experimentally righteous; all enmity between God and them is removed – they are reconciled.

In our last we also exposed the sophistry of the Socinian contention that if the propitiatory character of Christ's sacrifice be insisted upon, then we repudiate the uncaused love and free grace of God. We sought to show that while the shedding of Christ's blood was an appeasement of the Divine wrath against God's people, it was not an inducement of His love unto them. Thus, in the latter half of our foregoing chapter we dealt more with the negative side in showing what the oblation of Christ was not designed to accomplish, namely, to procure God's good will unto sinners. Now we must turn to the positive side and point out what the Atonement was designed to effect. We need to be constantly on our guard against exalting the wondrous love of God to the deprecation of His ineffable holiness. If on the one hand it is blessed to continually bear in mind that never has there been such love as the love of God — so pure, so intense, so satisfying; it is equally necessary not to forget there has never been a law like unto the Law of God — so spiritual, so holy, so inexorable.

Divine love unto sinners originated reconciliation, but the Divine Law required that love to flow in a righteous channel. The method which it has pleased God to employ is one in which there is no compromise between love and law, but rather one where each has found full expression. At the cross we see the exceeding sinfulness of sin, the spotless purity of the Law, the unbending character of God's government, and the righteous outflow of His mercy unto Hell-deserving transgressors. The same conjunction of Divine light and love appears in connection with our receiving blessings in response to Christ's intercession, as is clear from His words, *"I say not unto you that I will pray the Father for you, for the Father Himself loves you"* (John 16:26,27) — which was to assure us that we not only have the benefit of Christ's prayers but the Father Himself so loves us that that alone is sufficient to obtain anything at His hands. Think not that the Father is hard to be exhorted and that blessings have to be wrung from Him by My supplications. No, they issue from His love, but in an honorable way, and that we may appreciate them the more.

But in our day it is necessary to consider reconciliation more from the standpoint of God's holiness and justice, for during the last two or three generations there has been an entirely disproportionate emphasis on His love. While it is true that at the cross we behold the highest expression of God's love to sinners, yet it is equally true that there we also witness the supreme manifestation of God's hatred of sin, and the one should never be allowed to crowd out or obscure the other. The apostle hesitated not to affirm that God *"set forth* (His Son) *to be a propitiation through faith in His blood, to declare* (or demonstrate) *His righteousness"* (Rom. 3:25) — observe well how those words *"to declare His righteousness"* are repeated in the very next verse. If the question is asked, Why did God give His Son to die for sinners rather than have them to perish in their sins? the answer is, Because He loved them. But the answer to: Why did He give His Son to be a propitiation for sinners rather than save them without one? is Because He loved righteousness and hated iniquity.

To any who have followed us closely through these chapters up to the present point it should be quite clear, we think, that they err gravely who contend that reconciliation is entirely one-sided, that it is sinners who need to be reconciled to God, that in nowise did God require reconciling to His people, seeing that He changes not, that He loves them with an everlasting love, and that it was entirely His good-will and benevolence which provided the Atonement for them. Yet since it is at this very point that so many have departed from the Truth, we must labor it and enter into more detail. It is sin which has caused the breach between the Holy One and His fallen creatures, and since He was the One wronged and injured by sin, surely it is self-evident that reparation must be made unto Him for that offence and outrage. Why, every passage in which *"propitiation"* occurs is proof that God needed to be reconciled to sinners, that His wrath must be averted before peace could be made.

It is of first importance to recognize that *"reconciliation"* necessarily implies alienation, and that both reconciliation and alienation connote a relationship between God and us. Alienation signifies that a state of enmity and hostility exists between two parties, reconciliation that the cause and ground of the alienation has been removed, so that amity now obtains between them. It is therefore essential that we define carefully and accurately the changed relationship between God and His people which was brought about by the entrance of sin. Though the everlasting objects of God's eternal favor have been chosen in Christ from all eternity and blest with all spiritual blessings in Him, nevertheless the elect (in Adam) apostatized from God, and in consequence of the Fall fell under the curse of His Law. Considered as the Judge of all, God became antagonistic to them; considered as fallen creatures (what they were in themselves) they were by nature enmity against Him. The entrance of sin into this world brought the Church into a condition of guilt before the Holy One, yet because of the Lamb being slain in the purpose of God, the Father's love never ceased unto His people, without any injury unto His justice.

There could be no thought of reconciliation between a holy God and a polluted rebel until full satisfaction had been made to His broken Law. Sin raised a barrier between God and us which we could in no wise surmount. *"Your iniquities have separated between you and your God, and your sins have hid His face from you"* (Isa. 59:2). Sin resulted in alienation between God and man. This was made unmistakably plain right after the Fall, in Eden itself, for we are told, *"God drove out the man: and He placed at the east of the garden of Eden cherubim, and a flaming sword which turned every way, to keep the way of the tree of life"* (Gen. 3:24). Let it be carefully remembered that God was not there dealing with Adam simply as a private person, but as the federal head of the race, as the legal representative of all his posterity – both of the elect and the non-elect. The *"flaming sword"* was emblematic of the vindictive justice of God. The natural man as such was excluded from Paradise and effectually barred from the tree of life. That it turned *"every way"* precluded any avenue of approach.

The reconciliation must be mutual because the alienation was mutual. Christ had to remove God's wrath from us, as well as our sins from before God. If God were not reconciled to us, it would avail us nothing to lay aside our enmity against Him. The fact that the flaming sword *"turned every way"* to bar man's access to the tree of life signified that by no effort of his could the sinner repair the damage which his capital offence had wrought, and declared in the language of the N.T. that *"they that are in the flesh cannot please God"* (Rom. 8:8). By nature we are *"the children of wrath"* (Eph. 2:3), and by practice *"alienated and enemies in our mind by wicked works"* (Col. 1:21), and unless peace be made and reconciliation effected we should neither have any encouragement to go to Him for mercy nor any hope for acceptance with Him. The throwing down of the weapons of our rebellion would avail nothing while we were obnoxious to the curse of the Divine Law. How then shall we be delivered from the wrath to come is thus the all-important question, for His wrath is *"revealed from heaven against all ungodliness and unrighteousness of men"* (Rom. 1:18).

The fallen sons of men have not only removed themselves to a guilty distance from God, but He has judicially and morally removed Himself from them. *"The Lord is far from the wicked"* (Prov. 15:29). And men have wickedly departed from Him, God has righteously withdrawn from them, and thus the distance is mutual, and ever increasing. While Adam remained obedient, his Creator admitted him to near communion with Him, as is intimated by His *"walking in the garden in the cool of the day;"* but when he transgressed the commandment, He withdrew His favor and thrust him out of Paradise. Had no Atonement been provided there had never again been any communion with God – any more than there is between Him and the fallen angels. This awful state of distance from God is still the condition of all the unregenerate – elect or non-elect, the interposition of Christ availing them not while they continue rejecting Him, as is made unmistakably plain by *"he that believes not the Son shall not see life, but the wrath of God abides on him"* (John 3:36).

While they remain in a state of nature the elect, equally with the non-elect lie under the guilt of sin and the condemnation of the Law, and are therefore obnoxious to God – considered as the moral Governor and Judge of all. "God hates sinners as they hate Him, for we are children of wrath from the womb, and that wrath abides on us till we enter into God's peace; and the more wicked we are, the more we increase His wrath. *'He is angry with the wicked every day'* (Ps. 7:11); they are under His curse. Whatever be the secret purposes of His grace, yet so they are by the sentence of His Law, and according to that we must judge of our condition" (Manton vol. 13, p. 257). So too, J. Owen: "Reconciliation is the renewing of friendship between parties before at variance, both parties being properly said to be reconciled, even both he that offended and he that was offended. God and man were set at distance, at enmity, and variance by sin, man was the party offending, God offended, and the alienation was mutual on every side" (*"The Death of Death"* chap. 6, 2nd para.).

But how may God be said to love or hate believers before their reconciliation since He is the Author of it? Let us give a condensation of Charnock's reply. "First, God loves them with a love of purpose or election, but till grace be wrought in them not with a love of acceptation. We are within the love of His purpose as we are designed to be the servants of Christ, but not within the love of His acceptance till we are actually His servants – *'He that in these things serves Christ is acceptable to God'* (Rom. 14:18). They are alienated from God while in a state of nature and not accepted by God till in a state of grace. There is in God a love of good-will and a love of delight. The love of good-will is the root, the love of delight is love in the flower. The love of good-will looks upon us as afar off, the love of delight is itself in us, draws near to us. By peace with God we have access to Him, by His love of delight He has access to us. God wills well to them before grace, but is not well pleased with them till grace.

"Second, God does hate His elect in some sense before their actual reconciliation. (A) Not their persons, though He takes no pleasure in them, neither their persons nor services. (B) But He hates their sins. Sin is always odious to God, let the person be what it will. God never hated, nor ever could, the person of Christ, yet He hated and testified in the highest measure His hatred of those iniquities He stood charged with as our Surety. He hates the sins of believers, though pardoned and mortified. (C) God hates their state. The elect before conversion are in a state of enmity, of darkness, of slavery, and that state is odious to God, and makes them uncapable while in that state to *'inherit the kingdom of God'* (1 Cor. 6:9-11). The state of the elect before actual reconciliation is odious because it is a state of alienation from God. Whatever grows up from the root of the old Adam cannot be delightful to Him. (D) God hates them as to withholding the effects of His love. His frown rather than His smile is upon them."

In Eph. 2 the apostle informs us how this mutual alienation is removed, namely, by Christ *"Having abolished in His flesh the enmity, even the law of commandments contained in ordinances, for to make in Himself of twain one new man, so making peace, and that He might reconcile both unto God in one body by the cross, having slain the enmity by that means"* (vers. 15,16). As Owen pointed out, "It is evident the reconciliation here mentioned consists in slaying the enmity so making peace. Now what is the enmity intended? Not that in our hearts to God, but the legal enmity that lay against us on the part of God." This passage will come before us again when we consider the scope of reconciliation, suffice it now to point out while vers. 14,15, refer to that which was effected between believing Jews and Gentiles, ver. 16 has in view that which relates to God Himself, and as Owen well pointed out this enmity of God against Jews and Gentiles alike was a legal one, that which the Divine Law entailed.

"And having made peace through the blood of His cross to reconcile all things unto Himself. . . and you, that were sometime alienated and enemies in your mind by wicked works, yet now has He reconciled in the body of His flesh through death, to present you holy and unblameable and unreproveable in His sight" (Col. 1:20-22). Since *"peace"* was made, there must have been enmity or hostility, and since the peace was made *"through the blood of His cross"* then the shedding of it was in order to the placating of God, by offering a satisfaction to His outraged Law. Thus, when theologians use the expression *"a reconciled God"* they signify that a change in His relationship and attitude toward us has been effected, from one of wrath to favor. It is the removal of that estrangement which was produced by our offence. In consequence of His atonement Christ has pacified God toward all who believe and brought them to God. Our reconciliation unto God is the same thing as our conversion, when we surrendered to His just claims upon us, and in heart desired and purposed to forsake all that is opposed to Him.

CHAPTER XVI

In our last chapter we pointed out that reconciliation is an attitude or relation, and dwelt upon the fact that it is a mutual affair. This is so obvious that it should need no arguing, yet since so many have denied that God required to be reconciled unto sinners, we must perforce dwell upon it. Where one has wronged another and a break ensues between then, then just as surely as *"it takes two to make a quarrel"* so it takes two for a friendship to be restored again. If the one who committed the injury confesses his fault and the other refuses to accept his apology and forgive him, there is no reconciliation effected between them; equally so if the injured party be willing to overlook the fault, desiring peace at any price, yet if the wrong-doer continues to bear enmity against the other, the breach still remains. There must be a mutual good-will before a state of amity prevails. That holds good in connection with God and His sinning creatures.

We dwelt upon the fact that the entrance of sin brought about a changed relationship between God and man. Since Adam stood as the federal head of the race and transacted as the legal representative of all his posterity, when he fell, the whole of mankind apostatised from God. In consequence of the fall, all mankind came under the curse of the Law, and therefore the elect equally with the non-elect are *"by nature the children of wrath, even as others"* (Eph. 2:3). Loved by God with regard to His eternal good-will, but born under His wrath in regard of His Law and its administration — let those words be carefully pondered. *"Accepted in the Beloved"* (Eph. 1:6) from all eternity, yet entering this time-state under Divine condemnation. Holy and without blame in Christ by election, yet guilty and depraved in ourselves by sin. We must distinguish, as Scripture does, between how God viewed His people in Christ in the glass of His decrees, and how He regards them as in Adam, participating in the consequences of his transgression and continuing in sin by their own course of constant rebellion against Him until they are regenerated.

"There is therefore now no condemnation to them which are in Christ Jesus" (Rom. 8:1) clearly implies that before they came to be *"in Christ Jesus"* the elect were under condemnation. As Rom. 5:18 declares *"by the offence of one judgment came upon all men to condemnation."* If it is asked, But were not the elect *"in Christ"* from all eternity? The Answer is, In one sense yes, in another sense no. *"In Christ"* always has reference to union with Him. The elect were mystically united to Christ, being *"chosen in Him before the foundation of the world"* (Eph. 1:4), yet until that decree is actualized, they are *"without Christ"* (Eph. 2:13). At regeneration the elect are vitally united to Christ: *"he that is joined to the Lord is one spirit"* (1 Cor. 6:19 and 2 Cor. 5:17). Therefore Paul speaks of those who *"were in Christ before me"* (Rom. 16:7). Having been brought from death unto life, the elect embrace the Gospel offer and become fiducially united to Christ (*"fiducial"* is from the Latin *"fido"* to trust) for they then savingly *"believe in Him"* (John 3:15). *"But He that believes is not condemned already"* (John 3:18). The members of Christ's body the Church, are in a state of guilt and condemnation until they personally exercise faith in the atoning blood of Christ. We have labored this point because some of our readers have been taught the contrary.

It was the entrance of sin which caused the breach between God and us, but in this connection particularly it is important to remember what sin essentially consists of. While in some passages sin is regarded as a *"debt"* and God in connection with it as the Creditor, in other places as an *"offence"* and God in connection with it as the injured Party, and in still other verses as a *"disease"* and God in connection with it as the great Physician, yet none of those terms bring before us the primary element in and basic character of sin. The fundamental idea of sin is that it is *"a transgression of God's Law"* (1 John 3:4) the Rule which He has commanded us to observe, and this should therefore be the leading aspect in which it is contemplated when we consider how God deals with it. Proof of that is found in connection with the origin of human sin, in Gen. 2 and 3. God gave man a commandment which he transgressed: *"by one man's disobedience many were made sinners"* (Rom. 5:19).

Now as the essential idea of sin is not that it is merely a debt or injury, but a violation of our Rule of conduct, then it follows that the particular character in which God ought to be contemplating when we consider Him dealing with sin is not that of a Creditor or injured Party, who may remit the debt or forgive the injury as He pleases, but in His office as supreme Lord. Sin as transgression of the Divine Law has for its necessary corollary God as the Judge. Since He has promulgated a Divine Law which prohibits sin under pain of death, He is bound by His veracity to maintain the honor of His Law and establish His government by strict justice, and thus He cannot pardon sin unless adequate provision is made for accomplishing those objects. As the Judge of all the earth and Rector of the universe, His own perfections require Him to insist that if the penalty of the Law is remitted it must be by another suffering it vicariously, in that way meeting the claims of His Law.

There could be no reconciliation between an offended God and His apostate people until the breach between them had been healed, until His righteous wrath as the Governor of this world had been appeased, and until they also throw down the weapons of their warfare against Him. As the Judge of all, His honor required that His Law should receive full satisfaction, and since His fallen people were unable to make reparation, He graciously provided a Surety for them, who magnified His Law by rendering to it a perfect obedience and by dying in their stead, and thus enduring for them its unmitigated curse. In this way God's legal *"enmity"* or wrath was appeased and the sins of His people were blotted out, so God was propitiated and their guilt expiated. Though His atoning sacrifice Christ removed every legal obstacle which stood in the way of God's being merciful unto transgressors and receiving them into His favor, and by His merits Christ procured the Holy Spirit (Acts 2:33) who, by His effectual operations in the elect, slays their enmity against God, and brings them into loving and loyal subjection to Him, and thus (at their conversion) they are reconciled to God.

Socinians have objected that it was neither necessary nor just that Christ should both obey the Law in His people's stead and yet suffer punishment on the account of their transgressions, seeing that obedience is all that the Law requires. Such a demur would be valid had Christ been acting as the Surety of an innocent people who were under probation, but since He entered the Lawplace of transgressors the objection is entirely without point. Obedience is not all that the Law requires of guilty creatures, for they are not only obliged to be obedient for the future, but to make satisfaction for the past. the covenant which the Lord God made with Adam had two branches: obey and live (*"the commandment which was ordained to life"* (Rom. 7:10): sin and die (Gen. 2:17). And therefore since Christ was *"made under the law"* (Gal. 4:4) — which, in the final analysis, signified *"under the Covenant of Works"* — and since He was acting and transacting as *"the last Adam"* and *"the Second Man"* (1 Cor. 15:45,47) it devolved upon Him to meet the requirements of both branches of the Covenant. As we discussed that at length earlier there is no need to further enlarge upon it.

Since the will of God changes not and the requirements of His government remain the same forever, then if a Surety engaged Himself to discharge all the obligations of God's elect, He must necessarily meet all those requirements on their behalf. The Son therefore became incarnate and subjected Himself unto the full demands of the Law and was dealt with according to its high spirituality and rigorous justice. First He honored the preceptive part of the Covenant by rendering a perfect obedience to every detail. But that of itself would make no satisfaction for His people's transgressions nor afford any expression of the Divine displeasure against sin; and therefore after a life spent in unremittingly doing the will of God, must also needs lay down His life. *"Such a high Priest became us, who is holy, harmless, undefiled and separate from sinners"* (Heb. 7:24). His compliance with the precepts was preparatory to His enduring the penalty of the Law, when He stood at the bar of God in the room of the guilty, and before God as the offended Lawgiver and angry Judge, executing upon Him what was due them.

Some are likely to still have a difficulty at this point. How could Christ be the gift of God's love if that Gift had for its first end the removing of His judicial *"enmity"* and the placating of His wrath? But such a difficulty arises from failure to distinguish between things that differ: between God in His essential and in His official character, between the elect as He views them in Christ and as He sees them as the fallen descendents of Adam. To affirm that God both loved and hated them at the same time and in the same respect, would indeed be a palpable contradiction; but this we do not. God loved His people in respect of His eternal purpose, but He was angry against them with respect to His violated Law and provoked justice by sin. There is no inconsistency whatever between God's loving the saints with a love of good-will and the hindrances to the outflow and the effects of it which their sins and His holiness interposed in the way of peace and friendship. Though the holiness of God's nature, the righteousness of His government, and the veracity of His Word, placed barriers in the way of His taking sinners into communion with Himself without full satisfaction being made to His Law, yet they did not hinder His love from providing the means to remove those barriers, and they were recovered from their apostasy.

"I have loved you with an everlasting love, therefore with lovingkindness have I drawn you" (Jer. 31:3); *"I will call them My people, which were not My people; and her, Beloved, which was not beloved"* (Rom. 9:25). It should be quite evident to every candid reader that if we are to avoid a contradiction in those two passages we must make a distinction in the interpretation of them, that in them the love of God is viewed in entirely different aspects. In other words, we must ascertain the precise meaning of the terms used. The former speaks of His paternal love or good-will towards them, the latter of His judicial favor or love of

acceptance; the one concerns His eternal counsels, the other relates to His dealings with us in a time-state. The former is His love of philanthropy or benevolence, the latter of His love of approbation. The one has to do with His loving us in Christ, the other with His loving us for our own sakes – because of what the Holy Spirit wrought in us at regeneration and conversion. The one concerns our predestination, the other our reconciliation. That distinction reveals the confusion in the piece from Mr. Philpot, quoted in *"The Introduction"* of this series.

The same distinction has to be observed again when we contemplate God's dual attitude toward Christ, the Son of His love, whom He both loved and poured out His wrath upon – yes, and at the same time, though in entirely different relations. When the Father declared, *"This is My beloved Son, in whom I am well pleased"* (Matt. 3:17), He was expressing Himself paternally, as well as testifying to His approbation of both Christ's person and work. But when we are told that *"It pleased the Lord to bruise Him"* (Isa. 53:10) and cried *"Awake, O sword, against My Shepherd and against the Man that is My Fellow, says the Lord of Hosts"* (Zech. 13:7), it was as the Law-administrator or Judge He was acting. Never was God more *"well pleased"* with His beloved Son than when He hung upon the cross in obedience to Him (Phil 2:10), yet He withdrew from Him every effect or manifestation of His love during those three hours of awful darkness, yea, poured out His wrath upon Him as our sin-bearer, so that He exclaimed *"Your wrath lies hard upon Me and You have afficted Me with all Your waves"* (Ps. 88:7).

The very men who object to God's loving and yet being antagonistic to the same person at one and the same time, perceive no antagonism between those things when they are adumbrated before their eyes and illustrated in their own experience on this lower plane. Love and anger are perfectly consistent at the same moment and may in different respects be terminated on the same subject. A father should feel a double affection or emotion toward a rebellious son. He loves him as his offspring, but is angry with him as disobedient. Have we not read of a judge who was called upon to pass sentence on his own child? Or of a military officer who was required to court-martial his son for insubordination in the ranks? Why then should we have difficulty in perceiving that, while in their lapsed state, God loved His people with a love of good-will, yet loathed and was angry with them as rebels against His government. As the injured Father He laid aside His anger, but as the Preserver of Justice He demanded full satisfaction from them or their Surety.

Equally pointless is another objection made by Socinians and Arminians, namely, that such a doctrine as we are propounding represents God as changeable, as a fickle Being – first angry and then pacified. But precisely the same objection might be well brought against repentance! If it be granted that sin is displeasing to God, then obviously He is no longer displeased when the sinner repents and He forgives him! "The atonement did not make God hate sin less than He did before, or excite feelings of compassion towards us which did not formerly exist. He loved us before He gave His Son; and sin still is, and ever will be, the object of His utmost aversion. The effect of the atonement was a change of dispensation, which is consistent with immutability of nature" (J. Dick). The fact is that God demanded an atonement because He does not change, and would not recind or modify His Law, revoke His threatening, nor lay aside His abhorrence of sin. They who represent God as being mutable are the very ones who assert that He pardons sin without satisfaction to His justice.

The precise nature of *"reconciliation"* can be ascertained clearly from the Levitical offerings. Unless those O.T. types were misleading, then they definitely exhibited the fact that the sacrifice of Christ pacified God, made peace and procuring His favor. Personally we unhesitatingly adopt the words of Principal Cunningham when he said, "The whole institution of Levitical sacrifices and the place which they occupied is the Mosaic economy, were regulated and determined by a regard to the one sacrifice of Christ." Those sacrifices set forth the principles on which the effects of the Redeemer's work depended, and provide the surest and best materials for interpreting and illustrating the character and bearing of the Atonement. Those typical sacrifices demonstrated beyond any doubt that the sacrifice of Christ was vicarious and expiatory, that it was presented and accepted in the room and stead of others, that it propitiated God and averted His wrath, and therefore that it procured the exemption of His people from the penal consequences of their sins and effected their reconciliation unto God.

Earlier we quoted Num. 16:46 in proof that *"an atonement"* is made in order to turn away the *"wrath of the Lord;"* let us now allude to further examples. *"And David built there an altar unto the Lord and offered burnt offerings and peace offerings. So the Lord was entreated for the land and the plague was stayed from Israel"* (2 Sam. 24.25) — the occasion being when *"the anger of the Lord was kindled against Israel"* because David had numbered the people (v. 1). The same incident is mentioned again in 1 Chron. 21, where we are told that *"God sent an angel unto Jerusalem to destroy it"* (v. 15), which was in addition to the *"pestilence"* or *"plague"* which slew seventy thousand Israelites mentioned in 2 Sam. 24. Then, after David had built an altar there unto the Lord and had offered appropriate sacrifices and *"called upon the Lord,"* and He had *"answered him from heaven by fire upon the altar"* (in token of His acceptance of the same), we read that *"the Lord commanded the angel, and he put up His sword again into the sheath"* (vers. 26,27). What anointed eye can fail to see in that incident a vivid anticipation and adumbration of what occurred at Calvary.

There is a striking case of alienated friends being reconciled by means of sacrifice recorded in Job 42. *"The Lord said to Eliphaz the Temanite, My wrath is kindled against you and against your two friends, for you have not spoke of Me the thing that is right, as My servant Job has. Therefore take unto you now seven bulls and seven rams and go to My servant Job and offer up for yourselves a burnt offering, and My servant Job shall pray for you, for him will I accept, lest I deal with you after your folly"* (vers. 7,8). Upon which Owen pointed out: "The offenders are Eliphaz and his two friends, the offence is their folly in not speaking aright of God. The issue of the breach is, that the wrath or anger of God was towards them; reconciliation is the turning away of that wrath; the means by which this was done, appointed by God, is the sacrifice of Job for atonement. This then is that which we ascribe to the death of Christ when we say that as a sacrifice we were reconciled to God. Having made God our Enemy by sin, Christ by His sacrifice appeased His wrath and brought us into favor again with God."

The more closely that example in Job 42:7,8 is examined the more clearly should we perceive the meaning and significance of the antitype. There was a declaration of God's anger against those three men, yet also a revelation of His love to them, by directing them to the means by which His anger might be put away and they restored to His favor. Clearly, He had good-will unto them before He directed them what to do, yet He was not then reconciled to them — otherwise there was no need of an atonement for appeasing Him. There was a cloud upon God's face, yet the sun of mercy peeped out through that cloud: as He acquaints them with His anger, so He also shows them the way to pacify it. Though His wrath was truly kindled, yet He was ready for it to be quenched by the means of His prescribing. God could not find complacency in them till He was reconciled to them. In acting on their behalf, Job was a type of Christ, whose propiatory sacrifice God both appointed and accepted.

CHAPTER XVII.

A beautiful type of what we have contended for in these articles is found in Gen. 8. In the preceding chapter we behold the fearful judgment of God under the antediluvian world because of its wickedness – solemn figure of what our Sinbearer endured for us as He was *"made a curse,"* when He cried *"deep calls unto deep at the noise of Your waterspouts. All Your waves and billows are gone over Me"* (Ps. 42:7). After the storm of wrath had done its awful work, Noah (who represented the company of God's elect in the place of safety, exempted from the Divine vengeance) opened the window of the ark and *"sent forth a dove."* Later, he sent her forth again, and *"the dove came unto him in the evening, and lo, in her mouth was an olive leaf"* – *"the emblem of peace"* (v. 11). Christ was the Pacifier of God and He is *"our Peace"* (Eph. 2:14). He is the former, because He is *"to make reconciliation for iniquity"* (Dan. 9:24). He is the latter, because He has satisfied every claim of God upon us. Therefore He designated *"shiloh"* (Gen. 49:10) – an appellation which signifies *"the Peacemaker"* – and *"the Prince of peace"* (Isa. 9:6).

Reconciliation was one of the effects which resulted from the atonement which Christ made unto God, and in our last we pointed out that the simplest and surest way of ascertaining the significance of the antitype is to attend closely to the types. Now the Levitical offerings were not designed to produce any change within the offerer, but were presented for the express purpose of placating and propitiating God Himself. The Israelites did not offer them with the object of turning away their own enmity from Jehovah, but rather to turn away His anger from them, and since the sacrifices which they presented were emblems of the one great Sacrifice of Christ, it necessarily follows that the chief end of His oblation was to divert God's wrath from those on whose behalf it was made. The great fact – the terrible thing – brought out by this doctrine is, that God is the offended Party; while the central fact – the grand thing – proclaimed by it is, that Christ is the all-sufficient Pacifier of God.

We are afraid that some of our friends will feel that we have drawn out these articles on the meaning of Reconciliation to a rather wearisome length, and for their sakes we regret that it was necessary for us to do so. But while they may not have been troubled by the errors we have refuted or the objections answered, yet a considerable number of our readers have been much bewildered by them, and therefore as a servant of God it was part of our duty to *"prepare a way, take up the stumbling-block out of the way of My people"* (Isa. 57:14). At the beginning of our first article on this branch of the subject we stated that we proposed to do much more than barely furnish a definition of the word reconciliation. Having sought to make good that promise, we must now look more closely at the term itself and ponder carefully how it is used in Scripture.

Reconciliation presupposes alienation and therefore it results from the removal of hindrance to concord, and is the act of uniting parties which have been at variance. It is the putting an end to strife and changing enemies into friends. Sin has placed God and man apart from one another – all harmony between them being disrupted. Therefore satisfaction must be made for sin before peace can be restored. Consequently, to be *"reconciled to God by the death of His Son"* is to be restored to His favor. It is the reconciliation of the King to His rebellious

94

subjects, of the Judge to offenders against Himself. To reconcile is to bring to agreement, to unite those who were divided, to restore to unity and amity. Reconciliation is a relation, a mutual one. On God's part it denotes a change from wrath to favor; on ours, from one of contempt and opposition to loyal and loving obedience. It is therefore a change from hostility to tranquility, from strife to fellowship.

The *"peace"* which Christ procured for His people was effected through chastisement. *"But He was wounded for our transgressions, He was bruised for our iniquities: the chastisement of our peace was upon Him, and with His stripes we are healed"* (Isa. 53:5). There are three things here. First, the history of Christ's sufferings: set out by wounds, bruises, chastisements and stripes — the expressions being multiplied to impress our hearts more deeply. The cause of those sufferings: our transgressions and iniquities — the difference between sins of commission and omission. The fruits or benefits of them: peace and healing — a summary of the objective and subjective results of them. The punishment due our sins was borne by Christ that we might have *"peace with God."* "He, by submitting to those chastisements, slew the enmity and settled an amity between God and man; He made peace by the blood of His cross. Whereas by sin we were become odious to God's holiness and obnoxious to His justice, through Christ God is reconciled to us, and not only forgives our sins and saves us from ruin, but takes us into friendship and fellowship with Himself (Matt. Henry).

"The chastisement of our peace was upon Him" is explained by *"therefore being justified by faith we have peace with God through our Lord Jesus Christ"* (Rom. 5:1), where the reference is not to a state of heart, but to a relation with God. *"Peace with God"* does not have reference to anything that is subjective, but only to what is objective: not to an inward peace of conscience (though that follows if repentance and faith are in exercise), nor to that *"peace of God which passes all understanding"* which keeps our hearts and minds through Christ Jesus (Phil. 4:7), but to *"peace with God"* — in other words, to reconciliation. It means we are no longer the objects of His displeasure, and have no more reason to dread the Divine vengeance. It is that blessed relation which results from the expiation of our sins: because Christ endured the penalty of them, we are no longer God's enemies in the objective sense, but the subjects of His favor. Every one that is *"justified"* does not enjoy peace of conscience (though he should); but every justified person has *"peace with God"* (whether he knows it or not) for His quarrel against him is ended, Christ having made God (judicially) his Friend.

There is an interesting passage in 1 Sam. 29 which makes quite clear the meaning of this controverted word and shows it signifies the very opposite of what the Socinians understand by it. While a fugitive from Saul, David and a company of his devoted followers found refuge in Gath of Philistia, where Achish its *"king"* (*"lord"* or *"chief"*) showing kindness to him (1 Sam. 27:2,3). While he was there, the Philistines planned a concerted attack upon Israel, and Achish proposed that David and his men should accompany him (28:1,2), to which he acceded. But when the other lords of the Philistines discovered the presence of David and his men among the forces of Achish they were angry, for they feared he would not be loyal to their cause, saying *"Let him not go down to battle with us, lest in the battle he be an adversary to us, for wherewith shall he reconcile himself unto his master? Shall it not be with the heads of these men?"* (29:4).

"*Reconcile*" there means not, How shall he remove his own anger against Saul, but Saul's against him. How shall he restore himself again to his master's favor.

The great thing to be clear upon in connection with reconciliation is, that it is objective in its significance and action. In other words, it terminates upon the object and not upon the subject. The offender does not reconcile himself, but the person whom he has wronged, and that, by making suitable amends or reparation. Socinians and Arminians have sought to make capital out of the fact that in the Scriptures it is never said in so many words that "*God is reconciled to us,*" but that they uniformly speak of "*our being reconciled to Him.*" The explanation of that is very simple. God is the Party offended, we the parties offending, and it is always the offending party who is said to be the one reconciled and not the offended. Another clear proof is found in Matt. 5:23,24, "*Therefore if you bring your gift to the altar and there remember that your brother has aught against you, Leave there your gift before the altar and go your way, first be reconciled to your brother, and then come and offer your gift.*"

There we have a brother offended, a grievance against one who has injured him. Aware of that, the duty of the wrong-doer is clear, he must do all in his power to right the wrong, remove the ground of grievance and secure amity between them, for until that is done a holy God will not receive his worship. "*Be reconciled to your brother*" does not refer to any state of mind or feeling in the emotions of the wrong-doer, but signifies, makes reparation to him, pacify him. The offender is not bidden to lay aside his own enmity, though that is understood, but is to go to the aggrieved one and seek to turn away his wrath from him, by means of an humble and frank confession of his sin, in that way gaining an entrance again into his good-will and favor. Nothing could be plainer. "*Be reconciled to your brother*" means, put right what is wrong, conciliate him and thus heal the breach between you which is hindering your communion with God.

Before going further we want the reader to be thoroughly clear upon what has been said. At first sight "*with which he shall reconcile himself unto his master?*" (1 Sam. 29:4) seems to mean David's laying aside his own ill-will and healing a breach he had made. Yet the very opposite is its actual sense. It was Saul who hated him! The Philistines feared that David and his men would slay them and take their heads to Saul and thus cause him to look favorably again on David. So too a careless reader of Matt. 5:24 would conclude "*be reconciled to your brother*" signifies that the one addressed was the offended party, who needed to change his own feelings toward the other. But again, the very opposite is the case. It was the brother who had something against him, because of a wrong he had done him, and thus the one addressed is the offender and so "*be reconciled to your brother*" means, go and confess your fault and appease him. The sense of the words is the reverse of their sound.

Matt. 5:24 contains the initial occurrence of our term, and in accordance with the law of first mention intimates how the word is used throughout the N.T. It definitely establishes the fact that to be reconciled to another connotes the pacifying of the offended party so that a state of concord is the result, and it has precisely the same force whenever it is used in connection with God. We are reconciled to Him as we are to an injured brother — reparation having been made to Him, we are restored to His favor. This is plain, again, from the next occurrence of the word in Rom. 5:10. There the whole context makes it plain that God is the offended one, that the cause of His indignation against us was our sins, that Christ offered a sufficient satisfaction unto Him, thereby removing His wrath and conciliating Him unto us. Christ's sacrifice averted God's displeasure as our Govenor and Judge. His relation and judicial attitude toward us was changed by a great historical transaction. *"For if, when we were enemies, we were reconciled to God by the death of His Son; much more, being reconciled, we shall be saved by His life."*

Here then is the issue. Do those words *"reconciled to God by the death of His Son"* signify that Christ pacified God so that He has laid aside His judicial wrath against His people, or, that Christ moves us to lay aside our enmity and hostility against God? We contend that it means the former, that, in the language of Wm. Shedd, "Here the reconciliation is described from the side of the offending party — man is said to be reconciled. Yet this does not mean the subjective reconciliation of the sinner toward God, but the objective reconciliation of God towards the sinner. For the preceding verse speaks of God as a Being from whose wrath the believer is saved by the death of Christ. This shows that the reconciliation effected by Christ's atoning death is that of the Divine anger against sin." The reconciliation which is here mentioned is prior to conversion and therefore quite distinct from conversion (which is when we lay aside our enmity), for occurred when Christ laid down His life for us and not when the Holy Spirit quickened us.

We submit that, from the following considerations, *"reconciled to God by the death of His Son"* refers to God's reconciliation to His people. First, from the relation which that clause bears to *"while we were yet sinners Christ died for us"* (v. 8). The one being parallel with the other. Why did Christ die for sinners? Was it not in order to deliver them from the curse of God and to secure everlasting felicity for them! Second, from the fact that the same expression is described as *"being justified by His blood"* (v. 9), for in the previous verse the apostle speaks of Christ's dying for sinners or rebels against God. The consequence of His death is that believers are *"justified by His blood"* and, as every Scripturally-enlightened person knows, to be *"justified"* is to be received into God's favor (being His acceptance of us, and not ours of Him), which is precisely what *"reconciliation"* is. Third, from the fact that the *"when we were enemies"* refers to the relation we stood in to God — the objects of His displeasure. *"Sinners...justified by His blood"* and *"enemies...reconciled to God by Christ's death"* correspond exactly the one to the other.

Fourth, from the obvious sense of the verse the apostle is arguing (as his *"if"* and *"much more"* shows) from the less to the greater. If when we had no love for God, Christ's sacrifice procured His favor, much more, now that we are converted, will His mediation on high deliver us from our sins as Christians. Fifth, from the reconciliation being ascribed to Christ's death, which was definitely and solely Godward. Had it been the removing of our enmity and turning us to love God, it had been attributed to Christ's Spirit. Sixth, from the obvious meaning of the term: as we have shown from 1 Sam. 29:4 and Matt. 5:23,24, it is the injured party who is the one needing to be reconciled to the offender. Seventh, from the fact that our reconciliation is something which is tendered to us. *"we have now received the reconciliation"* (v. 11): we received the reconciliation effected by Christ and then presented for our acceptance in the Gospel. It would be the height of absurdity to say that we *"received"* the laying down of the weapons of our warfare against God. *"All things are of God, who has reconciled us to Himself by Jesus Christ, and has given us the ministry of reconciliation. To wit, that God was in Christ reconciling the world unto Himself, not imputing their trespasses unto them"* (2 Cor. 5:18,19). That His reconciling of *"us"* *"the world"* unto Himself refers to God's placation unto and favor toward us is clear. First, because it was effected by *"Jesus Christ"* and therefore signifies the removing of God's anger. Second, because had it meant His work of grace within us, subduing our enmity, it had said *"God is in Christ"* or more precisely *"God by His Spirit is reconciling the world unto Himself."* Third, because *"God was in Christ reconciling the world unto Himself"* means, God appointed and anointed Christ to procure His reconciliation. He was in Christ as the Surety — God out of Christ is *"a consuming fire"* to the wicked. Fourth, because the term is here formally defined as *"not imputing their trespasses unto them,"* which is God's act and not the creature's — *"not imputing"* etc. means, not dealing with us as justice required for our sins, on account of Christ's atonement. Fifth, because the *"ministry"* and *"word of reconciliation"* was committed to the apostles — that is, the Atonement was the grand theme of their preaching (1 Cor. 2:2). Sixth, because on that ground sinners are exhorted to be *"reconciled to God"* (v. 20). Since God has changed His attitude unto you, change yours toward Him. Seventh, because our sins were imputed to Christ, and since He atoned for them His righteousness is imputed to us (v. 21).

"And that He (Christ Jesus) *might be reconciled both unto God in one body by the cross, having slain the enmity by it, and came and preached peace to you"* (Eph. 2:16,17). As these verses and their context will come before us again we will confine ourselves now to that which concerns our present purpose. The *"both"* refers to Jews and Gentiles *"in one body"* signifies the Saviour's humanity — compare *"in the body of His flesh"* (Col. 1:22). *"By the cross"* speaks of a definite historical action in the past, and not a protracted process throughout the whole Gospel era. *"Having slain the enmity by it"* signifies not that between Jew and Gentile (which is mentioned in the former verse), but of God's judicial disapprobation against both. This is confirmed in the next verse, where the *"preached peace"* means preached the peace made with God, as the *"access"* in v. 18 clearly indicates. Having effected peace, Christ, after His resurrection, ministerially (2 Cor. 5:18-20) announced it.

"And having made peace through the blood of His cross, by Him to reconcile all things unto Himself" (Col. 1:20). This passage we also hope to enter into more fully in a later chapter, suffice it now to point out that: since peace was *"made"* there must previously have been hostility, and since that peace was made through *"the blood of His cross,"* then the shedding of it was the placating of God, by offering a satisfaction to His violated Law. In Scripture man is never represented as making reconciliation Godward. It is what he experiences or embraces, and not what he makes. It should also be pointed out that never is reconciliation ascribed to the risen Christ, any more than that we are *"justified in a risen Christ."* It is His blood that justifies (Rom. 5:9), which brings redemption (Eph. 1:7), by which we are brought nigh (Eph. 2:13), which sanctifies (Heb. 13:12), which gives us the right of approach to God (Heb. 10:19).

We have been contending for a great truth and not merely for a word or sylla-ble. When Socinians object that Scripture nowhere says in so many words that *"God is reconciled to us,"* they are guilty of mere trifling, for equivalent express-ions most certainly do occur. If it be admitted that sin is displeasing to God and that His vengeance is proclaimed against the sinner, it must also be admitted that if God's anger has been turned away from sinners by a propitiatory sacrifice, then He must have been reconciled to them. "He who once threatened to punish another but has since pardoned him and now treats him with kindness, has cer-tainly been reconciled to him" (J. Dick). The emphasis is thrown upon our re-conciliation to God because we were first in the breach. We fell out with God, before He fell out with us; and because the averseness is on our side. The Gospel makes known His willingness to receive us (because of Christ's sacrifice) if we are prepared to cease our fighting against Him.

If it be asked, Was God reconciled to all the elect and they to Him the moment Christ cried *"it is finished,"* the answer is both yes and no. We must distinguish between (1) reconciliation in the eternal purpose of God (2) as it was effected by Christ (3) as it is offered to us in the Gospel (4) as it actually becomes ours when we believe.

CHAPTER XVIII.

ITS SCOPE

Who are the ones from whom the wrath of God has been turned away and to whom He is reconciled? Who are they whose enmity against God has been slain and are actually reconciled to Him? Though those questions are quite distinct, yet are they intimately allied the one to the other; though they relate to separate transactions, yet really they are but parts of one whole. Those inquiries signify much the same as though we asked, On whose behalf did Christ satisfy God? Who are the ones who must eventually partake of the saving benefits of His mediation? Theologians have been by no means agreed in the answers they have returned, for those questions necessarily raise the fundamental issues which have divided Christendom into Calvinists and Arminians. That issue may be more clearly drawn if we make our question yet more definite and specific. For whom did Christ act as Surety and Substitute? For all the human race, or for the Church only? What was the scope of the Everlasting Covenant? Did it embrace the whole of Adam's posterity or did it respect only a chosen remnant of them?

Who are the ones who will eternally benefit from the great Propitiation? Probably most of our readers would reply, all who truly exercise faith in the blood of Christ. Nor would their answer be incorrect, though it would be more satisfactory to frame it from the Divine side of things rather than from the human side. As it is made from the latter, we have to push the inquiry further back and ask, Who are the ones who savingly trust in the blood of Christ? Not all who hear the Gospel, for even the majority of them turn a deaf ear unto it, so that its preachers have to exclaim *"who has believed our report?"* (Isa. 53:1). Perhaps the reader will return answer to this last inquiry, Those who are willing to receive Christ as their Lord and Saviour. Correct: but who are they? By nature none are willing to do that. *"No man can come to Me except the Father which has sent Me draw him"* (John 6:44) that is overcome his reluctance. *"Your people shall be willing in the day of Your power"* (Ps. 110:3) gives the Scriptural answer. From the Divine side, the reply to our opening question is, Those on whose behalf the great propitiation was made — God's people.

If there were no explicit statements in Scripture there are many implicit ones in it from which we may determine with certainty the precise scope of reconciliation. The ordination, impetration, (accomplishment) and application (bestowal of the benefits) of Christ's work must of necessity be co-extensive. We say *"of necessity"* for otherwise we should be affirming that the ways of God were *"unequal"* — inconsistent, inharmonious. What God the Father purposed that God the Son effected, and what He effected God the Spirit applies and bestows. The only other possible alternative is to predicate a defeated Father, a disappointed Christ, and a disgraced Holy Spirit — which is the kind of *"God"* the Arminians believe in. But there are clear and decisive statements in Scripture which reveal to us the extent of the Father's purpose and the scope of the Son's purchase. Says the Father concerning His Son, *"for the transgression of My people was He stricken"* (Isa. 53:8). *"You shall call His name Jesus for He shall save His people from their sins"* (Matt. 1:21). Said the Son *"the good Shepherd gives His life for the sheep"* (John 10:11) — and not the goats.

The idea of a mere conditional *"provision"* for the reconciliation of all mankind is a theory which sets aside the absolute purpose of God respecting the work of Christ. That theory renders of no account the promises of God concerning the death of His Son, for by pleading that it made the salvation of all men possible, in actuality it denies that it made the salvation of any man certain. God the Father promised His Son a definite reward upon the successful accomplishment of His work. *"He shall see His seed, He shall prolong His days, and the pleasure of the Lord shall prosper in His hands. He shall see of the travail of His soul, and shall be satisfied"* (Isa. 53:10,11). How could He be satisfied if any of those for whom He was their sin-offering were finally lost? *"By the blood of Your covenant I have sent forth Your prisoners out of the pit in which is no water"* (Zech. 9:11). But what security could there be for the fulfilment of those promises if no infallible provision was made for the regeneration of those persons, and instead, everything was left contingent on the wills of men!

Consider the special character in which Christ died. *"Now the God of peace that brought again from the dead that great Shepherd of the sheep through the blood of the everlasting covenant make you perfect in every good work to do His will, working in you that which is well pleasing in His sight through Jesus Christ"* (Heb. 13:20,21). In serving as the Shepherd Christ died for the sheep and not for the goats. Said He *"I am the good Shepherd, the good Shepherd gives His life for the sheep"* (John 10:11), and mark it well, they are represented as being His *"sheep"* before they believe. *"And other sheep I have* (as the Father's gift and charge), *which are not of this* (Jewish) *fold. Them also I must bring, and they shall hear My voice* (when the Spirit quickens them) *and they shall be one fold, one Shepherd"* (John 10:16). But all men pertain not to the *"sheep"* of Christ: said He to those who rejected Him *"you believe not, because you are not of My sheep"* (John 10:26). The *"sheep"* are the elect, God's chosen people. Christ Himself declared that His *"flock"* is a little one (Luke 12:32), and therefore not the whole human race.

Christ laid down His life as a Husband. *"Your Maker is your Husband, The Lord of hosts is His name, and your Redeemer the Holy One of Israel; The God of the whole earth shall He be called"* (Isa. 54:5). Note this comes right after Isa. 53! Equally clear is the teaching of the N.T.: *"Husbands love your wives even as Christ also loved the Church and gave Himself for it, that He might sanctify and cleanse it with the washing of water by the Word, that He might present it to Himself a glorious Church"* (Eph. 5:25-27). As the Husband He died for His Wife (Rev. 19:7). It was His love which caused Him to do so, and it was a discriminating love — set upon a definite object. And again we say, note this well, that the Church for whom Christ gave Himself is not here viewed as a regenerated and believing company, but as one whose members needed to be *"sanctified and cleansed."* He died not for believers as such, but *"while we were yet enemies"* (Rom. 5:10). Nor can Christ be foiled of His design, for He will yet present the Church to Himself *"a glorious Church"* and not a mutilated one — as it would be if any of its members were finally missing.

Christ served as a Surety. He is expressly denominated the *"Surety"* of a better covenant (Heb. 7:22), and unless we are prepared to believe that Christ is defeated in His undertaking, then we cannot extend the persons for whom He was Sponsor beyond those who are finally saved. To speak of a *"surety"* failing is surely a contradiction in terms. If he does not, with certainty, prevent loss how can he be a *"surety!"* To remove any doubt on this point Scripture declares *"He shall not fail"* (Isa. 42:4). He shall yet triumphantly exclaim, *"Behold I and the children which God has given Me"* (Heb. 2:13). Christ's suretyship was no fictitious one, but real. Under that office He engaged Himself to make satisfaction for certain people, and by His engagement to cancel all their debt and fulfill all righteousness in their stead, and since He has perfectly performed this, as much and as truly as though those for whom He acted had themselves endured all the punishment due their sins and had rendered to the Law all the obedience it required, the consequence is clear and unescapable. Those for whom He engaged and satisfied are they who are actually saved from their sins and pronounced righteous by God, and none else.

The very nature of Christ's satisfaction determines to a demonstration those who are the beneficiaries of it. It was a federal work. There was both a covenant and legal oneness between Christ and those for whom He transacted. The Saviour stood as the Bondsman of a particular people, and if a single one of those whose obligations He assumed received not a full discharge, then Divine justice would be reduced to a farce. It was a substitutionary work. Christ acted not only on the behalf of, but in the stead of, those who had been given to Him by the Father; therefore all those whose sins He bore must of necessity have their sins remitted – God cannot punish twice. First the Substitute and then the subject. It was a legal work. Every requirement of the Divine law, both preceptive and punitive was fulfilled by Christ. Therefore all for whom He acted must receive the reward of His obedience, which is everlasting life. It was a priestly work. He presented Himself as an offering to God, and since God accepted His sacrifice its efficacy and merits must be imputed unto all those for whom it was offered.

The intercession of Christ defines the scope of His atoning sacrifice. The death and intercession of Christ are co-extensive. Define the extent of the one and you determine the extent of the other. That must be so, for the latter is based upon the former and is expressive of its grand design. Scripture is too plain on this point to allow of any uncertainty or mistake. *"Who shall lay anything to the charge of God's elect? It is God that justifies. Who is he that condemns? It is Christ that dies, yea rather that is risen again, who is even at the right hand of God, who also makes intercession for us"* (Rom. 8:33,34). *"Wherefore He is able also to save those to the uttermost that come unto God by Him, seeing He ever lives to make intercession for them"* (Heb. 7:25). To make assurance doubly sure on this important matter our great High Priest has expressly declared *"I pray not for the world"* (John 17:9). Thus there must be a *"world"* for whom He did not die. For whom did He say He prays? *"But for them which You have given Me, for they are Yours."*

There are those who suppose that the doctrine of particular redemption detracts from the goodness and grace of God and from the merits of Christ, and therefore conclude it cannot be true. But this mistake becomes manifest if we examine the alternative view. Surely it is not honoring the goodness and grace of God to affirm that the whole human race has nothing but a bare possibility of salvation, yea, a great probability of perishing, notwithstanding all that He has done to save them. Yet that is exactly what is involved in the Arminian scheme, which avers that Christ died to make the salvation of all men possible. That love and grace must indeed be greater which infallibly secures the salvation of some, even though a minority, than that which only provides a mere contingency for all. To us it seems to indicate coldness and indifference for God to leave it a second time to the mutable will of man to secure his salvation, when man's will at its best estate ruined Adam and all his posterity.

If infinite love and goodness was shown to all men in giving Christ to die for them, would it not also give the Holy Spirit to all of them to effectually apply salvation – to subdue their lusts, overcome their enmity, make them willing to comply with the terms of the Gospel and fix their adherence to it? The Scriptures set forth the love and kindness of God as one which makes not merely a bare offer of salvation to sinners, but as actually saving *"by the washing of regeneration and renewing of the Holy Spirit"* (Titus 3:4,5). The Word of Truth declares that the *"God who is rich in mercy, for His great love with which He loved us, even when we were dead in sins, has quickened us together with Christ. By grace you are saved"* (Eph. 2:4,5). How would God's love and mercy toward men appear if He gave Christ for all only to make it possible that they might be saved, and then left by far the greater part of them ignorant of even the knowledge of salvation, and a large number of those who are acquainted with it, not made willing to embrace it in a day of His power?

But over against all that has been set forth in the above paragraphs some will quote *"God was in Christ reconciling the world unto Himself"* (2 Cor. 5:19), and suppose that by so doing they have completely overthrown the whole of what has been brought out. But surely the candid reader can perceive for himself that what has been presented in the whole of the foregoing is not the theories of Calvinistic theologians, nor the subtle reasonins of metaphysicians, but rather the plain and simple teaching of Holy Writ itself. Thus, whatever 2 Cor. 5:19 does or does not mean, it cannot annul all the other passages which have been appealed to. God's Word does not contradict itself, and it is positively sinful for any of us to pit those verses we like against those we dislike. If we humbly look to God for wisdom and patiently search His Word, it should be found that 2 Cor. 5:19 can be interpreted in perfect harmony with all other Scripture, and that, without any wresting or straining, namely, by the same principles of exegesis which we apply to all other passages.

Like every other portion of the Word 2 Cor. 5:29 needs interpreting, by which is meant, its terms explained. Perhaps some demur and say, No explanation is necessary. The verse says what it means and means what it says. We fully agree that it means what it says, but are we sure that we understand what it means? The meaning of a verse is not obtainable from the sound of its words, but rather from the sense of them, and that can only be ascertained from the way in which they are used and by comparing other passages where the same subject is in view. If we take general and indefinite terms and understand them in an unlimited sense, then we soon land ourselves in the grossest absurdities. For instance, when the apostle said, *"I am made all things to all men that I might by all means save some"* (1 Cor. 9:22), he surely did not include duplicity, unfaithfulness, or the use of carnal means. When we are exhorting *"in every thing give thanks"* (1 Thess. 5:18) we must exclude a course of sinning, for God condemns the one who blesses himself in a wicked way (Deut. 29:19).

Now just as all things and all means in 1 Cor. 9:22 are general expressions, which other passages (and considerations), require us to qualify, so the term *"world"* in 2 Cor. 5:19 is an indefinite one, and its scope is to be determined by the tenor of the passage in which it occurs and its meaning understood in a way harmonious with the teaching of Holy Writ. Any one who has taken the trouble to make a concordant study of the word *"world"* will have discovered that it is a most ambiguous term, that it has widely different significations in Scripture, and therefore no definition of its extent can be framed from the bare mention of the term itself. Sometimes the *"world"* has reference to the material world, and sometimes to its inhabitant; it is used in both these senses in John 1:10. In some cases it refers to only a very small part of its inhabitant, as in *"show Yourself to the world"* (John 17:4) and *"the world is gone after Him"* (John 12:19), where the references are to only a portion of Judea, and cannot signify *"all mankind."* Other passages will be noticed in the article which immediately follows, where further proof is given that the term *"world"* is far from being used with one uniform significance, and that it rarely means the whole human race.

CHAPTER XIX.

Some times the *"world"* signifies the Gentiles in general, in contrast from the Jews in particular, as in *"If the fall of them* (unbelieving Israel) *be the riches of the world,"* which is explained in the next clause — *"and the diminishing of them* (Jews) *the riches of the Gentiles;"* and *"if the casting away of them be the reconciling of the world"* (Rom. 11:12,15). In other places the *"world"* refers to the non-elect, as in *"the Spirit of truth whom the world cannot receive, because it sees Him not, neither knows Him"* (John 14:17), and *"I pray not for the world."* In Luke 2:1 it is the profane world that is in view: *"there went out a decree from Caesar Augustus that the world should be taxed"* — yet even that included only those parts of the earth which were subject to the Romans: whereas in John 15:18-25 it is the professing world — it was the religious sections of Judaism Christ alluded to when He said *"if the world hate you, you know that it hated Me before it hated you."*

In Rom. 4:13 the *"world"* signifies the Church, for when Abram is there said to be *"the heir of the world"* it manifestly expresses the same idea as when he is termed *"the father of all them that believe"* and *"the father of many nations"* (Rom. 4:11,18). When Christ said of Himself *"the Bread of God is He which comes down from heaven and gives* (not merely offers) *life unto the world"* (John 6:33). He must have meant His Church, for all who are not members of it remain dead in sins until the end of their careers. We have just as much right to cite the words *"the world knew Him not"* (John 1:10) as a proof that not a single member of Adam's race knew Christ — when aged Simeon did (Luke 1:28-30) — as we have to argue that *"Behold the Lamb of God, which takes away the sin of the world"* (John 1:29) means the sin of all mankind. When it is said *"the whole world lies in the Wicked one"* (1 John 5:19) it cannot mean every one alive on earth, for all the saints are excluded; and *"all the world wondered after the Beast"* (Rev. 13:4) excepts the faithful remnant!

It should be quite clear to any candid and careful reader that, taken by itself, the word *"world"* in 2 Cor. 5:19 supplies no proof and furnishes nothing decisive in enabling us to determine the scope or extent of reconciliation, for that term is an indefinite and general one: more so than usual here, for in the Greek there is no definite article — literally *"reconciling world unto Himself."* It should also be obvious that this verse calls for a careful and detailed exposition: pointing out its relation to what precedes and its connection with what follows, seeking also to define each separate expression in it. To the best of our ability we will now set ourself to this task, and in so doing seek to show that everything in it and the setting in which it is found obliges us to regard the *"world"* reconciled to God as connoting His Church, and not the entire human family.

Under our next main division when we shall deal with our reception of the Reconciliation, or our response to the Gospel call *"Be reconciled to God"* (2 Cor. 5:20), we hope to enter more fully into the scope of the whole context (from v. 11 onwards): suffice it now to begin at v. 17. Nor shall we even attempt an exposition of that much misunderstood verse, rather will we limit ourselves to its central truth, namely, that of regeneration. *"Therefore if any man is in Christ he is a new creature"* — literally *"a new creation"* (v. 17). That is, if anyone is favored to be *"in Christ,"* first, by federal constitution or legal representation, then it will sooner or later follow that he is *"in Christ,"* second, by vital union or regeneration. Whatever is meant by *"old things are passed away; behold, all things are become new"* no explanation of those words can possibly be right if it clashes with Rom. 7:21-25 and Gal. 5:17, for Scripture is perfectly harmonious.

"And all things are of God who has reconciled us to Himself by Jesus Christ." When expounding the *"all things are of God"* Chas. Hodge rightly pointed out that, "this is not spoken of the universe as proceeding from God as its Author, nor does it refer to the providential agency of God by which all events are controlled. The meaning is: *'but all is of God,'* that is the entire change of which he had been speaking. The new creation experienced by those in Christ is *'out of God'* (Greek), proceeding from Him as its efficient cause. It is His work." Proof that it is His work and that *"God"* here refers to the Father in His official character, appears in what immediately follows: *"who has reconciled us to Himself by Jesus Christ."* But that last clause does something more than supply evidence that the glorious work of regeneration issues from the Father as its originating source. It also explains to us the meritorious cause by which the new creation is brought into existence – regeneration is the effect of reconciliation.

The connection then between vers• 17 and 18 is plain. Having spoken of the new creation in the former, the apostle proceeded to point out the legal foundation on which that new creation rests, namely, God's having been pacified by the work of His Son and that work having purchased rich blessings for His people. It is not simply as our Maker, but as a reconciled God, that He quickens His people into newness of life. On vers 17,18 the eminent Puritan, Stephen Charnock declared, "God is first the God of peace before He is the God of sanctification: *'and the very God of peace sanctify you wholly'* (1 Thess. 5:23). The destruction of the enmity of our nature (against Him) was founded upon the removing of enmity in God (against us). There had been no sanctification of our natures had there not been a reconciliation of our persons." Thus, there had been no regenerating of us by God until He had been reconciled to us. "All the powerful effects and operations of the Gospel in the hearts of men are from God as reconciled by Christ, not from God as Creator" (Charnock).

What has just been before us in the immediate context of 2 Cor. 5:19 provides a clear index to the scope of reconciliation, being of equal extent with the new creation! It may be stated either way: the ones whom God regenerates are those to whom He has been reconciled; all to whom He was reconciled, in due course He makes new creatures. If the one is universal, the other is; if the one is limited, the other must be. *"And has given us the ministry of reconciliation"* (v. 18). The *"us"* refers first to the apostles, and second to all whom God has specially called and qualified to act as His heralds. *"The ministry of reconciliation"* is but another name for the proclamation of the Gospel, except that it is more specific, having in view that particular aspect of the Gospel which is concerned with the doctrine of reconciliation. Exactly what that consists of in its essential elements is stated in v. 19-21. First, *"To wit* (or 'namely') *that God was in Christ reconciling the world unto Himself"* (v. 19).

The relation of v. 19 to v. 18 is also quite clear. In the former the apostle said *"All things are of God, who has reconciled us to Himself by Jesus Christ,"* which signifies (as shown in an earlier article) has turned away His wrath from His fallen people and received them into His favor by virtue of the mediation of His

Son. But here he informs us, that transaction was not one which began of late to be done by Him, but rather had engaged His mind and will in His eternal counsels. *"God was in Christ reconciling the world unto Himself."* As the Church was in Christ from everlasting, as her Surety and Head, so God was in Him from everlasting as His ambassador, making peace for those who had revolted against Him. The reference is not to a present process by which God is little by little winning the world back into allegiance with Himself, but to something actually accomplished. God is already propitiated. *"God in Christ"* signifies the covenant-God of His people, for out of Christ *"our God is a consuming fire"* (Heb. 12:29). *"God was in Christ"* speaks then in the language of the *"everlasting covenant,"* and that embraced none but the elect.

Definite light is thrown upon what *"world"* it was unto which God is reconciled by ascertaining the force of that clause *"God was in Christ reconciling"* it. In His ancient designs He formed the purpose of reconciliation in, by and through the Mediator. The identical idea is conveyed whether it be said we are *"in Christ"* or God was *"in Christ acting toward us,"* namely that He designed to show favor unto us as a covenant God. God never was and never will be *"in Christ"* toward any other persons but His Church. Redemption was not the work of the Son only. The Father appointed the Mediator, receiving the stipulated price from Him, and imputes the full value of it to His believing people. The Saviour distinctly affirmed *"the Father is in Me"* (John 10:38). As the elect were in Christ mystically, federally, legally, the Father was in Him authoritatively and efficiently as His Plenipotentiary. Yet the ultimate reference is to God's being in Christ imminently by His eternal decree.

"God was in Christ reconciling the world unto Himself, not imputing their trespasses unto them." It is in that last clause we have the most decisive proof of all that the *"world"* there cannot possibly signify mankind in general, for most certainly God does impute their trespasses unto all who are without Christ. The great problem which confronted the Divine government was how sin could be remitted without righteousness being compromised, but since God has received full satisfaction to His broken law, He has laid aside His official wrath and justice can no longer clamor for punishment. The pardon of sin is one of the main branches and fruits of reconciliation. Not to impute sin is to forgive it. *"Blessed is he whose transgression is forgiven whose sin is covered. Blessed is the man unto whom the Lord imputes not iniquity"* (Ps. 32:1,2). Here then is the *"world"* to which God is reconciled -- the pardoned, the justified, the elect (Rom. 8:33).

Not only do the verses preceding, not only do all the terms used in 2 Cor. 5:19 oblige us to understand the *"world"* there as an indefinite term, including all *"the children of God that were scattered abroad"* (John 11:52), but the closing words of the passage compel us to take the same view. *"For He has made Him to be sin for us who knew no sin, that we might be made the righteousness of God in Him"* (v. 21). Here we learn why God does not impute their trespasses unto His believing people. It is because they were transferred and imputed to their Surety, and accordingly vengeance was executed upon Him. Here too we learn that not only is there no charge laid to the account of God's elect, but that, positively, they are constituted the righteousness of God in Christ -- all the merits of His obedience being charged to them. Thus the *"reconciled us"* of v. 18, the *"their"* of v. 19, and the *"us"* and *"we"* of v. 21 all refer to the same company, and that company is one and the same as *"world"* in v. 19.

If it is inquired, since it is the Church, the mystical body of Christ, that is in view in 2 Cor. 5:19, why did the Holy Spirit designate her by the term *"world?"* First, to show it was not the fallen angels. No Mediator nor Reconciler was provided for them. Second, to show that the love of God in Christ was not restricted unto the Jews (as they supposed) but included also a people to be *"taken out of the Gentiles for His name"* (Acts 15:14). Third, to represent the freeness of God's grace. *"The whole world lies in the Wicked one"* (1 John 5:19). *"In themselves God's elect differ nothing from the rest of the world till grace prevent them. They were as bad as any in the world, of the same race as cursed mankind."* Fourth, "to awaken all that are concerned to look after their privilege, which is come to all nations. The offer is made indifferently to all sorts of persons where the Gospel comes, and this grace is effectually applied to all the elect of all nations" (T. Manton).

None should be stumbled by a particular redemption which pertains only to the Church of God being expressed in such extended terms as *"the world"* and *"all men"* in the N.T. The employment of such language is fully accounted for by the change of dispensation, from the local religion of Judaism to the international reach of Christianity. The Mosaic economy was entirely exclusive, whereas that of the Gospel is inclusive. In anticipation of that, we should note the indefinite language used by the Prophets when predicting the blessings of Messiah, as extending beyond Judea and bestowing indiscriminately. *"The Desire of all nations shall come"* (Hagg. 2:8). *"All kings shall fall down before Him and all nations shall serve Him"* (Ps. 72:1). *"O You that hear prayer, unto You shall all flesh come"* (Ps. 65:2). *"I will pour out My Spirit upon all flesh"* (Joel 2:25) — interpreted by Peter as accomplished on the day of Pentecost (Acts 2:16)! Such language was as universal as any employed by Christ and His apostles, yet it certainly did not signify that every individual the earth over would become a subject of Christ's kingdom and a partaker of His saving benefits.

There are other general terms used in the N.T. besides *"world"* which cannot be taken in an unlimited sense. For example *"every man."* We read of one to whom the Lord gave sight that he *"saw every man clearly"* (Mark 8:28). The kingdom of God was preached *"and every man presses into it"* (Luke 16:16). The early Christians sold their possessions and goods *"and parted them to all, as every man had need"* (Acts 2:45). *"God has dealt to every man the measure of faith"* (Rom. 12:3 but see 2 Thess. 3:2). *"Then shall every man have praise of God"* (1 Cor. 4:5). Other passages could be quoted where *"every man"* cannot be understood without qualification. *"The Gentiles"* is another general expression which is restricted by what is predicated of them in each case. For instance *"on the Gentiles also was poured out the gift of the Holy Spirit"* (Acts. 10:45). And again *"God also to the Gentiles granted repentance unto life"* (Acts 11:18). *"Declaring the conversion of the Gentiles"* (Acts 15:3). *"The salvation of God is sent unto the Gentiles, and they will hear it"* (Acts 28:28). Let those who say of John 3:16 or 2 Cor. 5:19 *"we keep by the plain declaration of the passage,"* apply the same principle to the verses quoted in this paragraph!

"And having made peace through the blood of His cross, by Him to reconcile all things unto Himself; by Him, whether they are things in earth or things in

heaven" (Col. 1:20). These words bring before us another aspect of our theme, and one which has been generally overlooked by writers on this subject. By means of His mediatory work Christ has not only effected a reconciliation between God and the whole election of grace, but He has also closed the breach which existed between the celestial hosts and the Church. At the creation of the world the holy angels sang together and even shouted for joy (Job 38:7), "because though it was not made for them, but for the children of men, and though it would increase their work and service, yet they knew that the eternal Wisdom and Word whom they were to worship (Heb. 1:6), would *'rejoice in the habitable parts of the earth'* and that a large part of *'His delight would be with the sons of men'* (Prov. 8:31)." (Matt. Henry). Likewise, when the grand foundation of the new creation was laid, we read of *"the heavenly host praising God, and saying, Glory to God in the highest, and on earth, peace, good will toward men"* (Luke 2:13,14).

When God made the earth and placed man in it the angels rejoiced in the work of their Creator's hands, and so far from being jealous at the appearing of a further order of beings, they took delight in them. But upon man's revolt from his Maker and Lord, they would be filled with disgust and holy indignation. The sin of Adam (and of the race in him) not only alienated man from God, but also from the holy ones on high. No sooner did our first parents fall from their original state, followed by their expulsion from Paradise, than God employed the holy angels as the executors of His vengeance against them: represented by the cherubim with the flaming sword (for He *"makes His angels spirits and His ministers a flame of fire"* Heb. 1:7) to keep them out of Eden and from the tree of life (Gen. 3:24). Yet now they are *"all ministering spirits, sent forth to minister for them who shall be heirs of salvation"* (Heb. 1:14). And, my reader, it is the blood of the cross which has brought about that blessed change. The atonement of Christ has made the celestial hosts the friends and helpers of His people.

It was not that *"the things in heaven"* were alienated from God, but that Adam's fall introduced disruption into the universe, so that the inhabitants of heaven were alienated from those on earth; but Christ has restored perfect concord again. His sacrifice has repaired the breach between the elect and the holy angels; He has restored the broken harmony of the universe. As one has well pointed out, "If Paul could address the Corinthians concerning one of their excluded members, who had been brought to repentance, *'To whom you forgive anything, I also'* (2 Cor. 2:10), much more would the friends of righteousness (the angels) say in their addresses to the great Supreme, concerning an excluded member from the moral system, *'to whom You forgive anything, we also.'"* For this reason we find *"there is joy in the presence of the angels of God over one sinner that repents"* (Luke 15:10), for another has been joined to their company as worshippers of the Most High.

CHAPTER XX

"And having made peace through the blood of His cross, by Him to reconcile all things unto Himself, whether things in earth or things in heaven" (Col. 1:20). In the final paragraphs of our last we touched upon this aspect of our subject, pointing out that the mediatory work of Christ not only effected a reconciliation between God and the whole election of grace, but also closed the breach which existed between the celestial hosts and the Church. But our remarks on it were all too brief for a subject so blessed, so important, so honoring to Christ, yet so little understood. The relation which exists between the holy angels and the Church which is the mystical body of Christ has not received the attention that it deserves, and failure to perceive that the basis of this fellowship lies in the person and work of Christ obscures one of the distinctive honors which God has placed upon His beloved Son and loses sight of one of His mediatorial glories. *"On His head are many crowns"* (Rev. 19:12), and that which is now engaging our attention is by no means the least of them.

According to the principle of *"the process of doctrine"* or the orderly unfolding of the Truth (first the blade, then the ear, etc.), in the earlier epistles of Paul (Thess., Rom., Cor., Gal.,) we see more the individual effects and blessings of Redemption. The truth of justification, so prominent in it, brings each person face to face with his own sin and salvation. In that supreme crisis of the soul, the crisis of spiritual life and death, there is consciousness of but two existences — God and self. But when we come to the prison epistles (Eph., Phil., Col., etc.), it is no longer the individual as such which is prominent, but rather as he is part of a greater whole — a member of the body of Christ. True, in the earlier epistles the Church is recognized, as in later epistles the individual believer is never for a moment ignored. But the proportion of the two aspects is changed — what is prominent in the first becomes secondary in the other. This is the natural order in the development of Truth. The Christian unity is directly the unity of each soul with Christ, the Head, and indirectly the unity of the various members in the one Body.

When the Gospel of salvation speaks it must speak to the individual, but when the Saviour has been found by each soul as the Christ *"who lives in me"* (Gal. 2:20), then the question arises, What is my relation to other believers? The answer to which is, fellow-members of the Church, fellow-members of the family of God. Accordingly, when taking up the doctrine of reconciliation, the apostles first placed the emphasis upon *"be reconciled to God"* (2 Cor. 5:20), though even there he indicated the basis on which the call is made. But it was reserved for his later epistles to bring out the reconciliation or unity which Christ has effected between believing Jews and Gentiles — which he shows at some length in Eph. 2; while in Col. he goes still further and presents Christ as the Head of all created beings and the new relation which He has established between the Church and the celestial hosts. It is much to their loss that so many Christians advance no further than the epistle to the Romans in their apprehension of the Truth; I must beware of being so wrapped up in what Christ has done for me, that I fail to glory in the wider results of His work.

There was a particular reason why this reference to the larger scope of reconciliation was made in the epistle to the Colossians (rather than in Eph. or Phil.) for as the Judaisers were corrupting the Galations, so the Gnostics were seeking to seduce the saints at Colosse. The word Gnostic means *"one who knows"* (the opposite of agnostic) and that which characterized this sect (which to a considerable extent exerted a powerful and pernicious influence upon early Christianity) was an Orientalized form of Grecian philosophy – a modern though more Buddhistic species of which is *"Theosophy."* Gnosticism was an attempt of carnal reason to show the relation between the Infinite and the finite, the Absolute and the phenomenal, the *"first Cause"* and the universe. They argued that the gulf could only be bridged by a series of creatures rising in the scale of being, the highest of them being semi-personal emanations, of which Christ was the first (yet only a creature), and then many orders of angels which intervened between God and men.

Therefore it was that in the Colossian epistles the apostle insisted that by Christ *"were all things created that are in heaven and that are in earth, visible and invisible, whether thrones or dominions, or principalities or powers, all things were created by Him and for Him. And He is before all things, and by Him all things consist"* (1:16,17), and that he bids the saints there *"beware lest any man spoil you through philosophy and vain deceit"* (2:8). Here too he insisted that *"in Christ dwells all the fulness of the Godhead bodily,"* and again warned them *"that no man beguile you of your reward in a voluntary humility and worshipping of angels, intruding into those things which he has not seen, vainly puffed up by his fleshly mind"* (2:9,18). Having stated in 1:16 that the angels were created by Christ, he then went on to show how they were also the gainers by the blood of His cross, for that blood had *"made peace"* not only with God, but it had also restored to amicable relationship the two great branches of His family – the angelic hosts and the Church.

There was originally a union between the holy angels and unfallen men, for they existed as fellow-citizens in the kingdom of God, but upon Adam's apostasy that union was broken. Sin is rebellion, and the holy angels could have no fellowship with rebels against their God. *"Things in earth"* and *"things in heaven"* became at variance through sin. When men became the enemies of God, they became at the same time the enemies of all His faithful subjects. Take this analogy on a lower plane. Suppose that one country in England should cast off allegiance to King George and disown his government at Westminster, then all lawful communion between the inhabitants of that country and the loyal subjects of the crown in all other parts of the country would be at an end. A line of moral and patriotic separation would at once be drawn between the two companies, and all friendly intercourse would be forbidden. Nor would it less accord with their inclination than the duty of all the friends of the throne to withdraw their communion and connection from those who were in revolt against the supreme authority and the general good.

But now suppose one possessing the necessary dignity and qualifications, say a member of the royal house, should voluntarily undertake to make adequate reparation unto his majesty for the injury done him by the rebellious country, and that he was pleased to acknowledge that reparation as a full satisfaction to his honor. And suppose that his plenipotentiary succeeded in removing all enmity against their king from the members of that county, so that they sincerely repented of their insubordination and threw down the weapons of their hostility against the throne and government; as soon as it became generally known that company had been restored to reality, would not the remainder of the country rejoice and all the loyal subjects of the crown be ready to resume fellowship with them again? That is as close a parallel as we can think of. Having made peace between God and the Church by the blood of His cross, Christ has also united the Church unto all who love God throughout the whole extent of creation. Things or creatures on earth have been reconciled to things or creatures in heaven.

The redemptive work of Christ has done something more than *"gather together in one the children of God that were scattered abroad"* by the fall (John 11:52). It has also united a disrupted universe. As we are informed in Eph. 1:9,10 it was God's eternal purpose *"that in the dispensation of the fulness of times He might gather together in one* (kingdom and family) *all things in Christ, both which are in heaven and which are on earth, in Him."* It was unto the accomplishment of this end that God was working all through the preceding dispensations. He had ordained that unto the last Adam should pertain the honor and glory of repairing the great breach made by the first Adam's sin. Christ could say *"I restored that which I took not away"* (Ps. 69:4). He restored honor to God in the scene where He had been so grievously dishonored, He restored glory to the Law in the very place where it had been trampled underfoot. He brought blessing to the fallen Church by restoring it to the judicial favor of the Judge of all, He restored harmony to the broken universe by reconciling the two most important sections or members of it.

Eph. 1:9,10 makes known to us the entire range of God's eternal purpose of grace. It was to gather together in Christ not only the elect from the sons of men on earth, but also the elect from among the angels in heaven, uniting all into one harmonious whole, and this with the grand design of making more manifest the glory of the God-man Mediator. Under His eternal foreview of the entrance of sin, God purposed the reunion of the two great portions of the moral universe, bringing them into one holy and happy commonwealth under Christ as their glorious Sovereign. If it is asked, Why are the persons of angels and men referred to as *"things?"* The answer is, This is the Scriptural form of expressing them. As when the apostle said *"all things are yours whether Paul or Apollos or Cephas"* (1 Cor. 3:21,22), or, *"the Scripture shuts up all things under sin"* (Gal. 3:22) which is explained by *"God has shut them all up in unbelief"* (Rom. 11:32). As the *"all men"* of 2 Tim. 2:1,2 signifies men of all stations, so the *"all things in heaven"* of Eph. 1:10 means angels of all ranks — *"thrones or dominions, or principalities or powers,"* etc. (Col. 1:16).

The word for *"dispensation"* (oikonomia) contains no time element and has no reference to an age or era. Literally it means *"the arrangement of a house"* (Young's Concordance), or as we should say today, the administration or management of a household. Its force may be clearly ascertained from its first occurrence in the N.T.: *"give an account of your stewardship"* (Luke 16:2), that is of your administration of my household — the same Greek word is again translated *"stewardship"* in the next two verses. Thus the *"Dispensationalists"* have no warrant whatever for their arbitrary partitioning of the Scriptures. When Paul said *"a dispensation of the Gospel is committed unto me"* (1 Cor. 9:17), obviously he is to be understood as meaning, an administration or dispensing of the

Gospel is entrusted to me in my apostolic labors. The *"fulness of times"* signifies the termination of the times or *"seasons,"* namely, this final Christian season, which is the culmination and termination of all preceding ones – as Heb. 1:1,2; 1 John 2:18 make evident.

The *"gathering together of one"* is a single (compound) word in the Greek occurring nowhere else in the N.T. except Rom. 13:8, where it is rendered *"briefly comprehended."* There, after quoting several of the Commandments – *"You shall not commit adultery, you shall not steal,"* etc., – the apostle added and if any other commandment, it is briefly comprehended in this saying namely, *"you shall love your neighbor as yourself,"* that is, all these precepts of the second table are summed up in that single injunction. It is an arithmetical term, where many items are added together in one total sum. It is also a rhetorical term, to recapitulate, as an orator does at the close of his discourse. Thus it contains (in its prefix) the idea of repetition, as *"gathering together"* implies an original unity and then a scattering, before the unity is restored. In Christ God has regathered and re-established in a new condition of stability and blessedness the previously disrupted elements, forming them into one kingdom, under one Head, having restored to harmony and mutual love the alienated portions of His empire.

Christ is not only *"the Head of the Church"* (Eph. 4:23), but He is also *"the Head of all principality and power"* (Col. 2:10), *"angels and authorities and powers being made subject unto Him"* (1 Pet. 3:22). Thus He is *"the Head over all"* (Eph. 1:22). Christ is the gathering Center of all holy creatures, they being united into one great commonwealth under His sovereignty. Elect angels and elect men make up one household. This is clearly brought out in, *"I bow my knees unto the Father of our Lord Jesus Christ, of whom the whole family in heaven and earth is named"* (Eph. 3:14,15). Since Christ is the Head of all (Eph. 1:22), the whole family receive its name from Him. They all own Him, and He owns them all. So too, together they make up one City, the new Jerusalem, of which Christ is the Governor and King. *"You are come unto Zion and unto the City of the living God, the heavenly Jerusalem"* (Heb. 12:22). There is the general description, but who are the inhabitants? The same verse goes on to tell us *"and to an innumerable company of angels, to the General Assembly and Church of the Firstborn"* they all make up one united company of worshippers, for the angels worship Christ as the redeemed do.

As Goodwin showed at length in his masterly exposition of Eph. 1:10, this honor was due Christ. First, as the God-man and *"Heir of all things"* (Heb. 1:2) it was right that He should be the Head over the highest of God's creatures – of the celestial hosts as well as the Church. Second, this unity of the holy angels with the redeemed into one family and commonwealth is greatly to the honor and spendor of the Church. Third, angels and men are capable of being thus knit together under one Head, for they each have an understanding, affection, will and spiritual nature, and therefore are suited to the same happiness, dwelling together in the same place. As Matt. 22:30 tells us *"In the resurrection they...are as the angels of God in heaven!"* Fourth, by this arrangement there is constituted a complete parallel in opposition to Satan, who is the head both of wicked men and demons. The Devil is the head of the evil angels (Rev. 12:7), called *"the Prince of the Demons"* (Matt. 12:24), and he is the head of the wicked (1 John. 5:19) and termed *"the Prince of this world"* (John 12:31). Answerably to this,

God has made Christ the Head of the Church and of angels.

"You are come unto...an innumerable company of angels" (Heb. 12:22). We are come to them as our fellow-citizens, in consequence of our faith in Christ. Our access to them is spiritual. We come to them now, while we are on earth and they in heaven. But we come to them not with our prayers, which is the doting superstition of Rome, and utterly destructive of the communion here asserted. For altought there is a difference and distinction between their persons and ours as to dignity and power, yet as to this fellowship we are equal in it with them; as one of them expressly declared to the apostle John *"I am your fellow-servant and of your brethren that have the testimony of Jesus"* (Rev. 19:10). Upon which John Owen said "nothing could be more groundless than that fellow-servants should worship one another" — nor absurd. We have access to all of them, not simply to this or that tutelar angel, but to the whole company of them. We are come to them by virtue of the recapitulation of them and us in Christ, they and we being members of the same heavenly family and associated together in a common worship.

"What was the reason that the tabernacle was so full of *'cherubim?'* Read Exodus 25:19 and observe there were two of them over the mercy-seat in the holy of holies. Read. Ex. 26:1 and mark how all the curtains of the tabernacle had cherubim wrought on them. Cherubim are angels (1 Pet. 1:12). Go from there to the temple of Solomon. There you have the cherubim again — on the mercy-seat, all the walls of the house, and its very doors (1 Kings 6:23,29,32). All this indicated that angels still fill the temple as well as men. Little do we think it, but the angels, as well as human beings, fill our churches and are present in our assemblies. Therefore are the women bidden to be modest and have their heads covered — the sign of their subordination — not only because of men, but because of the angels (1 Cor. 11:10), for surely that is the meaning of it. Because we are to be with them hereafter and to worship God together, therefore they come down and are present at the worship of God here with us" (T. Goodwin — slightly changed).

In Rev. 5, under the representative emblem of the *"twenty-four elders,"* we behold the Church worshipping, singing a new song: "You are worthy to take the book and to open the seals of it, for You were slain and have redeemed us to God by Your blood, out of every kindred and tongue and people and nation, and have made us unto our God kings and priests, and we shall reign on the earth." Immediately after which the apostle tells us *"And I behold, and I heard the voice of many angels, round the throne and the living creatures and the elders...saying with a loud voice, Worthy is the Lamb that was slain to receive power and riches and wisdom and strength and honor and glory and blessing"* (vers. 9-12). The ascription of praise from the angels is mingled with the praise of the Church so as to comprise one entire worship. Thus the *"gather together in one"* of Eph. 1:10 also included one great Choir or company of worshippers.

The holy angels are the adversaries of the wicked, for since such are the enemies of God they are their enemies too. Thus we read of the angel of the Lord standing in the way of perverse Balaam as *"an adversary against him"* (Num. 22:22). They were sent to destroy wicked Sodom (Gen. 19:1,13). One of them smote the camp of the Assyrians and slew nearly two hundred thousand of them in a night (2 Kings 19:35). Another slew the blasphemous Herod (Acts 12:23) in N.T. times. Observe how prominently they figure in the Apocalypse as the agents of God's judgments and the executioners of His vengeance. See Rev. 8:7-13; 15:1; 16:1-12. So also at the day of judgment *"The Son of man shall send forth His angels and they shall gather out of His kingdom all things that offend and them which do iniquity, and shall cast them into a furnace of fire"* (Matt. 13:41,42).

How blessed the contrast to behold the ministrations of the angels unto the saints! *"He shall give His angels charge over you, to keep you in all your ways"* (Ps. 91:11) – a promise not only to Christ personally, but also to all the members of His mystical body. When the beggar died, his soul was *"carried by angels into Abraham's bosom"* (Luke 16:22). An angel delivered Peter from prison (Acts 12:7-10). In the Day to come Christ *"shall send His angels with a great sound of a trumpet, and they shall gather together His elect from the four winds"* (Matt. 24:31). In an earlier paragraph we called attention to the cherubim with the flaming sword barring our first parents from the tree of life (Gen. 3:24). But, in consequence of Col. 1:20 and Eph. 1:10, they now stand at the entrance of Paradise to admit the redeemed into it! The holy Jerusalem has *"twelve gates, and at the gates twelve angels"* (Rev. 21:12) and in that city is *"the tree of life."* (22:2).

"Behold, a ladder set up on earth and the top of it reached to heaven. And, behold, the angels of God ascending and descending on it" (Gen. 28:12). *"Hereafter shall you see* (with the eyes of faith – enlightened from the Scriptures) *the heaven open, and the angels of God ascending and desending upon the Son of man"* (John 1:51). Here we are shown plainly the grand Medium for uniting heaven and earth, the Foundation on which rests the intercourse between the angels and the redeemed. *"The Son of man"* views Christ as the last Adam, and is the Mediator's title of humiliation, while bearing sin. It is brought in here to emphasize the fact that it is His atonement, *"the blood of His cross"* (Col. 1:20) which is the meritorious ground of the restoration of the long-forfeited fellowship between the two branches of the one family in Christ. "If the partition wall between Jews and Gentiles is removed by the cross, and the enmity slain by it, the same thing holds true in reference to angels and men" (Geo. Smeaton).

CHAPTER XXI.

It is not sufficiently realized that sin is the one great divisive, disrupting and destructive agency at work in every part and strafum of our world. It was sin that separated man from God, which produced a breach between him and the holy angels, and which operates to the alienating of one man from another. Among the many and dreadful effects of the Fall (which was itself an expression of enmity against God) is the enmity between man and man which has issued from it. That abominable thing which caused Adam to be driven out of Eden swiftly exhibited itself in the murderous hatred of Cain for Abel. Sin has not bred a quarrel with God, but between man and man, between brother and brother, between nation and nation. Not only do the unregenerate hate the regenerate, but they *"live in malice and envy, hateful and hating one another"* (Titus 3:3). The whole of human history is little more than a sad record of man's enmity against man — modified (though not eradicated) only where the Gospel has taken root.

As one has truly said, "There is in every man, if his nature were let out to the full, that in him which is *'against every man'* as was said of Ishmael." Self-love is the greatest monopolist and dictator in this world, *"for men shall be lovers of their own selves."* What immediately follows? *"Covetous...disobedient to parents... without natural affection, truce breakers, false accusers, incontinent, fierce, despisers of them that are good"* (2 Tim. 3:2,3). Self-love is the regulating principle in every natural man. Self-love breaks all bonds and overrides all other considerations. And self-love is but another name for sin, for so far from seeking God's glory or the good of my fellows, it selfishly considers only my own interests. Since each nation is but an aggregate of individual sinners, self-interests regulate it, and therefore the nations are kept in a state of continual suspicion, jealousy and enmity one against another.

Now since Christ is the Saviour, and the only Saviour from sin, to Him was appointed the honor of healing the breaches made by sin. We have already seen how He reconciled God unto the Church and the Church unto Him, as we also dwelt at some length on His reconciliation of the Church to the celestial hosts, forming them into one holy and harmonious company. We are now to consider how He brought into the Church, welding them into one Body, two diverse peoples who had for many centuries been widely separated, and bitterly hostile to each other. That was indeed a miracle of grace, constituting as it does one of the greatest and grandest triumphs of the Atonement. We refer of course to the making of the Gentiles *"fellow-heirs and of same Body and partakers of God's promise in Christ by the Gospel"* (Eph. 3:6) with Jews. To appreciate that marvel let us carefully behold the awful and age-long alienation that existed between them.

We begin by contemplating that of the Jews against the Gentiles, for the quarrel originated with them. This is clearly intimated by *"Gentiles in the flesh, who are called Uncircumcision by that which is called the Circumcision"* (Eph. 2:12), for the word *"called"* there signified *"dubbed."* It was the Jews who first began

116

using nick-names! Out of their carnal pride, they misused the privilege bestowed upon them by God as His peculiar people, to scorn the poor Gentiles, and this almost from the beginning. The sons of Jacob said, *"To give our sister to one that is uncircumcised, that were a reproach to us"* (Gen. 34:14), and afterwards the whole race of Jews, good and bad, used the term *"uncircumcised"* as a stigma. As by Samson (Judges 15:18), by Jonathan (1 Sam. 14:6), David (17:26,36), Saul (31:4). Yea, they regarded it as worse than death itself to *"die by the hands of the uncircumcised"* or have *"the daughters of the uncircumcised triumph"* (2 Sam. 1:20). When they would accurse to the most degraded death, it was, Let him die the death of the uncircumcised.

This enmity of the Jews was expressed in their attitude toward and dealings with the Gentiles. Not only was there no communion between them in sacred things, but they deemed it an abomination to have any social intercourse with the Gentiles. In the latter they erred grievously, through perverting a particular precept, given upon a special ground, and making it of general application. Concerning the Ammonites and Moabites the Lord had said *"You shall not seek their peace nor prosperity all your days forever"* (Deut. 23:6), but as though foreseeing that the evil spirit in them would develop into a hatred of all nations and to prevent a wrong use of that precept, in the very next verse God bade them, *"You shall not abhor an Edmonite, for he is your brother; you shall not abhor an Egyptian, because you were a stranger in his land"* (v. 7). Yet the Jews ever carried themselves toward the Gentiles as though they were the scum of the earth.

It was for this reason that when our Saviour asked water from the woman at the well, she was astonished and said, *"How is it that you, being a Jew, ask drink of me, which am a woman of Samaria, for the Jews have no dealings with the Samaritans"* (John 4:9). Yea, so intense was their animosity against the Gentiles, that the Jews would have killed Paul for no other crime than this that he *"brought Greeks also into the temple and has defiled this holy place"* (Acts 21:28,31). Malice could not rise higher in any people against another than it did in the Jews for the Gentiles. They carried it so far that the apostle tells us *"they please not God and are contrary to all men, forbidding us to preach to the Gentiles that they might be saved"* (1 Thess. 2:15,16). What hope was there of such enmity being removed, and of peace, love and concord displacing it?

How strong the Jewish prejudice was, how powerful the working of his enmity against the Gentiles, appears in him even after his conversion. This is forcibly illustrated in Acts 10, where we find God giving Peter a special vision in order to overcome his disinclination to carry the Gospel to those outside the pale of Judaism. When he arrived at the house of Cornelius he frankly admitted, *"You know how that it is unlawful for a man that is a Jew to keep company, or come into one of another nation, but God has shown me that I should not call any man common or unclean"* (v. 28). When this good news reached Jerusalem that *"the Gentiles had also received the Word of God"* and Peter returned to the brethren there, we are told that, so far from rejoicing over these new trophies of Divine grace, *"they that were of the circumcision contended with him, saying, you went into men uncircumcised and did eat with them"* (11:1-3).

Naturally the Gentiles resented their being held in such contempt by the Jews and were not slow to retaliate, though it must be confessed they were the more moderate of the two. And this was a righteous judgment upon them from God: *"I will deliver them to be removed into all the kingdoms of the earth for their hurt: to be a reproach, and a proverb, and a taunt, and a curse in all places where I shall drive them"* (Jer. 24:9). In the days of Ahasuerus, who ruled over one hundred and twenty-seven provinces, amongst which the Jews were scattered and in which they had enemies in all, it was only by special letters of appeal from the king that the Gentiles were restraining from falling on them (Esther 8:9). They were accused of being *"hurtful unto kings and provinces, and that they have moved sedition within the same of old time"* (Ezra 4:15). When the apostles were arrested in Phillippi the charge preferred against them was *"these men, being Jews, do exceedingly trouble our city"* (Acts. 16:20).

But more. God Himself has made a distinction and difference between them, having dealt with and favored Israel as no other nation upon earth (Amos 3:2). He had assigned them their own special land, giving them a particular code of laws — moral, civil and religion — and set up His own exclusive worship in their midst. He had made of them a peculiar polity, having great privileges exclusive to itself, such as no other people ever enjoyed. From all of that the Gentiles were Divinely barred. As the apostle declares, they were *"without Christ, being aliens from the commonwealth of Israel and strangers from the covenants of promise having no hope, and without God in the world"* (Eph. 2:12). Those consequences followed from their being *"without Christ,"* for He is both the substance and end of the covenants of Israel and the Revealer of God, and so of spiritual life. But in Christ all fleshly distinctions disappear, and through His mediation the Gentiles have been made partakers of Israel's *"spiritual things"* (Rom. 15:27). This is shown at length in Eph. 2:14-22, unto which we now turn.

In approaching that passage it needs to be borne in mind that, the Spirit's principal design in it, as in all His ministrations, is to exalt Christ in our esteem. The incarnate Son glorified the Father on earth as He was never glorified here before or since, and therefore He was entitled to ask *"Father, glorify Your Son"* (John 17:1). That request received answer not only in His exaltation on High, not only in a redeemed people being quickened and united to Him to show forth His praises, but also in the further revelation made of Him in the N.T. An illustration of that is now to be before us. The Spirit's object in it is to give us an eminent instance of the efficacy of Christ's mediation by bringing to pass that which the united efforts of all men could never have accomplished, namely, the slaying of an age-long and inveterate enmity which existed between the two great branches of the human family, from each of which God takes a remnant to exemplify His sovereign grace. Eph. 2 shows us how Christ abolished that which was the means or occasion of alienation between them.

"For He is our peace" (v. 14) objectively, what He is in Himself: as He is *"our righteousness"* (Jer. 23:6), *"our life"* (Col. 3:3), *"our hope"* (1 Tim. 1:1) — though there is that which is correspondent to each wrought in us. He is *"our peace"* because He is Himself *"the Prince of peace"* and because He is the great and glorious Peacemaker. Christ is at once the Author, the Substance, and Center of peace. In what follows the apostle supplies proofs or exemplifications. Christ is our peace between ourselves mutually, and He is our peace between God and us. The key to a right understanding of what follows lies in bearing in mind that duality. As vers. 11-13 exhibit a dual alienation — of Gentiles from

Jews, of both from God, so vers. 14-17 treat of a double reconciliation opposite to it. And accordingly in vers. 18-22 we are shown the grand twofold privilege which results from it: access into the favor of God (v. 18), the introduction of a new and united worship of Himself (vers.19-22).

"For He is our peace: who has made both one and has broken down the middle wall of partition" (v. 14). He who is not only the Giver of Peace, but the Peace itself, has united together believing Jews and Gentiles. Those who previously were alienated, are reconciled by Him, because He has broken down that which divided and separated them. Of old God had *"fenced"* His vineyard (Isa. 5:1,2; Ps. 80:8; Matt. 21:33-43), or as the margin reads it *"made a wall about it"* which had barred the Gentiles from an entrance into Israel's spiritual things. The *"middle wall of partition"* is an expression which connotes the separating cause which existed between Jew and Gentile, but which was demolished by Christ when He had — as the Representative and Surety of each alike — *"made both one"* in Himself. As Christ's death rent the veil of the temple — the innermost barrier to God — so it destroyed the middle wall of partition.

"Having abolished in His flesh the enmity — the law of commandments contained in ordinances" (v. 15). This tells us how Christ broke down that which divided. The middle wall of partition is now designated *"the enmity,"* and that in turn, is described as *"the law of commandments, etc."* Here, too, there is a double reference: first to the ceremonial law of Moses which excluded Gentiles from the Jews. Second to the Covenant of works which excluded both from God. *"In His flesh"* is the same as *"by His blood"* (v. 13) and *"by the cross"* (v. 16). By His sacrificial and atoning death the Law — both as a ceremonial system and as a rule of justification — was annulled. In the parallel passage (Col. 2:14) the word ordinances is connected with *"the handwriting that was against us,"* that is, to a legal bond of indictment, which Christ took out of the way *"nailing it to His cross."*

"For to make in Himself of twain one new man, so making peace" (v. 15). In 2:10 the believer is declared to be *"the workmanship of God,"* but there the glory of the creation is directly attributed to Christ, who is its Head and Life. The *"twain"* or *"two"* were the Jews and Gentiles, who were separate and hostile bodies, alike the children of wrath and dead in trespasses and sins. They are created anew so as to become *"one new man"* (collectively) and this by virtue of their federal union with Christ — therefore the *"in Himself."* *"So making peace:"* the present participle is used because the operation is a continuous one the work is done, but the fruit of it is progressive. The long feud in the human family is healed. In Christ *"there is neither Jew nor Greek"* (Gal. 3:28) — both disappearing when the *"enmity"* that sundered them was abolished. There is now one fold, one Shepherd.

"And that He might reconcile both unto God in one body by the cross, having slain the enmity in this way" (v. 16). Here the *"enmity"* which Christ slew is the barrier which existed between God and men — created by sin; and not the enmity in our hearts against God, for it was slain by Christ's death and not by the working of His Spirit. To *"reconcile"* is to effect peace and unity between parties at variance. Christ reconciled both Jews and Gentiles unto God by propitiating Him, by satisfying the demands of His Law, in this way making it possible for Him to be just and yet the Justifier of the ungodly. There is no room

for any uncertainty here. It was *"by the cross"* that Christ effected the reconciliation. The proximate design of a sacrifice is to appease God, and not to convert those for whom the offering is made. *"Having slain the enmity"* both amplifies and explains *"by the cross."* Christ's death removed God's wrath or judicial enmity from sinners.

And came and preached to you that were afar off (the Gentiles) and to them that were (in outward privileges) near (v. 17). As the *"enmity"* of v. 16 is the legal enmity of God, so the *"peace"* here is that *"peace with God"* (Rom. 5:1) into which Christ has brought all His redeemed. His *"preaching"* of it is after the cross, and therefore through His apostles (see 2 Cor. 5:20). It is the proclamation to those who savingly believe the Gospel that since the Law has been satisfied God is no longer hostile to us. Proof of that is *"For through Him we both have access by one Spirit unto the Father"* (v. 18) — which had been impossible unless His wrath had been removed or His enmity slain. Christ has done something very much more than simply *"open a way to God"* He has actually brought us to God (1 Pet. 3:18), inducted us into His grace or favor (Rom. 5:2).

As God determined to magnify the exceeding riches of His grace by permitting the most heinous sins in the lives of some of those whom He chose unto salvation for the glory of His Son He suffered the strongest and bitterest animosity to possess the hearts of Jews and Gentiles, that the efficacy of His mediation might be displayed in constituting them one new man in Himself — blessedly exemplified when those, who formerly would not eat with one another, sit down together to partake of the Lord's Supper!

CHAPTER XXII.

ITS RECEPTION.

This brings us to the manward side of the subject, and that will present more or less a difficulty unto some of our readers; not because of its abstruseness, but in seeking to ascertain its consistency and harmony with some other aspects presented previously. It concerns the ever-recurring problem of adjusting in our minds the conjunction of the Divine and human elements. Because that conjunction cannot always be stated with mathematical exactitude or in language fully intelligible to the average mind, the great majority are inclined to cut the knot and reject either the one or the other of those elements or factors. But if both be clearly set forth in the Word, whether or not we can perceive the precise relation between them or the definite point at which they meet, it is our bounden duty to believe and hold fast to both. If on the one hand Scripture teaches that Christ has effected reconciliation with God, Scripture just as plainly calls upon us to *"be reconciled to Him."* And it speaks of our *"receiving the reconciliation."* It is this latter aspect we must now be occupied with: what God requires from the sinner if he is to enter into the good of what Christ did for sinners.

There ought to be no need to labor this point at any length, and there had been none had not certain men — true servants of God we doubt not, who were thoroughly sound on almost every other part of that Faith once delivered to the saints, and whose ministry has deservedly been held in high esteem by the generations who succeeded them — departed from the Truth thereon and influenced many since their day to perpetuate a serious error. As we have previously pointed out, mutual alienation requires mutual reconciliation. The reconciliation of God to us and of us to God must answer the one to the other, for unless each party lay aside his enmity no real amity is possible. If peace were on one side only and hostility on the other, there would still be a breach. God must be propitiated; we must be converted: the one is as requisite as the other. As we have already shown at length how Christ reconciled God unto us, we must now enter into some detail of how we may be reconciled to God. That we are not about to depart from *"the old paths"* (Jer. 6:16) will appear from the following quotations.

"Although God the Father has transacted all these things from eternity and Jesus Christ has long since performed all that which might pacify and reconcile His Father and procure our atonement with His Father, yet it was withal agreed mutually then by Them that not a man, no, not any elect man, should have benefit by either, until they came to be reconciled . . . He that will be reconciled to God must part with and forsake all other friends and lovers, renounce and break off all interests and correspondence with them, and choose God for his sole Friend and Portion — he must choose God forever, to cleave to Him with full purpose of heart" (T. Goodwin vol. 6, pp. 122, 129). "We are actually justified, pardoned, and reconciled when we repent and believe. Whatever thoughts and purposes of grace God in Christ may have towards us from all eternity, yet we are under the fruits of sin till we become penitent believers . . . That these are conditions which alone make us capable of pardon is evident" (T. Manton, vol. 12, 266).

"This reconciliation, purchased by the blood of Christ, is offered unto men by the Gospel upon certain articles and conditions, upon the performance whereof it actually becomes theirs, and without which, notwithstanding all that Christ has done and suffered, the breach still continues between them and God. And let no man think this a derogation from the freeness and riches of grace, for those things serve singularly to illustrate and commend the grace of God to sinners. As He consulted His own glory in the terms on which He offers us our peace, so it is His grace which brings our souls to these terms of reconciliation. And surely He has not suspended the mercy of our reconciliation upon unreasonable or impossible conditions. He has not said, If you will do as much for Me as you have done against Me I will be at peace with you; but the two grand articles of peace with God are repentance and faith" (J. Flavell vol. 1, p. 476).

"To make perfect reconciliation (which Christ is said in many places to do) it is required, first, that the wrath of God be turned away, His anger removed and all the effects of enmity on His part toward us. Secondly, that we be turned away from our opposition to Him and brought into voluntary obedience. Until both these be effected reconciliation is not perfected" (J. Owen, *"The Death of Death."* bk. 3, chap. 6, para. 1 on *"Reconciliation"*) "A mediator must be accepted by both parties that are at variance, and they must stand to what the mediator does. As where two princes are at difference and a third interposes to make an agreement between them, they must both consent to accept of that prince for mediator and both put their concerns in his hand: he can be no mediator for him that does not accept of him in that relation . . . God has declared Himself fully contented and has complied with all the conditions of the first agreement (the everlasting covenant); it only remains now that man will accept of Him for those purposes for which God did constitute Him and comply with those conditions which God has settled. This is necessary: God saves no man against his will" (S. Charnock, vol. 3, p. 164).

Those excerpts supply a clear if brief idea of what was the almost uniform teaching of the Puritans on this subject. Probably they will come as a real surprise unto a considerable number of our readers who are wont to regard those men as the champions of orthodoxy and as the best-instructed scribes of the Gospel since the days of the apostles. If so, it is because they have imbibed subversive teaching which came from other men that followed the Puritans in the eighteenth century, men who though they upheld the banner of Truth, previously erected, yet in other things departed from the foundations laid down by their better-balanced predecessors. Though we highly respect these men too and freely acknowledge our indebtedness to many good things in their writings, yet we dare not and cannot follow them in those things wherein they relied more on logical reasoning than on the teaching of Holy Writ. And for the sake of those who have been misled by the errors of men who otherwise taught the Truth, it devolves upon us to at least make an attempt to lead them back into *"the good way"* (Jer. 6:16).

"Now then we are ambassadors for Christ, as though God did beseech by us: we pray in Christ's stead, be reconciled to God" (2 Cor. 5:20). That is the ringing call of the Gospel as it is addressed unto the unsaved. *"Be reconciled to God:"* cease your hostility against Him, throw down the weapons of your rebellion, turn from your wicked ways, abandon your idols, repent of your sins,

sue for mercy in the name of Christ, receive forgiveness through His blood. But in certain more or less influential circles that is flatly rejected. It is blankly denied that the Gospel called upon the unsaved to be reconciled to God, or that He requires anything from sinners in order to the forgiveness of their sins. Nay it is argued that such an assertion as ours repudiates the free grace of God and denies the finished work of Christ, by inculcating salvation by works and making man in part his own Saviour. If that were so, then it would necessarily follow that the most eminent and godly of the Puritans (quoted above) were guilty of those very crimes! But we deny that any such conclusion follows.

"Be reconciled to God" is both the demand of Divine holiness and the enforcement of human responsibility. But because that Gospel call clashed with the views of certain men, they attempted to explain away its real force, insisting that those words are addressed to saints and not to the unconverted. A certain air of plausibility is given to that view by an appeal to the fact that this verse is found in a church epistle, but if due attention be paid to its setting, and the scope of the apostle in the whole passage be rightly ascertained, then the seeming *"plausibility"* disappears and the untenability of such an interpretation is at once exposed. But in order to discover and exhibit the scope or design of the apostle here, careful attention has to be paid to the context and considerable ground must be covered by the expositor to make the same clear. We fear this may prove rather tedious to some of our friends, yet beg them to bear with us for the sake of others who need and for those who earnestly long for the opening-up of this passage.

Let us give first, in few and simple words, what we are convinced is the force of 2 Cor. 5:20 and then state why we so understand it, setting forth the grounds on which our conviction rests. When the apostle wrote those words *"Be reconciled to God"* he was not exhorting saved or unsaved: rather was he giving a brief account of the evangelical message which he had been called to deliver to the latter. In the light of the immediate context we can come to no other conclusion. In the second half of v. 18 the apostle expressly declares that there had been given to him and his fellow-evangelists *"the ministry of reconciliation,"* and then in vers. 19-21 (and 6:1,2!) he tells us — as the opening *"to wit"* unequivocally shows — what that *"ministry of reconciliation"* consisted of, what were its principal elements and contents. Before proceeding further, let the reader carefully ponder vers. 18-21 for himself, and see if he does not concur. If the meaning of v. 20 is still not clear to him, let him read again from v. 18 and omit the repeated *"you"* in v. 20, and all should be plain. But we will attempt a more thorough analysis of the passage.

As we pointed out in the opening paragraphs of the chapters on *"the Prayers of the Apostles,"* certain false teachers were very active against Paul at Corinth, seeking to undermine his apostolic authority and destroy his influence and usefulness. It is that which accounts for what he says in 1 Cor. 4:1; 9:1-5; 15:9-11, and 2 Cor. 5:1,2; 10:2; 11:5, 12-16. It is that which explains why he was forced (by his adversaries) to vindicate his apostleship and point out that in authority, knowledge and effective grace, none excelled him: see 11:22-23 for his credentials. It seems quite evident from a close reading of those two epistles that his enemies had succeeded so far as to shake confidence in himself of some of his own converts there, and thus his appeals in 1 Cor. 5:14-16; 2 Cor. 3:1-4, 13:3

124

etc. From those passages it will be seen that Paul was on the defensive and obliged to justify himself and do what his modesty and humility detested – say much about himself and appear to resort unto boasting and self-laudation (2 Cor. 11:16-18). In the light of those references the apostles's scope in the epistle should be more easily perceived.

Throughout the third chapter he gives an account of how he had discharged the commission which he had received from his Master, acknowledging, tacitly, that he was no Judaiser (as were his opponents), but rather an able minister of the new testament or covenant (v. 6). In the fourth he continues the same subject, and makes mention of some of the trials which a faithful discharge of his commission had entailed (vers. 1, 8-14). Then, as was so often the case, his heart and mind (so to speak) ran away with him and he digressed to describe the rich compensation which God had provided for His servants and people in general – their afflictions being abundantly counterbalanced and recompensed by the glory awaiting them, which he continues to 5:10. But in 5:11 he returns to the subject of his own ministerial labors, making known the springs from which they issued. Having alluded to *"the judgment-seat of Christ,"* he declared *"knowing therefore the terror of the Lord, we persuade men."* Nothing is more calculated to stir the soul of Christ's minister and make him earnest and faithful in dealing with his fellows than the solemn realization that naught but the *"everlasting burnings"* await all who die out of Christ. It is that which makes him cry to his hearers *"flee from the wrath to come."*

(1) *"Knowing therefore the terror of the Lord* (1) we persuade men:" the one was the cause, the other the effect. The *"terror of the Lord"* was not something of which the apostle stood in any doubt of, but a thing he knew – of which he was fully assured. And therefore he *"persuaded men"* at large, reasoning with, pleading with, urging them to flee for refuge and personally lay hold of the hope which he set before them in the Gospel. An illustration that this was the course which he followed, is supplied us in Acts 24:25, where we are told that, even when before one of his judges, *"he reasoned of righteousness, temperance and judgment to come,"* so that *"Felix trembled."* Alas, how little of such zeal and fidelity is there today on the part of those who profess to be the servants of God; how little is there in their preaching which makes the hearer *"tremble!"* How little does the twentieth-century evangelist resemble those of the first. If the reader of this paragraph is a preacher, let him honestly measure himself by this verse and ask, Is the awful truth of the eternal punishment of the wicked in the Lake of Fire impelling me to so preach that in the day to come I shall be *"pure from the blood of all,"* or am I deliberately withholding what I know would be unpalatable unto my congregation?

"But we are made manifest unto God" (v. 11). That was a solemn appeal by the apostle unto the Searcher of hearts of his sincerity and fidelity. And then he added, *"and I trust also are made manifest in your consciences"* (5:11): I cherish the hope that such zeal and honest dealing with souls will make it evident, to your conscience at least, that I am indeed and in truth an accredited servant of God. Can the reader, if he be a preacher, make the same appeal both to the Omniscient One and the conscience of his auditors? *"For we commend not ourselves unto you, but give you occasion to glory on our behalf, that you may have somewhat to answer them which glory in appearance and not in heart"* (v. 12).

It was not that the apostle would seek to ingratiate himself in the esteem of these unstable Corinthians, but that he reminded them of what they had already witnessed and experienced when he labored among them, and that, in order that they could effectually close the mouths of his detractors, who sought to take advantage of his absence by destroying the confidence of those who were his own children in the Faith.

"For whether we be beside ourselves, it is to God: or whether we be sober, it is for your cause" (v. 13). Here he replies to one of the charges which his adversaries had brought against him – that he was a wild fanatic. Says the apostle, even if I am mad, it is for God's glory that I have been so zealous; and if I had restrained myself within the bounds of sobriety, it was for your sakes. Whether he succeeded the limits of discretion as his enemies asserted, or whether he conducted himself decorously as men judged, it was not for himself: he had in mind only the glory of God and the good of His Church. *"For the love of Christ constraines me"* (v. 14): that was the second dynamic or motive-power of his ministry. That was what caused him to set aside all considerations of ease or self-aggrandizement and made him willing to be counted *"the filth of the world, the offscouring of all things"* (1 Cor. 4:13). Here again we see a blessed balance: the *"terror of the Lord"* and *"the love of Christ"* inspiring him in all his ministerial labors. The love of Christ for sinners for himself: the love of Christ filling his heart and engendering a love for sinners, made him willing to *"spend and be spent"* in labors *"more abundant,"* and to get little more than misunderstanding and misrepresentation, jealousy, and bitter persecution for his pains.

Cannot the impartial reader see for himself the drift, the scope, the line of things of Paul in this passage? Having mentioned *"the love of Christ"* as constraining him to diligence in the ministry of the Gospel, he went on to enlarge upon the nature of that love: it was the One dying for the all (v. 14), and then to the end of v. 17 he describes some of the consequences and fruits of that love, upon which we must not now enlarge, as originally intended. The final fruits of Christ's love here enumerated are, that God *"has reconciled us unto Himself by Jesus Christ, and has given to us the ministry of reconciliation"* (v. 18). What that *"ministry"* consisted of he tells us in vers. 19-21. It "consists of two parts. 1. A reconciliation wrought on God's part toward us, in the effecting of which Christ was concurrent with Him (v. 19). 2. A reconciliation on our parts, enforced from what God and Christ had done (v. 21), and this is equally necessary unto man's salvation as that reconciliation on God's part and Christ's part" (T. Goodwin vol. 6, pp. 117). "The end of the ministry is to reconcile us to God, to prevail with us to lay down our enmity against Him and opposition to Him" (Owen on 2 Cor. 5:20).

"Now then we are ambassadors for Christ, as though God did beseech by us, we pray in Christ's stead, be reconciled to God" (v. 20). We trust it is now clear that in those words the apostle was "evidently giving an account of his commission and general ministry" (T. Scott). That he should here do so is quite in accord with what he had done in the previous epistle: see 1 Cor. 2:2 and 15:1-3. Thus in this instance we believe that that most able expositor J. Gill erred in his interpretation of this verse – following as he did James Hussey rather than the earlier Puritans. So far from exhorting the saints unto *"submission to providence and obedience to the discipline and ordinances of God,"* the apostle was stating

how he exhorted the unsaved when preaching the Gospel to them. Had Gill's interpretation been valid, the twice stated *"you"* had been in the text! If any supplement be needed, it should be *"men."* *"Be reconciled to God"* is the imperative demand of the Gospel to all who hear it being parallel with *"Let the wicked forsake his way, and the unrighteous man his thoughts, and let him return unto the Lord, and He will have mercy upon him"* (Isa. 55:7).

The apostle continues the same subject in chapter 6. "In this chapter (verses 1-10) the apostle gives an account of his general errand to all whom he preached to, with several arguments and methods he used" (M. Henry). It should be carefully noted that not until 6:11 did the apostle directly address himself to the Corinthians! Now if Paul had been addressing the saints in 5:20, then in the opening verses of 6 he must have been addressing their ministers, which is how Mr. Gill understood him. But in such case he would not have said *"approving ourselves as the ministers of God"* (v. 4) but *"yourselves!"* Thus it is manifest he was still vindicating himself and his fellow-apostles against the Judaisers. Not only were all who heard him preach the Gospel exhorted *"be reconciled to God,"* but to *"receive not the grace of God in vain,"* urging them not to procrastinate with the overtures of Divine mercy, but to recognize and realize that *"now is the accepted time"* (vers. 1,2). Having been favored with the Gospel, let them not spurn it.

On 2 Cor. 6:1 Owen said, "The grace of God may be considered two ways. 1. Objectively for the revelation or doctrine of grace, as in Titus 2:11, 12. So we are said to 'receive' when we believe and profess it, in opposition unto those by whom it is rejected. And this is the same with receiving the Word preached, so often mentioned in the Scriptures: Acts 2:41, James 1:21, which is by faith to give it entertainment in our hearts, which is the meaning of the word in this place." The *"we"* of 6:1 is the *"we are ambasadors"* of 5:20, and the *"you receive not the grace of God in vain"* (His gracious overture in the Gospel) are the same *"you"* as *"be you reconciled to God."* The meaning of *"giving no offence in any thing that the ministry be not blamed, but in all things approving ourselves as the ministers of God"* (6:2,4) is, that the apostles comported themselves in such a manner that there was nothing in their conduct which would hinder their Gospel preaching.

CHAPTER XXIII.

In our last we sought to show that the words *"be reconciled to God"* (2 Cor. 5:20) are not an exhortation unto saints to acquiesce in the Divine providences or to render submission to His discipline and ordinances, but instead, that they form part of an account which the apostle was giving of his evangelical commission, of what his message was to men at large, and therefore those words express the call which the Gospel makes to the unsaved. Before turning from that verse let us point out that there is an expression in it which supplies an incidental yet very real and strong confirmation of what has been frequently insisted upon in this series. Again and again we have pointed out that in connection with reconciliation God is viewed specifically in His official and governmental (rather than in His essential or paternal) character, as Rector or Judge. In full accord with this His servants are here referred to as *"ambassadors for Christ, as though God did beseech"* — in no other connection are ministers of the Gospel so designated!

After all that was pointed out under our fourth main division (its Arrangement), when we dwelt at length on the glorious provision of the Everlasting Covenant, and all that was brought forward under our fifth division (its Effectuation), when we showed how Christ carried out all He had engaged Himself to do under that Covenant and the reward He earned — a *"seed"* for the travail of His soul; it might be thought that the elect were absolved and reconciled to God the moment the Saviour triumphantly cried *"It is finished."* But not so. As Charnock pointed out, "We must distinguish between reconciliation designed by God, obtained by Christ, offered by the Gospel, and received by the soul." It is through failing to recognize and bear in mind those very real and necessary distinctions that we confuse ourselves, confounding what should be kept separate. It was their failure to distinguish between totally different aspects of the Truth which led some Arminians into teaching the gross error that the entire human race was reconciled to God by Jesus Christ, though most of them know it not.

For the purpose of simplification the fourfold distinction drawn by Charnock may be reduced unto a twofold one: A reconciliation which, in the language of lawyers, is de jure and one which is de facto, or in theological terms, the impetration or purchase of reconciliation by Christ and the application of it to us or our actual receiving of the same. This will be more intelligible to the average reader if we remind him of the difference between having a legal right to a thing and a right in it. Such is the case with a minor with reference to an inheritance. If but ten years old when his father died and willed an estate to him, as soon as the will was proved, he had a legal right to the estate — none else could claim it; but not until he was twenty-one could he enter into possession and enjoyment of it. The Holy Spirit uses that very figure in Gal. 4:1-7 when treating of dispensational differences of privilege under the old and new covenants.

It is by observing this fundamental distinction that we obviate a difficulty which a first reading of 2 Cor. 5 might occasion. There we read *"God has reconciled us to Himself by Jesus Christ"* (v. 18), and then the call is made *"be reconciled"* (v. 20). But there is nothing whatever inconsistent between those two statements, or anything in them which should puzzle us. Paul was not there essaying a systematic exposition of the doctrine of reconciliation, but instead, was giving an account of his evangelical ministry or message in connection with it. As was shown in our last — by the quotation from T. Goodwin — that "ministry" consists of two parts: a reconciliation wrought on God's part and a reconciliation on our part toward God. The latter being equally necessary as the former. It is necessary because since the alienation exists on each side, both parties must set aside their enmity before amity is possible. It is necessary in order to the enforcement of human responsibility. It is necessary for us to be reconciled to God because that is what He requires of us, as the way He has appointed. But let us amplify that a little.

While a great deal has been written to show that in the transactions between the Father and the Mediator God determined to take full satisfaction unto His justice, and therefore ordained that His Son should be offered a sacrifice, much less has been written to demonstrate that the holiness of God required we must cease our revolt against Him before He can be reconciled to us or receive us into His favor. Yet the one is as true, as important, as necessary, as essential as the other. God is as jealous in the vindication and glorifying of one of His attributes as He is of another, and therefore if on the one hand we read that Christ is set forth "a propitiation through faith in His blood, to declare His righteousness" and "that He might be just and the Justifier of him that believes in Jesus" (Rom. 3:25,26); on the other hand, we are told that He "has saved us and called us with a holy calling, not according to our works, but according to His own purpose and grace which was given us in Christ Jesus before the world began" (2 Tim. 1:9), addressing us thus: "as He which has called you is holy, so be holy in all manner of behavior."

In the wondrous and perfect salvation which God planned and provided for His people, infinite wisdom saw to it that each of His perfections should be owned and magnified, and if our presentation of the Gospel fails to exhibit that grand fact it is defective and partial. It is "to the praise of the glory of His grace in which He has made us accepted in the Beloved" (Eph. 1:6). It is "according to His mercy He saved us" (Titus 3:5). In order that the claims of His righteousness might be met He "spared not His own Son," abating not the least whit that justice demanded. Likewise He is resolved that "without holiness no man shall see the Lord" (Heb. 12:14). If He would not that the cup of death pass from Christ at His so earnest entreaty, most certain it is that He will not recede one iota from the requirements of His holiness in receiving us into His friendship, and therefore His inexorable demand is, "Let the wicked forsake his way, and the unrighteous man his thoughts, and let him return unto the Lord, and He will have mercy upon him, and to our God for He will abundantly pardon" (Isa. 55:7). For God to pardon those who persisted in their wicked ways would be to condone sin.

If there be a revolt in a kingdom, two things are required before peace can be restored and amity again prevail. The king must be willing to exercise clemency on a righteous basis and his subjects must cease their rebellion and become obedient to his sceptre. Orderly government would be reduced to a farce if a pardon was offered unto those who continued to oppose the throne. Now the King of kings has announced His willingness and readiness to pardon any rebel among men, but only on the condition that he first throw down the weapons of his warfare against Him. The carnal mind is enmity against God, and obviously that enmity must cease before we can be reconciled to Him.

By nature and practice we are *"alienated and enemies in our minds by wicked works"* (Col. 1:21), and clearly those works must be confessed and repented of, hated and abandoned, before there can be peace between us and the thrice Holy One. God does not save us in our sins, but *"from our sins"* (Matt. 1:21). *"But if while we seek to be justified by Christ, we ourselves also are found sinners, is therefore Christ the Minister of sin? God forbid"* (Gal. 2:17).

In his chapter on what God requires from us in order to our reconciliation with God, T. Goodwin pointed out that "1. For the preparing us to be reconciled it is necessary that we be convinced that we are enemies to God, and that He accounts us such; and that so long as we remain in that estate, He is also an enemy to us, and can be no other. This what God in Christ has done gives demonstration of. He would not save us upon Christ's bare entreaty, but He would have satisfaction, and have Christ feel what it was to stand in the room of sinners. Yea, one end why God saved us by way of satisfaction to His justice, was that sinners pardoned might, in what Christ suffered, see and thoroughly apprehend what sin had deserved. And is it not then requisite that they should at least lay to heart and be sensible of their own treason and rebellions, and that God and they are at odds? Traitors must be convicted and condemned before they are capable of a legal pardon, as sentence must be pronounced before a legal appeal can be made. It is so in man's courts, and it is so in God's proceedings also. Neither indeed will men be brought so to sue out for His favor and prize His love till then, for it was never heard any man did heartily sue to one for pardon and peace with whom he did not first apprehend himself at variance.

2. It is necessary also that men apprehend the danger of going on in this estate; for though one should know another and himself to be enemies, if he thought his enemy were either careless or weak, he would slight reconciliation with him, and though sought unto would not seek it. He who is mentioned in Luke 14:31,32 was to sit down and consider if he were able to go out and meet his enemy, else he would never have sought conditions of peace. So the soul, until it apprehends and considers (finding God and itself enemies) what a sore enemy He is and what a fearful thing it is to fall into His hands, will not till then care to seek out to Him. 3. If one apprehended God implacable, not inclinable to peace, or hard to be entreated, he would never come at Him either. Thus David, when Saul and he were at odds, suborned Jonathan secretly to observe what mind Saul bare towards him, and when he found him bent to kill him (1 Sam. 20:33), David came not at him.

4. The soul comes to be persuaded better things of God and things that accompany reconciliation, and conceives hope that reconciliation is to be had, and had for it. And therefore in all whom God means to reconcile to Himself, after He has humbled them He fixes a secret persuasion on their hearts that He is ready to be reconciled to them, if they will be reconciled to Him. God gives them a secret hint of His intended good will to them. He reveals what a gracious God He is, and how freely He pardons...the same God who from everlasting spake unto His Son and wooed Him for us, does speak likewise secretly (inwardly) to a man's heart to allure and woo him to come into him" (T. Goodwin). In this way overcoming his reluctance, quieting his fears, and making him willing in the day of His power. As He employs the Law to impart a knowledge of sin, to convict us

of our high-handed rebellion against the Most High, so He uses the Gospel to make known the wondrous provision He has made both to satisfy the claims of His Law and to meet deep need.

If it be asked, Since Christ has satisfied every requirement of God why are repentance and faith necessary from us? What has been said above should furnish a sufficient and satisfactory answer. It is because God is pleased to exercise pardoning mercy in such a way as is suited to all His perfections. It would be contrary to His wisdom to dispense the precious benefits of Christ's atonement to impenitent rebels. It would be contrary unto His governmental honor for Him to cast pearls before swine, to be trampled beneath their feet. It would be contrary unto His holiness for Him to bestow pardon upon one whom He knows would abuse such a favor — as though He granted a dispensatory power for him to sin with impunity. As it is no reflection upon the sufficiency of Christ's satisfaction that believers are called to suffer afflictions and death — for they are not penal inflictions for the satisfying of His justice, but are sent for the exercising of their graces (1 Pet. 1:7); so it in no way derogates from the perfections of Christ's satisfaction that sinners be required to repent and believe, for there is nothing meritorious about such exercises.

Goodwin then went on to point out, the sinner "must be set a-work to seek, as a condemned man, God and His favor in Christ, and peace and reconciliation through Him. He should pray to Him and He will be gracious . . . God is the party superior, and it is fit the inferior should seek to the superior. He also is the person wronged, and though He be willing and desirous to be reconciled, yet He will have His favor prized. David longed to be reconciled to Absalom, yet he would be sought unto, for he would have his favor prized to the utmost and not cast away. Yea, and because the favor of God is better than life. He will be sought to with more earnestness and constancy that a man seeks for his life, *'you shall seek Me and find when you shall search for me with all your heart'* (Jer. 29:13). *'If God has bidden us seek peace with men, yea, and to ensue it'* (Ps. 34:14; 1 Pet. 3:11), that is, though it fly away and though He seems to reject us, yet to press upon Him — as David says my soul follows hard after you (Ps. 63:8).

He will be sought unto with confession of and mourning for offending Him, for being in bitterness and mourning is joined with suplication for grace (Zech. 12:10). This is necessary to reconciliation because an acknowledgement is to be made (Jer. 3:13). God would be sought humbly unto by us, as those that are traitors and rebels. God will have men know when He pardons, that he knows what He pardons, and therefore will have them acknowledge what they deserve: *'that every mouth may be stopped and become guilty'* (Rom. 3:19). If a man will become wise he must become a fool (1 Cor. 3:18); so a man that will become a friend to God must turn enemy against himself and judge himself worthy of destruction (Ezek. 36:31)...Where mourning for offending God is wanting, there is no sign of any good will yet wrought in the heart to God nor love to Him, without which God will never accept of a man...God will not pardon till He sees hope of amendment. Now until a man confesses his sin, and that with bitterness, it is an evidence he loves it (Job 20:12-14). While he hides it, spares it, and forsakes it not, it is sweet in his mouth. A man will never leave sin till he finds bitterness in it.

He must renounce all other friendships. The nature of reconciliation requires this, for friendship with anything else is enmity with God. *'Yea adulterers and, adulteresses, know ye not that the friendship of the world is enmity with God?'* (James 4:4). As God will not have us serve other masters. so neither other friends. *'Whosoever does not forsake father and mother, etc., is unworthy of Me'* says Christ (Luke 14:26). A friendship not only with proclaimed enemies – open sins – but with all the things which the world has, is enmity with God. A believer may have a lordship over them, but not friendship with them. He may use them as strangers and servants, but not as friends, so as they have his heart. Friendship is entered into by choice – kindred is not so. So Jonathan chose David to be his friend (1 Sam. 20:30). As God did choose you, so also must you choose Him. As God chose you *'freely'* (Hos. 14:4), out of good will, so must you choose Him freely. As He chose you forever, never to cast you off, so you are to choose Him forever. As nothing can separate from His love, so let nothing separate Him from yours.

Let your heart resign up itself and all that it has and devote it all unto God forever, to be commanded and used by Him. Thus did God for us – if He spared not His own Son, but with Him also freely gives us all things, let all you have be God's, giving up yourselves first unto the Lord (2 Cor. 8:5). Let God have all your understanding, will, affections, and whatever else. And let all be His, to command in any thing as He pleases, and study how to set all a-work for Him. Likeness of disposition is the only sure and lasting foundation of friendship, being the soul of it, for it is impossible two should long be friends unless they be one in their minds and affections, liking and loving the same things. *'Can two walk together except they be agreed'* (Amos 3:3). Accordingly, a man that is thus reconciled must endeavor to walk and behave himself as a friend. The nature of reconciliation requires it. *'A man that has friends must show himself friendly'* (Prov. 18:24). Therefore Christ said, *'You are My friends, if you do whatsoever I command you'* (John 15:14). Watch over yourselves in all your ways and be fearful to displease Him and His goodness (Hos. 3:5).

God designed to set forth His love so as to attain the ends of loving. It is not to give forth peace only, but to manifest good will and kindness, as Luke 2:14 shows. Yea, the ground of His showing mercy is His love (Eph. 2:4). And although on our part our love and friendship to God is not the ground of His, yet it is the end or aim of His. Though He did not love us because we loved Him first, yet He loved us that we might love Him in return. Therefore in those He saves, if there were not wrought an inward principle of love and friendship, and good will mutual again to Him, that might answer His love to us, His love would not have its end, and would be finally cast away. For so we reckon love to be given away in loss when it is not answered in its kind, that is, with a true love in response. God would have His love valued and esteemed by those He saves, for love is the dearest thing that anyone has to bestow, because whoever has a man's love has all he has – for it commands all. If God's love be esteemed by us it will work holiness in us" (T. Goodwin, condensed and a few words altered).

We have quoted at such length from that excellent Puritan because while T. Goodwin was a high Calvinist (a supralapsarian) and magnified the free and sovereign grace of God as few have done, yet he was also an able evangelist, a faithful shepherd of souls. And though he was a strict particular-redemptionist, yet he also enforced human responsibility. And while he taught clearly the total depravity and utter ruin of fallen man, yet he also shunned not to state plainly and emphatically what God required from the unsaved. We could easily reproduce the same, in substance, from Owen, Manton, Bunyan, and others of the seventeenth century. How far some in the eighteenth and nineteenth centuries departed from their teaching we leave the reader to determine, as he may also decide how solemn and serious — or how unimportant — such departure was. Whether the unsaved in many a so-called *"place of truth"* have been lulled to sleep by a fatalistic presentation of the doctrine of election and by harping so much on the creature's inability to meet God's requirements, or whether they have been faithfully exhorted to repent and believe the Gospel.

Should the reader say, I mentally assent to most of what Goodwin wrote, but I find myself totally unable to comply with his directions, we ask, cannot you see that such a statement greatly aggravates your wickedness? Suppose I have grievously wronged and offended a dear friend of yours, and you came to me saying you deplored the breach between us, that your friend was willing to be friends again if I would put matters right and beg forgiveness. Suppose you pleaded with me to do the proper thing, and the only reply I made you was, I am unable to. What would you think? Would you not justly conclude that all I lacked was a willing heart? That the reason I would not seek unto the one I had injured was either because I hated him or because I was too proud to humble myself before him? You would judge rightly! So it is with the sinner and God. If we analyse his *"cannot"* it is because he is so wedded to his idols, so in love with sin, he will not forsake them. And anything in our preaching which comforts him in his *"will not"* is contrary to Truth.

CHAPTER XXIV.

On this occasion we propose to treat of the present aspect of our subject in connection with the Covenant. There is a pressing need for this today, for while on the one hand most professing Christians are woefully ignorant about the Covenant, some others have been very faultily instructed in them. As on almost every other doctrinal and practical subject, the Puritans were much sounder than many of the outstanding Calvinists of the nineteenth century, for the sermons of the latter were sadly lacking in perspective. Those of men like Joseph Irons, and Jas. Wells, were thoroughly lop-sided. While they rightly emphasized Divine sovereignty, they remissly ignored human responsibility; while they had much to say about God's grace, they had little to say about the demands of His holiness; while magnifying the finished work of Christ, they were silent upon what God required from sinners before the benefits of it were applied to them. They were very fond of quoting *"He has made with me an everlasting covenant, ordering in all things and sure"* (2 Sam. 23:5), but they scarcely ever cited, and never expounded, *"Incline your ear and come unto Me: hear and your soul shall live: and I will make an everlasting covenant with you"* (Isa. 55:3).

A covenant is a compact between two parties in which there is mutual stipulation and restipulation, the one promising certain benefits in return for the fulfilling of certain conditions by the other. Thus it was in the covenant or agreement entered into between Isaac and Abimelech (Gen. 26:28,29) and between Jonathan and David (1 Sam. 20:16,17). God entered into covenant with Christ as the Head of the elect, and to that covenant He attached the demand of repentance, faith, and obedience from them.

Let us first consider the passage we quoted above from Isa. 55 and which is so much ignored by many Calvinists. That chapter opens with a most blessed Gospel invitation, though there are one or two things in it which have been both misunderstood and disregarded. *"Ho everyone that thirsts, come you to the waters"* has been restricted unto a spiritual thirst, as though the invitation is made only unto souls Divinely quickened. That is an unwarrantable limitation. The Gospel call goes forth freely to all classes and conditions of men, addressing them simply as sinners – guilty, lost, needy sinners. Since they are sinners, they have no satisfying portion, yet they have a thirst for something more contenting, and therefore their quest for happiness. But since they are blinded by sin they know not what that satisfying portion consists of or where true happiness is found. They seek it, but seek it wrongly and in vain. Therefore the question is asked them, *"wherefore do you spend your money for that which is not bread? And your labor for that which satisfies not."* In this way is the Gospel called enforced.

"Come to the waters" which can quench your thirst and satisfy your heart. *"And he that has no money, come you, buy and eat."* The Inviter is a generous Benefactor who makes no charge for His benefits and bars not the poorest from a welcome to them. Nevertheless, those who would partake of them must *"buy."* That does not mean they must give something for those benefits and purchase them. But it does signify they must part with something, or otherwise the word *"buy"* would have no force. There are two things which the sinner must part with if he would be a participant of the Gospel feast: he must abandon his idols, and he must renounce his own goodness or righteousness. That which

133

his idols, and he must renounce his own goodness or righteousness. That which Christ requires from the sinner is that he come to Him empty handed. If on the one hand that means he must bring no price with him, nothing seeking to merit his acceptance; on the other hand, it also means he must drop the world, and no longer cherish and cling to those objects or pleasures in which until this time he has sought to delight himself.

"Come you, buy and eat; yea, come, buy wine and milk, without money and without price." Three times over in that first verse is the word *"come"* used. It is the respone which is required to the invitation made. It is a word calling for action, for voluntary action. It is a word too of clear yet necessary implication. One cannot come to a place without leaving another! The prodigal son had to quit the *"far country"* in order to turn unto the Father's house. The sinner must (in his affections and resolutions) turn his back upon the world if he would embrace Christ. Twice is the word *"buy"* found in it, to emphasize the fact that it is a definite and personal transaction which is here in view, and as we have already pointed out, to denote that something must be relinquished or parted with – whatever stand in opposition to Christ as seeking to hold the sinner's heart. While the *"no money,"* *"without money and without price"* stresses the truth that eternal life is not to be obtained by the works of the Law, but is a free gift, that we bring nothing with us to commend ourselves to God's favorable regard, but come simply as poverty-stricken beggars.

"Hearken diligently unto Me, and eat that which is good, and let your soul delight itself in fatness" (v. 2). Listen to the voice of Wisdom which pleads with you to waste no more of your money on that which ministers not to your spiritual and eternal needs and your efforts after what has no power to afford you real and lasting satisfaction. Appropriate unto yourselves the riches of Divine grace as they are spread before you in the Gospel, and let your soul delight itself in that which will bring no disappointment with it or regrets afterward. *"Incline your ear, and come unto Me."* Too long have you hearkened to the sirens of your lusts and to the false promises of this world. Too long have you been deaf to My counsels and precepts, to My expostulations and warnings. Incline your ear "as you do to that which you find yourselves concerned in, and pleased with. Bow the ear, and let the proud heart stoop to the humbling methods of the Gospel; bend the ear this way you may hear with attention" (Matt. Henry). *"Hear,"* that is, heed, respond, obey, comply with My demands. *"Hear, and your soul shall live; and I will make an everlasting covenant with you."* (v. 3).

Here, then, we learn plainly and definitely who are the characters with whom God proposes to make an everlasting covenant, and the terms with which they must comply if He is to do so. They are those who have freely sampled the lying vanities of this world and, like the poor prodigal, have found them to be naught but *"husks."* They are those who hitherto had closed their ears against Him, refusing to meet His requirements and steeling themselves against His admonitions. *"Incline your ear"* signifies, cease your rebellious attitude, submit yourselves to My righteous demand. They are those who are separated and alienated from the Holy One, at a guilty distance from Him – away in *"the far country."* *"Come unto Me"* means, throw down the weapons of your warfare and cast yourselves upon My mercy. They are those who are unquickened, destitute of spiritual life, as the *"hear, and your souls shall live"* clearly shows. Comply with those terms, says God, and I will make an everlasting covenant with you. It is human responsibility which is there being enforced. It is but another way of saying to sinners *"Be reconciled to God."*

As we pointed out in a former chapter, this enforcing of man's responsibility is most meet for the honor of God, and as the honor of the Father lies nearer to the heart of Christ than anything else, He will not dispense the benefits of His atonement except in that way which is most becoming to God's perfections. There is a complete accord between Christ's impetration of God's favor and the application of it. That is, between Christ's purchase of it and our actual entrance into the same. As the justice of God deemed it meet that His wrath should be appeased and His law vindicated by the satisfaction made by His Son, so His wisdom determined and His holiness ordered it that the sinner must be converted before pardon be bestowed upon him (Acts 3:19). We must be on our guard here, as everywhere, against extolling one of God's attributes above another. True, the Covenant is entirely of grace – pure, free, sovereign grace – nevertheless, here too grace reigns *"through righteousness"* (Rom. 5:21) and not at the expense of it. Christ died not to render any sinner secure in his carnality.

God will not disgrace his grace by entering into covenant with those who are impenitent and openly defying Him. To do so would make Him the Condoner of sin, instead of the implacable Hater of it. It is not that the sinner must do something in order to earn the grand blessings of the covenant, or that he must add his quota to the redemptive work of Christ. No, no he contributes not a mite to the procuring of them. That price, and infinitely costly it was, was fully paid by the Lord Jesus Himself. But though God requires naught from us by way of purchasing or meriting those blessings, He does in the matter of receiving them. "The honor of God would fall to the ground if we should be pardoned without our submission, without confession of past sin, or resolution of future obedience. For till then we neither know our true misery, nor are we willing to come out of it; for they that securely continue in their sins, despise both the curse of the Law and the grace of the Gospel." (Manton).

"And I will make an everlasting covenant with you, the sure mercies of David" (v. 3). It is of course the Messiah, the spiritual or antitypical David of whom God there speaks – as He is also called *"David"* in Ps. 89:3, Jer. 30:9, Ezek. 34:23,24; 37:24, Hos. 3:5). If proof is needed that it is the Lord Jesus who is in view, Acts 13:34-37 supplies it. *"The sure mercies of David"* are the special and distinguishing favors which are reserved for and in due time bestowed upon God's elect. They are the grand privileges and benefits of the Covenant which God pledged Himself to impart unto Christ and His seed upon the completion of His engagement. They are *"sure"* because the promises of One who cannot lie, and because they are now dispensed by the victorious and risen Redeemer. They are revealed in the Gospel and presented for the acceptance of faith. *"Behold I have given Him* (the spiritual David) *a Witness to the people, a Leader and Commander to the people"* (Isa. 55:4). That tells us those *"sure mercies"* are dispensed in a way of righteousness and holiness. The Gospel presents Christ to us not only as a Redeemer, but a Teacher and Ruler. We are required to surrender to Him as our absolute Lord and voluntarily take His yoke upon us before He becomes our Saviour and imparts rest unto our souls.

"For thus says the Lord, unto the eunuchs that keep my sabbaths and choose

the things that please Me, and take hold of My covenant; even unto them will I give in My house and within My walls a place and a name better than of sons and daughters. I will give them an everlasting name that shall not be cut off. Also the sons of the stranger that join themselves to the Lord, to serve Him, and to love the name of the Lord, to be His servants, every one that keeps the sabbath from polluting it and takes hold of My covenant" (Isa. 56:4-6). Here we have spiritual and eternal blessings presented under the imagery of the Mosaic economy. It was an O.T. prophecy announcing the distinctive favors of the N.T. dispensation. Under the Mosaic law *"eunuchs"* were barred from entering the congregation of the Lord, and the *"stranger"* or Gentile was barred by the middle wall of partition; but under the Gospel era these restrictions would no longer abstain, for the grace of God should flow forth unto all without distinction. That which we would specially observe is the clause placed in italics, which sets forth the human side of things.

Let us notice carefully what is here predicated of those who *"take hold of"* God's covenant. They *"keep the Sabbath from polluting it,"* that is, they have a concern for God's honor and a respect for His Law, and therefore keep holy that day which He has set apart unto Himself, requiring us to act as per the instructions of Isa. 58:13. They *"choose the things that please"* the Holy One. They are not self-pleasers, or gratifiers of the flesh, but earnestly endeavor to abstain from whatever God has prohibited and to perform whatever He has enjoined; and this not by constraint or fear, but freely and cheerfully. They *"join themselves to the Lord."* They seek unto and cleave to Him, they do so in order *"to serve Him and to love His name, to be servants." "Serve"* Him means to be subject unto Him, to take their orders from Him, to promote His interests. They are resolved to *"love His name."* Their service is that of friends and not slaves, their faith is one which works by love and their obedience prompted by gratitude. Unless our service proceeds from love it is valueless. They had given Him their hearts, and therefore their faculties, talents, time and strength are dedicated and devoted unto Him. Such are the ones who *"take hold of His covenant."*

"In every covenant there is something given and something required. To take hold of God's covenant is to lay claim to the privileges and benefits promised and offered in it. Now this cannot be done unless we choose the things that please Him. That is, voluntarily and deliberately, not by chance but by choice, enter into a course of obedience wherein we must be pleasing or acceptable to Him: this is the fixed determination of our hearts" (Manton). And we never enter upon that course of obedience and do the things which are pleasing unto God until we have first chosen Him as our absolute Lord, our Supreme End, our highest Good and our everlasting Portion. Negatively, they can be *"no taking hold of the covenant"* until we cease all opposition to God. Positively, it is to embrace the Gospel offer and to comply with its terms. The covenant of grace is proffered to us in the Gospel and to take hold of the former is to heartily consent unto the latter and meet its requirements, giving ourselves to the Lord (2 Cor. 8:5) – freely, unreservedly, for time and eternity. Consent there must be, for none can enjoy the privileges of a charter which they never accepted and agreed to.

What has just been before us in Isa. 56 is virtually parallel with 27:4,5. *"Fury is not in Me* (unless I am provoked by the rebellion of My creatures. In such case): *Who would set the briers and thorns against me in battle? I would go through them, and I would burn them together."* Such opposition against the Almighty is utterly futile. If they stir up His wrath, naught but the Lake of fire can be their portion, unless they avail themselves of His amnesty, throw down the weapons of their warfare against Him and be reconciled to Him, which is what is signified by *"Or* (as the only alternative to burning) *let him take hold of My strength."* Let him grasp My arm which is uplifted to smite and crush him. And how shall that be done? Thus, *"that he may make peace with Me."* That he may cease this sinful fighting against Me; *"and He shall make peace with Me."* God is ready and willing – on the ground of Christ's satisfaction – to lay aside His vengeance and be reconciled, if the sinner is willing to lay aside his awful enmity and become friends.

"This (Isa. 27:4,5) may very well be construed as a summary of the doctrine of the Gospel, with which the church is to be watered every moment. Here is a quarrel supposed between God and man: for here is a battle fought and peace to be made. It is an old quarrel, ever since sin first entered. It is on God's part a righteous quarrel but on man's part most unrighteous. Here is a gracious invitation given us to make up this quarrel. Let him that is desirous to be at peace with god take hold on God's strength, on His strong arm, which is lifted up against the sinner to strike him dead; let him by supplication keep back the stroke. Pardoning mercy is called the power of the Lord; let him take hold of that. Christ crucified is the power of God, let him by a lively faith take hold on Him, as a sinking man catches hold of a plank that is within his reach, or as the malefactor took hold on the horns of the altar...it is vain to think of contesting with Him. It is like setting briers and thorns before a consuming fire. We are not an equal match for Omnipotence. This is the only way, and it is a sure way to reconciliation. Let him take this way to make peace with Me, and he shall make peace" (From. M. Henry).

"In those days and in that time, says the Lord, the children of Israel shall come, they and the children of Judah together, going and weeping. They shall go, and seek the Lord their God. They shall ask the way to Zion with their faces toward it, saying, Come, and let us join ourselves to the Lord in a perpetual covenant that shall not be forgotten" (Jer. 50:4,5). The historical reference is to the liberty which Cyrus gave to the Hebrews to return unto their own land, consequent upon his overthrow of Belshazzar. Unacquainted with the road, the exiled Jews on leaving Babylon for Palestine, made inquiry about it. Their case supplied a type or adumbration of the spiritual experiences of God's people. *"In those days"* is an O.T. expression which pointed forward to this Christian era. It was therefore one of many evangelical prophecies couched in the language of an historical event. Whatever fulfilment that prophecy may or may not yet have for the Jewish people (and on that matter we refraim from any dogmatic statement) its present application is to sinners who have been awakened and convicted by the Spirit so that they are concerned about their spiritual and eternal interests.

Like those in the historical type, these seekers are issuing forth from a lifelong bondage – in sin. Convicted of their guilt and resolved to reform their ways, they are represented as *"going and weeping"* and determining to *"seek the Lord their God,"* which in N.T. langauge would be *"repenting"* and being *"converted."* As Matt. Henry says "This represents the return of poor sinners to God.

Heaven is the Zion they aim at as their end. On this they have set their hearts, toward this they have set their faces, and therefore they ask the way to it. They do not ask the way to heaven and set their faces to the world, nor set their faces toward heaven and go on at a venture without asking the way. In all true converts there are both a sincere desire to attain the end and a constant care to keep in the way." Their desire and design was to *"join themselves to the Lord in a perpetual covenant."* That was something they must do, and it is to that particular expression we would ask careful attention, for it has been totally ignored by hyper-Calvinists, who say nothing at all upon the human-responsibility side of the subject — what we must do before the benefits of the Covenant are actually made over to us.

CHAPTER XXV

There is a zeal which is not according to knowledge (Rom. 10:2), and the ecclesiastical history of the last three centuries supplies many sad examples of same. In opposing the Papist fiction of human merits, some went too far in the opposite direction and failed to enforce the necessity of good works. In protesting against a general or indefinite atonement and in contending for particular redemption, not a few hyper-Calvinists repudiated the free offer of the Gospel. Many handled the total depravity and spiritual inability of the natural man in such a manner that his responsibility was completely undermined. In their ardor to magnify the sovereign grace of God, men often lost sight of the moral requirements of His righteousness. There has been a lamentable lack of balance in presenting the inseparable truths of justification and sanctification, and the privileges and duties of believers. The perseverance of the saints in faith and holiness has not received nearly so much emphasis among Calvinists as has the Divine preservation of them, nor have they said one-tenth as much on repentance as on faith. The same grievous defect appears in many of the sermons preached on the Covenant. The Puritans were thoroughly sound and symmetrical on it, but some who followed them, though posing as the champions of Truth, were very lopsided.

"Gather My saints together unto Me: Those who have made a covenant with Me by sacrifice" (Ps. 50:5). This is still another verse which has been greatly if not totally neglected by those against whose partiality we complain. It also deals with the human side of things. There is a human side in connection with the Covenant. It is just as true that men must enter into covenant with God, as it is that He deigns to enter into covenant with them. In this verse we learn that one of the distinguishing marks of God's saints is that they have made a covenant with Him: That speaks of human action and not of Divine operations. The saints make a covenant with God *"by sacrifice,"* for no valid paction can be entered into with Him apart from the intervention of a sacrifice. At the beginning of their national history Israel entered into a solemn covenant with Jehovah, and they did so by sacrifice. A graphic account of the same is furnished in Ex. 24. There is much there of outstanding interest and importance which we cannot now dwell upon; only a bare notice of the salient features will here be in order.

After Moses had received the ten commandments from the Lord, he returned and *"told the people all the words of the Lord"* (v. 3) – that obedience which He required from them. Their response was prompt and proper: *"all the people answered with one voice and said, All the words which the Lord has said will we do."* Moses then gave orders for oxen to be sacrificed unto the Lord: half of the blood he sprinkled on the altar, half he put into basins. Having written the words of the Lord in what is specifically called *"the book of the covenant"* he then read it unto the whole of the congregation, and they again vowed to be obedient (v. 7). Next Moses *"took the blood and sprinkled it on the people and said, Behold the blood of the covenant."* Thus was the covenant formally ratified: God binding Himself to the fulfilling of His promises and they binding themselves to His precepts, that they might avoid the penalty threatened and obtain the blessings promised. To that transaction the apostle refers in Heb. 9:19,20 – *"testament"* should be *"covenant."* those slain oxen prefigured the sacrifice of

Christ and the benefits accruing from there. The congregation represented *"the Israel of God"* (Gal. 6:16), and their compact with the Lord adumbrated the full surrender which believers make of themselves unto God when they respond to the call of the Gospel.

Christians also make a covenant with God, and they do so *"by sacrifice."* Christ's death was a real and true sacrifice: see Eph. 5:2. In all the sacrifices there was a shedding of blood without which there was no remission of sins, and as their antitype Christ's blood was poured out. Christ's death was a mediatory sacrifice, a propitiatory sacrifice, an accepted sacrifice, and therefore an effectual one. It has all the virtues of a sacrifice. As the Rector and Judge of the universe God was pacified, as the party offended, by Christ's oblation. Christ made His soul an offering for sin and God accepted the same as a full satisfaction to His justice. So too His blood expiates the offences of His people: *"when He had by Himself purged our sins, sat down on the right hand of the Majesty on high."* When rightly appropriated His blood removes both the guilt and pollution of sin. So too it is adequate for the sinner himself, the offending party. When he avails himself of the proferred remedy and trusts in Christ's atonement, he is reconciled to God. No other sacrifice is needed by God nor is it by the sinner.

By His sacrifice Christ made and confirmed the new covenant. By virtue of His oblation Christ is authorized to offer the terms and dispense the benefits of it. *"Now the God of peace, that brought again from the dead the Lord Jesus, that great Shepherd of the sheep, through the blood of the everlasting covenant"* (Heb. 13:20). Observe carefully the *"blood of the everlasting covenant"* has a double reference there. First, to God, as *"The God of peace,"* that is, to God as pacified – His wrath appeased and His justice satisfied by a full recompense being made for our offences. Second, to Christ Himself: having satisfied to the uttermost farthing, God brought Him back from the dead and invested Him with His office of *"the great Shepherd of the sheep."* That is, as the One who had the right to rescue His strayed sheep out of the power of the roaring lion, and bring them into the fold to enjoy the privileges of the flock. And by Christ's sacrifice the benefits of the covenant are ratified and conveyed to us. That is evident from His own words at the institution of the Lord's supper: *"this is My blood of the new covenant, which is shed for many, for the remission of sins"* (Matt. 26:28) – the principal blessing. It is by the blood of the covenant we are pardoned, sactified and perfected forever.

As Manton showed, our manner of entering into covenant with God is by the same moral acts as which Israel of old were conversant about the sacrifices and what they imported. Those sacrifices represented the defilement they had contracted by sin: by the killing of the beast, they owned that they deserved to die themselves. The oblations they brought to the tabernacle or temple were public testifications of their guilt and pollution, an acknowledgement that their life was forfeit to God. As the apostle informs us *"in those sacrifices there is a remembrance again made of sins"* (Heb. 10:3); they kept before their offerers what they were as violators of the Law. Now the same obligation lies upon us if we would make a covenant with God by virtue of the great sacrifice of Christ. There must be the recognition that the curse of the law binds us over to eternal wrath and a subscription to that solemn fact by our conscience. There must be an acknowledgement of our guilt and pollution, and that, with broken heartedness.

Unless we be deeply affected by our sinfulness and ruin Christ will be little valued by us.

The sacrifices appointed by God in the O.T. era told forth His abundant mercy: that God had no pleasure in the death of the wicked, but rather that he turn from his wickedness and live. And in order that His mercy might be on a righteous basis, His love provided that which His justice demanded. That has been lost sight of by the dispensationalists, who erroneously represent the Mosaic economy as a stern regime of unrelieved justice. But it should ever be remembered that side by side with the moral law was the ceremonial, with its oblations and ablutions, where forgiveness and cleansing were obtainable for those who availed themselves of it. All through the O.T. era *"mercy rejoiced against judgment"* (Ex. 34:6,7; Ps. 103:8; Isa. 1:18). That *"The Lord is gracious and full of compassion, slow to anger, and of great mercy"* was shown and believed in David's time (Ps. 145:8), for those blessed attributes were clearly revealed in the sacrifices – types as they were of Christ. So today the sinner who would enter into covenant with God should realize that He is merciful and in Christ has made full provision for his deep need. This is to be acknowledged by us with thankfulness and joy.

Those O.T. sacrifices were also so many obligations unto duty, for they instructed the offerer of that worship and obedience which he owed unto God. Since God required propitiation for sin, they were shown the need for conforming to His law, and whereas His mercy made provision for their past failure, gratitude should prompt them unto future subjection. Moreover, by offering a ram or an ox unto the Lord the one who brought it did in effect devote himself, with all his strength, unto Him. In this way the offerer was taught to yield himself unto His service. And so unto those who would make or renew a covenant with God, the N.T. word is *"I beseech you, therefore, brethren, by the mercies of God, that you present your bodies a living sacrifice, holy, acceptable unto God, which is your reasonable service"* (Rom. 12:1). That, as we showed at some length in a recent article, supplies an interpretation of the rites of the Law and of the *"reasonable"* part of the O.T. order of things. Thus, he who would make a covenant with God is required to give up himself wholly unto God with a sincere and firm resolution unto a new life of obedience to Him. If there is any reservation the covenant is marred in the making of it: *"Their heart was not right with Him, neither were they steadfast in His covenant"* (Ps. 78:37).

As the Puritan Wm. Gurnall so faithfully remarked upon Ps. 50:5, "We are not Christians till we have subscribed this covenant, and that without any reservation. When we take upon us the profession of Christ's name, we enlist ourselves in His muster-roll and by it do promise that we will live and die with Him in opposition to all His enemies. He will not entertain us till we resign up ourselves freely to His disposal, that there may be no disputing with His commands afterwards, but as one under authority, go and come at His word." So too Manton: "You have no benefit by the covenant till you personally enter into the bond of it. It is true, God being pacified by Christ, offers pardon and acceptance on the condition of the covenant, but we do not actually partake of the benefits till we perform those conditions. Though the price is paid by Christ, accepted by the Father, yet we have not an actual interest, through our own default, for not accepting God's covenant. What shall we do? Bless God for His grace. Own

Christ as the Son of God, the Redeemer of the world, and the Fountain of our life and peace. Devote yourselves to God, to serve and please Him."

Not only are we required to take hold of God's covenant (Isa. 56:4,6), to make a covenant with God by sacrifice (Ps. 50:5), and to *"join ourselves to the Lord in a perpetual covenant"* (Jer. 50:5), but we are enjoined *"Take heed unto yourselves lest you forget the covenant of the Lord your God"* (Deut. 4:23) and *"Be mindful always of His covenant"* (1 Chron. 16:15). We are required to abide faithfully by the promises we made and the agreement we entered into when we chose Him to be our God and gave up ourselves unreservedly unto Him, for the promises of the covenant are made only unto such: *"All the paths of the Lord are mercy and truth unto such as keep His covenant and His testimonies"* (Ps. 25:10). Of old the Lord complained, *"His people have transgressed My covenant"* (Judges 2:20). *"Israel and Judah have broken My covenant"* (Jer. 11:10). They themselves acknowledged *"the children of Israel have forsaken Your covenant"* (1 Kings 19:10). *"They kept not the covenant of God"* (Ps. 78:10). So it is with the Christian when he departs from the Lord and enters upon a course of self-pleasing. Therefore, in order for a backslider to be restored, he must needs renew his covenant with God, for the recovery of such an one is a new *"conversion"* (Luke 22:32). And so he is required to *"do the first works"* (Rev. 2:5).

Now cannot certain of our readers see for themselves how unfair and unfaithful it is for preachers and writers to make so much of and quote so frequently such verses as 2 Sam. 23:5, Jer. 31:33,34; 32:40,41, and utterly ignore Isa. 56:4-6, Jer. 50:5, Ps. 50:5 and those cited in the preceding paragraph. Cannot they perceive it is handling God's word deceitfully, and utterly misleading unto souls to be constantly comforting them with the *"I wills"* of God, yet remaining silent upon the *"Be you,"* *"you shalls"* and failing to press such exhortations? Cannot they see how dishonest it is to treat only of that covenant which God enters into with the elect before time began in the person of their Head, and say nothing of the covenant which we must make with God during this time-state? We ourself should be guilty of the very partiality against which we inveigh were we to publish in booklet form the last four of our articles on Reconciliation in the 1944 vol. and the first four in 1945 entitling them *"The Covenant of Grace,"* if we failed to add to them what has been adduced in this chapter and the three preceding it, in which we have set before the reader the human side of things — what God requires from us.

God has appointed a *"due order"* or connection — a moral and righteous one — between the blessings purchased by Christ and the actual conveyance of them unto us, in which our responsibility is enforced. To quote from yet another of the able and godly Puritans: "Holiness is God's signature upon all heavenly doctrines, which distinguishes them from all carnal inventions. They have a direct tendency to promote His glory and the real benefit of the rational creature. Thus the way of salvation by Christ is most fit to reconcile God to man by securing His honor, and to reconcile man to God by encouraging his hope...The grace of the Gospel is so far from indulging sin that it gives the most deadly wound to it, especially since the tenor of the new covenant is that the condemned creature, in order to receive pardon and the benefits that are purchased, must receive the Benefactor with the most entire consent for his Prince and Saviour. Thus the Divine wisdom has so ordered the way of salvation that, as mercy and justice in

God, so holiness and comfort may be perfectly united in the reasonable creature" (Wm. Bates, *"The Harmony of the Divine Attributes"* 1660). The death of Christ is not only the surest ground of comfort, but the strongest incentive to obedience.

We are advocating no new or strange doctrine when we insist that the Everlasting Covenant and the Gospel requires from us repentance and faith, full surrender unto God and the steadfast performance of obedience unto the end of our lives. "The obligation on us unto holiness is equal as unto what it was under the Law, though a relief is provided where unavoidably we come short of it. There is, therefore, nothing more certain than that there is no relaxation given us as unto any duty of holiness by the Gospel, nor any indulgence unto the least sin. But yet upon the supposition of the acceptance of sincerity, and a perfection of parts instead of degrees, with mercy provided for our failings and sins, there is an argument to be taken from the command unto indispensable necessity of holiness, including in it the highest encouragement to endeavor after it. For together with the command there is also grace administered, enabling us unto the obedience which God will accept. Nothing therefore can avoid or evacuate the power of this command and argument from it but a stubborn contempt of God arising from the love of sin" (J. Owen).

Probably there is another class of our readers who have never heard anything on the subject, as well as those who are acquainted only with the Divine side of it, who are ready to exclaim, If it is an imperative condition of salvation that man enters into a definite covenant with God, then that cuts me off entirely, for I have never made one with Him! Alas, it is sadly true that, through the laziness or unfaithfulness of the preachers they have sat under, many of the Lord's people know nothing, or next to nothing, about the Covenant of Grace. On the other hand, it is blessedly true that, in the mercy of God, though all unconscious to themselves, they had been led to comply with the terms of the Covenant. Though they knew not that they were truly (though not formally) entering into Covenant with God when they repented, believed the Gospel and received Christ Jesus as their Lord and Saviour, yet such was the case. Each one who has really responded to the call in Isa. 55:3 with him God has *"made an everlasting covenant"* — Nevertheless his ignorance of that fact does not excuse the Christian's failure to have learned from the Scriptures what they teach on it.

Let us now seek to remove one or two difficulties which may have been raised in the minds of our friends. When we affirm that God's ministers are to make a free offer of the Gospel to every creature and that they are to call upon all who hear it *"be reconciled to God,"* that does not imply that the results of Christ's death are rendered uncertain, that the success of His redemptive work is suspended on the caprice of man's will. Not at all. It has been far too little recognised that God has more than one design in sending forth the Gospel. First, it is for the glory of Christ — a worldwide proclamation of His excellencies. God intends that a universal testimony shall be borne to the person and work of the One who so superlatively honored Him. Second, the preaching of the Gospel is made a further test of corrupt nature, demonstrating that men love darkness rather than light. Third, God uses the Gospel as a remedial agency in curbing the wickedness of the world, for many are reformed by it who are never savingly transformed in this way, making this scene a safer place for His people to pass through. It is also the means by which He calls out His elect: the sieve in which the wheat is separated from the chaff.

But if Christ be the Head and Representative of His people, and as their Surety fulfilled every requirement of the Law, in their stead and earned its reward, must not every one of them be made partakers of that reward? Most assuredly, yet still in the order or way God has appointed. We must have the requisite qualification to make us meet for that reward. "This qualification is faith. As grace in God qualified God (if I may use the expression) for effecting reconciliation, so faith in us qualifies us for applying and enjoying it. Though Christ be the Purchaser, yet faith is the means of instating us in it. *'Being justified by faith, we have peace with God through our Lord Jesus Christ.'* Not a man has peace with God till justified by faith. This inestimable favor is not conferred but upon men of good will, that value and consent to it. We must lay our hands upon the head of the sacrifice and own Him for ours. This is the bond which unites us to Christ the Purchaser, and by Him to God as the Author of reconciliation. It gives us a right to this peace, and at the last the comfort of it " (S. Charnock).

But does not God's requirement of faith from us leave the outcome of Christ's redemption uncertain? In no wise. Why not? Because Christ by His merits procured the Holy Spirit to work in His people what God requires from them to meet the terms of His covenant and to fulfill the conditions of the Gospel. "The purchase was made by Christ alone upon the cross, without any qualification in us; the application is not wrought without something in us concurring with it, though that also is wrought by the grace of God. God has ordained peace for us. There is a work to be wrought within us for the enjoyment of that peace: *'Lord, You will ordain peace for us, for You also have wrought all our works in us'* (Isa. 26:12). The one is the act of God in Christ, the other is the act of God by the Spirit. Though the fire burn, if I would be warmed I must not run from it, but approach it"(Charnock). It is that work of Christ's Spirit within the elect which capacitates and causes them to abandon their idols, put forth faith, and makes them willing to be wholly devoted to God.

That was admirably set forth in the Westminster Confession of Faith — the joint and studied production of many of the ablest of the Puritans. *"Man by his fall having made himself incapable of life by the first covenant, the Lord was pleased to make a second, commonly called the Covenant of Grace: by which He freely offered unto sinners life and salvation by Jesus Christ, requiring of them faith in Him that they might be saved, and promising to give unto all those who are ordained unto life His Holy Spirit, to make them willing and able to believe."* The grand change in our legal relation to God, secured by Christ's satisfaction, is infallibly followed by the great change in our experimental relation to God, as that is wrought in us by the Spirit's work of regeneration and sanctification, the one being the fruit of the other — the reward assured the Surety on behalf of those He represented. Our reconciliation to God (through the renewing of the Spirit) is the sure consequence of His reconciliation to us, and a faith which works by love, which goes out in acts of holy obedience, is the evidence of our new birth and of our having entered into covenant with God.

"We joy in God through our Lord Jesus Christ, by whom we have now received the reconciliation" (Rom. 5:11). It is through Him, by the working of His

Spirit, that we have, by faith, been enabled to *"receive the reconciliation"* which the Mediator wrought out for us. From the Divine side of things the evangelist goes forth on no uncertain errand, for the invincible operations of the Spirit God makes the Gospel effectual unto each hearer chosen unto salvation. Yet from the human side of things the evangelist is required to enforce the responsibility of his hearers, calling on them to *"be reconciled to God,"* to repent and believe the Gospel, to make a covenant with God, and so far from assuring them that God will work in their hearts what He requires of them (which would encourage them to remain in a state of inertia), he is to enforce God's righteous demands, press upon them the claims of Christ, and bid them flee for refuge to the hope set before them.

CHAPTER XXVI.
ITS NEED

In the previous chapters we have shown at some length the need for and the nature of reconciliation being effected between God and those who have broken His Law. We have dwelt upon the amazing fact that, though He was the One wronged, yet God took the initiative and is the Author of recovering the rebellious unto Himself. We have seen how that project engaged His eternal counsels in the Everlasting Covenant, and that therein His wisdom found a way by which His love might flow forth unto the guilty without any sullying of His holiness of flouting of His justice, and how that the Son fully concurred in the Father's counsels and voluntarily performed the stupendous work in order to their accomplishment. We have already considered that which God requires from sinners if they are to become actual participants of the good of Christ's mediation and personally *"receive the reconciliation"* (Rom. 5:11). We are therefore now ready to contemplate the *"results"* of fruits of that reconciliation – the consequences which follow from the new relation to God and His Law which the sinner enters into upon his repentance and saving acceptance of the Gospel.

Causes and their effects need ever to be distinguished if we are to obtain something more than a vague and general idea of the things with which they are concerned. It is by confounding principles and their products that so many are confused. As we have shown in previous chapters, reconciliation is one of the principal results which issue from the sacrifice of Christ. Strictly speaking it has a fourfold cause. The will of the Father, or His eternal counsels, was its originating cause. The mediation of the incarnate Son is its meritorious and procuring cause. The work of the Spirit in the souls of the elect is the efficient cause, for it is by His gracious and invincible operations they are capacitated to do that which God requires of them before they become actual partakers of the benefits of Christ's mediation. The repentance and faith of the awakened and convicted sinner is the instrumental cause by which he is reconciled to God. We say that reconciliation is one of the principal results from Christ's sacrifice – redemption, remission, sanctification are others, and they are so intimately related that it is not easy to prevent an overlapping of them in our thoughts. But in what follows we shall treat, mainly, not of the effect of Christ's redemptive work, but rather the results of reconciliation itself.

Perhaps the most comprehensive of any single statement in Holy Writ concerning the outcome of reconciliation is found in that brief but pregnant word *"Christ has also once suffered, the Just for the unjust, that He might bring us to God"* (1 Pet. 3:18). *"Bring us to God"* is a general expression for the whole benefit which ensues from reconciliation, including the removal of all obstacles and impediments and the bestowment of all requisites and blessings. Formerly there was a legal hostility and moral dissimilarity between God and us, with the want of intercourse and fellowship, but now those who were once *"far off"* are *"made nigh"* (Eph. 2:13). In consequence of what Christ did and suffered, His people have been enstated into life, brought into the favor of God, become partakers of the nature of God, have restored to them the image of God, are given access to God, are favored to have communion with Him and will yet enjoy the eternal and ineffable vision of Him. Let that serve as our outline.

1. The initial consequence of our reconciliation to God by Christ is that we

146

have life: a life in Law. That is an aspect of our subject which, fundamental though it be, has received scarcely any attention from theologians and Bible teachers. It is one which is familiar to few of God's people, and therefore calls for both explanation and elaboration. By our sin and fall in Adam we died legally, our life-in-law was lost, for we came under its curse. The Divine Judge had threatened our federal head *"In the day you eat of it, you shall surely die,"* and *"in Adam all die"* (1 Cor. 15:22). The case of each descendant of his upon entering this world is like that of a murderer in the condemned cell – awaiting the hour of execution unless he be reprieved. We are by nature *"the children of wrath"* (Eph. 2:3) and until we savingly believe in the Son *"the wrath of God abides on us"* (John 3:36). We have no life in Law, no title to its award, but are transgressors, and as such under its death sentence – *"condemned already"* (John 3:18).

The consequence of Adam's dying legally was that he also died spiritually: that is, his soul became vitiated and depraved. He lost the moral image of God and the capacity to enjoy Him or please Him. Legal death and spiritual death are quite distinct (John 5:24), the latter being entailed by the former. *"By one man sin entered into the world, and death by sin, and so death passed upon all men"* (Rom. 5:12) – not simply *"entered into"* all men, but *"passed upon"* them as a judicial sentence. *"By the offence of one judgment came upon all men to condemnation"* (Rom. 5:18). The guilt of the federal head was imputed unto all he represented – evidenced by so many dying in infancy, for since even physical death is part of the wages of sin and infants having not personally committed any, they must be suffering the consequences of the sin of another. But Adam died spiritually as well as legally, and his depravity is imparted to all his descendants, so that they enter this world both legally and spiritually *"alienated from the life of God, through the ignorance that is in them, because of the blindness of their heart"* (Eph. 4:18).

Now it is only by Christ, *"the last Adam,"* that we can regain life either legally or spiritually. That they obtain spiritual life from Christ, is well understood by the saints, but His having secured for them a life in Law, most of them are quite ignorant about. Yet Rom. 5 is very emphatic on the point: *"For if by one man's offence death reigned by one (i.e. a single transgression), much more they which receive abundance of grace (to meet not only the original but their own innumerable transgressions) and of the gift of righteousness (i.e. the inputed obedience of Christ) shall reign in life by One, Jesus Christ. Therefore as by the one offence judgment came on all men to condemnation, even so by the righteousness of One the free gift came upon all men to justification of life"* (Rom. 5:17,18) – note well that last clause: not *"the free gift entered into all men unto regeneration of life."* Justification is entirely a legal matter and concerns our status before the Lawgiver. As God's elect lost their life in law through the disobedience of their first federal head, so the obedience of their last Federal Head has secured for them a life in law.

Christ is the fountain of life unto all His spiritual seed, and that, not as the second Person in the Trinity, but as the God-man Mediator. *"For it pleased the Father that in Him should all fulness dwell"* (Col. 1:19), which has reference to Christ officially and not essentially. Failure to grasp that truth has resulted in some verses of Scripture being greviously misunderstood and misinterpreted, to the dishonoring of our blessed Lord. For instance, when He declared *"For as the*

Father has life in Himself, so has He given to the Son to have life in Himself" (John 5:26) He was there speaking of Himself as incarnate. As God the Son, co-essential and co-glorious with the Father, He always had *"life in Himself" – "in Him was life"* (John 1:4) which refers to His essential person before He became incarnate. But as God-man Mediator the Father gave Him *"to have life in Himself:"* He gave Him a mediatorial life and fulness for His people. *"As You have given Him power over all flesh, that He should give eternal life to as many as You have given Him."* (John 17:2) presents the same aspect of Truth – Christ was there speaking as the Mediator, as is evident from His high priestly prayer which immediately follows.

"As the living Father has sent Me and I live by the Father, so he that eats Me even he shall live by Me." (John 6:57). That title *"the living Father"* respects Him in connection with the economy of redemption and expresses His supremacy over the office of His Son, as the One who covenanted and sent Him forth on His grand mission. In His Godhead the Son has life – has it essentially, originally, independently in Himself, as a Person co-eternal with the Father. But as Mediator, the life which Christ lived and lives to God, and which in the discharge of His mediatorial office He bestows on His people, is derived from and is dependent upon the will of the Father, for in office the Son is lower than and inferior to the Father – in that respect, and in that only, *"My Father is greater than I"* (John 14:28), He declared. In affirming that *"I live·by the Father"* (John 6:57), Christ signified that His mediatorial life was sustained by the Father. Let it be clearly understood that in John 6:57 the Lord Jesus was speaking of Himself officially, mediatorially, and not essentially as God the Son.

"I live by the Father." The Father prepared a body for Him (Heb. 10:5) and all the days of His flesh was upholding Him by the right hand of His righteousness. Christ definitely acknowledged this again and again, by the Spirit of prophecy and by His ministerial utterances: *"Thou maintainest My lot...I have set the Lord always before Me. Because He is at My right hand, I shall not be moved"* (Psalm 16:5,8). *"I gave My back to the smiters and My cheeks to them that plucked off the hair. I hid not My face from shame and spitting. For the Lord God will help Me; therefore I shall not be confounded"* (Isa. 50:5,6). *"I came down from Heaven not to do My own will, but the will of Him that sent Me"* (John 6:38). *"Believest thou not that I am in the Father and the Father in Me? The words that I speak to you I speak not of Myself, but the Father that dwells in Me, He does the works"... "as the Father gave Me commandment, even so I do"* (John 14:10,31). In all these passages He spoke as the dependent One, the Mediator.

By purchase Christ ratified His title to the mediatorial life – *"Now the God of peace* (the propitiated and reconciled One) *that brought again from the dead* (not *"the,"* but *"our"*) *Lord Jesus, that great Shepherd of the sheep,"* nor as the God-man considered as a private person, that God raised Him – but as the God-man Mediator and Surety of His people – by His own essential power Christ emerged from the tomb (John 2:19; 10:17). By the right of conquest Christ secured the mediatorial life, being made a royal priest *"after the power of an endless life"* –*"He asked life of You* (cf. Ps. 2:8)! *Thou gavest it Him, even length of days forever and ever"* (Heb. 7:16; Ps. 21:5). He has an official right and title to life because He had *"magnified the Law and made it honorable"* (Isa.42:21)—magnified it by rendering to it a personal, perfect and perpetual obedience in thought, word and deed, and that as the God-man Mediator, *"For Moses described the righteous-*

ness which is of the Law; that the man who does these things shall live by them."

It has not been sufficiently recognized that the converse of *"the wages of sin is death"* is *"the award of obedience is life!"* The first man violated the Law and therefore suffered its penalty; but the last man fulfilled the Law and therefore obtained a right to its reward. Christ found the Commandment *"unto life"* (Rom. 7:10), and it was for that life (the reward of the Law) He *"asked"* (Ps. 21:5) and which He received (Heb. 6:16) after He had vanquished death. Christ *"reigns in life"* (Rom. 5:17, in *"justification of life"* (Rom. 5:18 and cf. Isa. 50:8, 1 Tim. 3:16). Christ now *"lives unto God"* (Rom. 6:10) and He does so as the last Adam, as our Representative. Christ's life in law is also that of His people: *"Christ our life"* (Col. 3:4). Christ is the sole fountain of life, the source from which our life – both legal and spiritual – flows. It is for this reason that the scroll on which are the names of God's elect is inscribed is called *"the Lamb's book of life"* (Rev. 21:27), it is the Mediator's book for *"the Lamb"* is always expressive of Christ as the Priest and sacrifice of His people, and it is His mediatorial life which He shares with us.

The antithesis of sin is righteousness, for as sin is the transgression of the Law (1 John 3:4) so righteousness is rightness or measuring up to the standard of right, and therefore consists of fulfilling the Law. And since the God-man Mediator perfectly obeyed it, we are told that *"He is the end of the Law for righteousness to everyone that believes"* (Rom. 10:4). Now just as sin and death cannot be separated, so righteousness and life are indivisible. A further appeal to Rom. 5 establishes that: *"they. which receive abundance of grace and of the gift of righteousness shall reign in life by One, Jesus Christ. . . by the righteousness of One the free gift came upon all men into justification of life. . . as sin has reigned unto death, even so might grace reign through righteousness unto eternal life by ("in") Jesus Christ our Lord"* (vv. 17,18,21) – in each case it is a premial life or one of reward from the Law. *"Christ our life"* (Col. 3:4): apart from Him we have no standing before the Law, no title to its award; but being federally and judicially one with Him, then that which was due Him in return for His perfect fulfilment of the Law's requirements is due those He represented.

Far too little attention has been paid to the first member in the antithesis presented in Deut. 28, namely, *"that these blessings shall come on you and overtake you if you shall listen diligently to the voice of the Lord your God. Blessed shall you be...blessed shall be...blessed shall be...blessed shall you be when you come in and blessed shall you be when you go out"* (verses 2-6); which is set over against *"But. . . if you will not hearken unto the voice of the Lord your God to observe to do all His commandments. . . that all these curses shall come upon you and overtake you"* etc. (v. 5 etc.). Just as surely as the Law pronounces a curse on those who break it, so the Law pronounces a blessing on those who keep it. The curse is death, and the blessing life, and that blessing the God-man Mediator obtained as the Surety of His people. As Christ is, objectively and by imputation, *"our righteousness,"* so He is objectively and by imputation *"our life."* By Christ those who are reconciled to God have life in law, and that is the foundation of all the other results or consequences of their restoration to His judicial favor.

2. Pardon from God. *"God was in Christ reconciling the world unto Himself, not imputing their trespasses unto them"* (2 Cor. 5:19). The trespasses of God's penitent and believing people are not charged against them, because His wisdom discovered a way by which He might be fully recompensed for the wrong which

our sins did unto His majesty – by imputing them to our Substitute and exacting vengenance upon Him for the same. Our iniquities were laid upon Him and because of them He suffered *"the Just for the unjust."* That which was the ground of reconciliation was likewise the ground of the pardon of our iniquities: *"In whom we have redemption through His blood the forgiveness of sins, according to the riches of His grace"* (Eph. 1:7). Remission was the ransom-price which Christ paid unto God's justice, and therefore a principal part of our reconciliation is the remission of our sins. Remission of sins means that the guilt demnation of them is cancelled, and therefore that we are released from the penalty and punishment of them, and that, because the punishment was borne by Christ and God's wrath appeased.

Now observe how inseparably connected is the pardon of the believer's sins with his possessing a life in law before God. As we have shown above, obedience to the Law (in the person of our Surety) is righteousness, and where there is righteousness the Law bestows blessing, as surely as it pronounces a curse on all unrighteousness. Now what does the blessing of the Law consist of? Negatively, that it has naught against us, and where that is the case none can truly *"lay anything to our charge."* Positively, that it pronounces us righteous, and as such, entitled to its award and blessing. Therefore we are told *"Blessed is he whose transgression is forgiven, whose sin is covered. Blessed is the man unto whom the Lord imputes not iniquity"* (Ps. 32:1,2). Yet we need to be on our guard against drawing a false inference from this. As Christians we still transgress and therefore need to beg for daily forgiveness – as well as for daily bread, as Matt. 6:12 plainly shows. As Christ is required to ask and sue out the fruits of His mediation (Ps. 2:7), so we are enjoined to humbly sue out our right of forgiveness – Jer. 3:12; 1 John 1:9.

3. **Peace with God.** *"Therefore being justified by faith, we have peace with God, through our Lord Jesus Christ"* (Rom. 5:1). This verse has been commonly misunderstood, through supposing the *"peace"* there mentioned to be that which is subjective rather than objective. The verse is not speaking about that peace of conscience when assured of Divine forgiveness, when the burden of our sin is removed and left at the foot of the cross, nor to that *"peace of God which passes all understanding,"* that keeps the hearts and minds of God's children when they are anxious for nothing, but in everything by prayer and supplication make known their requests unto God (Phil. 4:6,7); but to *"peace with God."* It is not a state of mind, but a relation to the Lawgiver which is in view. It is not tranquility of heart, but that relation which arises from the expiation of sin and consequent justification. *"Peace with God"* means that He no longer regards us as His enemies in the objective sense of the term, but are now the objects of His favor. It is that state of things which ensues from the cessation of hostilities. It means that the sword of Divine justice, which smote our Shepherd (Zech. 13:7), is now forever sheathed.

"Peace with God" means that we are no longer the objects of His displeasure, and therefore that we no more have any cause to dread the Divine vengeance. If due attention is paid to the first clause of Rom. 5:1 there should be no difficulty in understanding the second: the illative *"therefore"* pointing the connection. In the previous chapters the apostle had proved that all have sinned and come short of the glory of God, that they are guilty and under the condemnation of the Law. They are therefore viewed by Him as *"enemies"* and as such they are

"without strength" or ability to help themselves. In blessed contrast therefrom in 5:1-11 the apostle described at length the glorious status and state of those who are justified by faith. Justification imports the forgiveness of sins (Rom. 4:5-7) and that imports *"peace with God,"* that He is reconciled to us, that He no longer frowns but smiles upon us. To *"peace with God"* is added *"through our Lord Jesus Christ"* not *"by the operation of the Holy Spirit"* as had been the case if peace of conscience had been in view. As Christ is *"our life"* (Col. 3:4) objectively and legally, so He is *"our peace"* (Eph. 2:14) objectively and legally.

Just as spiritual life wrought in our souls through regeneration is the consequence of the legal life which we have in Christ, so inward peace or the purging of our consciences from dead works follows from the peace which Christ made (Col. 1:20) by the blood of His cross, though the measure of our inward peace is largely determined by the daily exercise of our faith (Rom. 15:13). Here again we may perceive how, intimately one result is linked with another. The antitypical Melchizedek is first *"King of righteousness"* and then *"King of peace"* (Heb. 7:2). *"The work of righteousness shall be peace."* That is, the mediatorial work of Christ shall produce *"peace with God,"* *"and the effect of righteousness* (as it is apprehended by faith), *quietness and assurance forever"* (Isa. 32:17). *"We have peace with God"* because *"the chastisement of our peace"* (Heb. peaces) *"was upon Him"* (Isa. 53:5). Peace here and hereafter, objectively and subjectively, with God and in the conscience the whole corrective or punishment which produced them was laid upon Christ. "By submitting to those chastisements Christ slew the enmity and settled the amity between God and man...and God not only saves us from ruin, but takes us into friendship. Christ was in pain, that we might be at ease" (Matt. Henry).

4. **Brought into God's favor.** By nature, and by practice Christians were *"the children of wrath, even as others"* (Eph. 2:3), being under the curse of the Law — all the threatenings of God in full force against them. But condemnation, awful as it is, is not damnation — the sentence is not yet executed, and until it is, it is not irrevocable. But once the sinner savingly believes in Christ he stands in a new relation to God as Lawgiver and Judge. He is no longer under the condemning power of the Law, but is *"under grace."* As the manslayer on having entered the city of refuge was, by a special constitution of mercy, secure from the avenger of blood (Num. 35:12), so the sinner who has *"fled for refuge to lay hold on the hope set before us"* in the Gospel (Heb. 6:18), is, by the gracious constitution of God, forever secured from the curse. All the threatenings which until this time belonged to him, no longer stand against him, but are reckoned by the Judge of all as having been executed on his Substitute, who was made a curse for His people. But more: the favor of God, Divine blessing, is now his status and portion.

When Christ reconciled the Church unto God He did more than put away her sins and avert the judicial wrath of God. He reinstated her in God's favor and opened the way for the full manifestation of His love unto her. The two things are clearly distinguished in Col. 1:20. *"Having made peace through the blood of His cross, by Him to reconcile all things unto Himself."* As we have so often pointed out in these articles, *"reconciliation"* consists of two things: the removal of enmity, and the restoring of amity — the two parts of Christ's mediatorial work, respectively, effecting them. His bloodshedding or enduring the curse of the Law removed the enmity or *"making peace,"* His obedience to the Law or bringing in *"an everlasting righteousness"* procuring the reward and entitling unto the Divine blessing. The shedding of Christ's atoning blood obtained for His people the remission or pardon of their sins. His meritorious obedience secured for them the justification of their persons in the high court of Heaven, or their admittance into God's judicial favor.

"Therefore being justified by faith, we have peace with God through our Lord Jesus Christ; by whom also we have access by faith into this grace wherein we stand" (Rom. 5:1,2). As we pointed out in the last, *"peace with God"* refers not to a subjective experience but to an objective fact, that it signifies not tranquility of soul but a relation to the Lawgiver. Hostilities between the Divine Judge and His believing people have ceased. His sword of justice is sheathed, and therefore they no longer have cause to dread His vengeance. But that is more or less a negative thing: there is something else, something positive, something more blessed. That additional benefit is introduced in Rom. 5:2 by the word *"also."* Suppose that one of the nobles of the land who stood high at court and enjoyed special privileges from his sovereign, should commit some grave offence against the throne, in fact turn traitor. We can imagine that, in his clemency the king might pardon the offender upon the acknowledgement of his crime and his suing for mercy, but we can scarcely conceive of the monarch restoring his subject to the intimacy and privileges he formerly enjoyed. Yet that is what Christ has done — restored apostate traitors to the full favor of God.

"By whom also we have access by faith into this grace wherein we stand." Christ has not only brought us into a legal state in which we are secure from God's wrath, but into one of intimate friendship with Him. It is indeed a great mercy that God has ceased to be offended with us, that He will never inflict any penal punishment upon us; but it is a far greater and grander blessing that He should regard us with pleasure and pour blessings upon us. *"By whom also we have access"* implies that by nature we did not, and that by our efforts we could not. Previous to conversion our standing was in disgrace, but now we are *"accepted in the Beloved,"* (Eph. 1:6), or as it might more literally be rendered *"graced in the Beloved."* Christ has reinstated His people int he good will and perfect acceptance of God: *"this is the true grace of God wherein you stand"* (1 Pet. 5:12). We stand in the full favor of God, with not a single cloud between us.

By the mediatorial work of Christ the believer has full right of approach to the Divine mercyseat, to gaze upon the face of a reconciled God, to dwell in His glorious presence for evermore. For this is no transient blessing which the obedience and bloodshedding of Christ has procured for His people, but a permanent and unalienable one. It is not only that they are admitted into God's favor, but it is *"this grace wherein we stand"* — in which you are eternally settled and established. It is not only that God will never again be at judicial enmity against them, but that He is forever their Friend. The blessings which Christ has obtained for His redeemed are not contingent or evanescent ones, for they are dependent upon nothing whatever in or from them, but are the unforfeitable procurements of His infinitely-meritorious righteousness. And therefore has the Father made a covenant-promise to His Son concerning those He transacted for, *"I will not turn away from them to do them good"* (Jer. 32:40). We have been received into the most cordial good will and everlasting favor of the Father.

5. Given access to God. The very first message from Heaven after the advent of the Prince of peace revealed the purpose for which the Son had become incarnate and made known what He would accomplish from His mission. *"There was with the angel a multitude of the heavenly host praising God, and saying, Glory to God in the highest, and on earth peace, good will toward men"* (Luke 2:13,14). That brief word contained a broad outline of the whole subject of reconciliation. First, it declared that the glory of God was its grand design, for that ever takes precedence of all other considerations. Second, it proclaimed that the issue of it would be peace on earth — not *"in the earth,"* but a revolted province restored to fealty. Third, it announced, as the *"and"* connecting the first and second clauses shows, that God's glory and the good of His people go hand in hand. Though He would show Himself a Friend to them, yet He would conserve His own interests and maintain His own honor. Fourth, it published the grand outcome: *"good will toward men"* — they brought into God's favor. The final clause may also be rendered *"good will among men"* — Jew and Gentile made one!

Now no sooner had the Peacemaker exemplified God's holiness, magnified His law, and pacified His wrath, in this way glorifying Him to the superlative degree, than we are told *"Behold, the veil of the temple was rent in twain from the top to the bottom"* (Matt. 27:51). That was a parable in action, and one possessed of profound spiritual significance. There were several other remarkable phenomena which immediately followed the death of Christ, but the Holy Spirit has placed first the rending of the temple veil. He calls our attention to that miraculous happening with the word *"Behold"* — bidding us pause and consider this marvel, be awed by it, amazed over it. That *"veil"* was a magnificent curtain hung between the holy place and the holy of holies, separating the one from the other, barring an entrance into the innermost chamber and shutting out from view its holy furniture from the sight of those in the second compartment. It was rent asunder at the moment Christ expired. Immediately the soul and spirit were separated from Christ's body, an invisible hand separated the veil.

Amazing synchronisation was that! Christ was the true Tabernacle or Temple (John 1:14), and therefore when His flesh was rent (Heb. 10:20), there was an answering rending of the structure which typed forth His flesh. Well may we reverently inquire, What was signified by that? First, though subordinately, it signified a revelation of the O.T. mysteries. The veil of the temple was for concealment. Out of all the congregation of Israel only one man was ever permitted to enter the holy of holies, and he but once a year, and then in a cloud of incense — symbolizing the darkness of that dispensation. But now, by the death of Christ, all is laid open: the shadows give place to the substance, the mysteries are unveiled. Second, and dispensationally, the uniting of Jew and Gentile by the removal of the partition wall — the ceremonial law (Eph. 2:14,15) — which had separated them. But third, and chiefly, that a new and living way had been opened unto God: the rending of the veil opened the door into the holiest, where He abode between the cherubim. The rending of the veil signified and announced free access unto God.

First, for Christ Himself. During the three hours of darkness the Redeemer was cut off from God. But when the veil was rent there was an anticipation of what is recorded in Heb. 9:11,12. Though Christ did not officially enter Heaven till forty days after his resurrection, yet He acquired the right to enter immediately (as our Surety) when He cried *"It is finished,"* and had a virtual admission. Therein we may perceive the conformity between the Head and the members of His Body: the moment a sinner savingly believes in Christ he has a title to enter heaven, yet he has to wait his appointed time ere he does so in the fullest sense. Second, for the redeemed. Christ has procured an entrance for them in spirit and by faith even now: *"Having therefore, brethren boldness to enter into the Holiest by the blood of Christ, by a new and living way, which He has consecrated for us, through the veil, that is say His flesh"* (Heb. 10:19,20). We have a free access to the throne of grace. *"Through Christ we both* (believing Jews and Gentiles) *have access by one Spirit unto the Father"* (Eph. 2:18).

It was sin which estranged us from the Holy One. Upon his first transgression Adam was driven out of paradise. The whole congregation of Israel at Sinai were commanded to keep their distance. The unclean in Israel were debarred from the camp and tabernacle. By so many different emblems did the Lord signify that sin had obstructed our access to Him. *"But now in Christ Jesus, you who sometime were far off are made nigh by the blood of Christ"* (Eph. 2:13), because His blood put away our sins. The efficacy of His sacrifice and the virtue of His meritorious obedience conferred upon His believing people the right to draw near unto God. All legal distance is removed: reconciliation has been effected: access to God is their consequent privilege and right. What a wonder of wonders is this! that one who is by nature a depraved creature may by grace, and through the Mediator, not only approach unto God without servile fear, but may have blessed fellowship with Him. To come into His very presence as a consciously accepted worshipper is the distinguishing blessing of Christianity in contrast from Judaism, Romanism and all false religions..

6. Endowed with the sanctifying gifts of the Spirit. *"For through Him we both have access by one Spirit unto the Father."* The mighty work of the Spirit in us is as indispensable as the meritorious work of Christ for us in order to appear before God as acceptable worshippers. As it is by the obedience and sufferings of Christ we have the title of access to God, so it is by the regenerating and sanctifying operations of the Spirit we have personal meetness for the same. That was typed out of old under the Mosaic economy. Those who drew near unto Jehovah in the services of His house were required to have not only the consecrating blood applied to their persons, but to be sprinkled with the anointing oil (Lev. 8:24,30). Three things are required if we are to worship God right. There must be knowledge in the understanding that we may be informed of what God approves and accepts, grace in the heart so that our communion with Him may be a real and spiritual one and not merely a bodily and formal one, strength in the soul for the exercise of faith, love, reverence and delight. By the Spirit alone are those three essentials imparted.

Now it is from a reconciled God, in virtue of Christ's meritorious work, that we receive the sanctifying Spirit. This is evident from the particular character in which the apostle addressed Deity in the following prayers: *"And the very God of peace sanctify you wholly"* (1 Thess. 5:23); *"Now the God of peace, that brought again from the dead our Lord Jesus, that great Shepherd of the sheep, through the blood of the everlasting covenant, make you perfect in every good* work to do His will, working in you that which is wellpleasing in His sight" (Heb. 13:20,21). The "God of peace" is the pacified and reconciled God, and the blessings which the apostle requested are bestowed or wrought in us by the Spirit. Christ prayed that His redeemed might be loved as He was loved of the Father (John 17) — not in degree, but in kind; and the sanctifying graces of the Spirit are the tokens and evidences of His love, the manifestations of His heart toward His people. Or, as Manton so beautifully expressed it, they are "the jewels of the covenant, with which the Spouse of Christ is decked."

Even the regenerate, harassed as they are by indwelling sin and hindered by their infirmities, can no more spiritually approach unto the Father without the gracious operations of the Spirit than they could without the mediation of Christ. The One supplies the experimental enablement, as the Other has the legal right. The Spirit's operations within us are imperative if our leaden hearts are to be raised above the things of time and sense, if our affections are to flow forth unto their rightful Object, if faith is to be duly acted upon Him, if a sense of His presence is to be felt in our souls. He alone can empower us experimentally to have real fellowship with God, so that He is glorified and we edified. How shall we ask for those things which are according to the Divine will unless the Spirit prompts us (Rom. 8:26)? How shall we "sing with grace in our hearts to the Lord" (Col. 3:16) without the Spirit's quickenings? How shall we bring forth fruit to the glory of God without the Spirit energizing us? And our enduement with the Spirit is one of the bestowments — the chief of them — of a reconciled God.

7. God's acceptance of our services. Those "services" may be broadly and briefly summed up as our obedience and worship. But says the self-emptied Christian, What can a poor, sinful creature like me possibly offer unto God which would be acceptable unto Him? The proud religionist may boast of his performances and plume his fine feathers, but not so one whose eyes have been anointed by the Spirit so that he sees himself in God's light. The one who is really "poor in spirit," realizes not only that his very righteousnesses as a natural man are as "filthy rags," but that his most spiritual works as a regenerate man are defective and defiled. How then shall such services be received by the Holy One? Some may experience a difficulty at this point and ask, Since the spiritual works of a Christian are wrought by the Holy Spirit, how can they be defiled? Answer: they are wrought by His agency and yet are performed by us. The purest water is fouled when it passes through a soiled pipe. The most brilliant lamp is blurred if it shines through a smoky chimney. Thus it is with what the Spirit produces through us.

But since our obedience and worship are so faulty and polluted, how can God accept them? Turn back to the first worshipper on this sin-cursed earth: "Abel ...brought of the firstlings of his flock and of the fat of them. And the Lord had respect unto Abel and to his offering" (Gen. 4:4). It was by faith Abel offered that "excellent sacrifice" (Heb. 11:4) which so blessedly foreshadowed the Lamb of God, and "the Lord had respect unto Abel and to his offering." The worshipper himself was first accepted and then his worship! Thus it has been ever since. The person is first taken into God's favor, and then his services are acknowledged as well-pleasing unto Him. Yet that does not furnish a complete answer to the question. Other types have to be taken note of if we are to obtain a complete picture. On the forehead of Israel's high priest was a plate of pure gold bearing the inscription *"Holiness to the Lord."* He wore it that he might *"bear the iniquity of the holy things which the children of Israel shall hallow in all their holy gifts, and it shall be always upon his forehead, that they may be accepted before the Lord"* (Ex. 28:36-38). Christ bore the defects of our *"holy things"* and because of His holiness God accepts from us whatever is sincere.

"The sinful failings of our best actions are hid and covered: they are not examined by a severe Judge, but accepted by a loving Father" (Manton). That is true, but it fails to show how the Father is righteously able to act so graciously. It is not because there has been any relating of His holiness or lowering of His standard, but because our Surety made full satisfaction to God's holiness for the sinful failings of their best actions. But even that is not all, for it is largely negative: our sincere obedience and reverent worship is accepted by the Father because the same ascends to God perfumed with the merits of Christ. In Rev. 8:3 He is seen as the Angel of the Covenant, *"And there was given unto Him much incense that He should add it to the prayers of all saints!"* Thus it is *"by Him"* that we offer the sacrifice of praise to God (Heb. 13:15). As those made *"priests unto God"* (Rev. 1:6) we are to *"offer up spiritual sacrifices,"* and they are *"acceptable to God by Jesus Christ"* (1 Pet. 2:5), and they are acceptable because He has effected a perfect reconciliation between God and the Church.

8. Our eternal security. In view of all that has been brought out under the previous heads, there is little need for us to enlarge upon this one. So perfect was the sacrifice which Christ offered to God on behalf of His Church that there is a perpetuity annexed to it: *"by one offering He has perfected forever them that are sanctified"* (Heb. 10:14). Its efficacy is of everlasting force and its merits are imputed to the believer without cessation. Christ made an end of sins, effected reconciliation for iniquity and brought in an everlasting righteousness (Dan. 9:24). That righteousness is imputed to His people and placed upon them as a robe (Isa. 61:10), and such is its virtue and vitality that it never wears out. But more: the risen Christ now serves continually as the Advocate of His people, pleading His sacrifice on their behalf, and suing out the benefits of it. *"If when we were enemies we were reconciled to God by the death of His Son, much more being reconciled we shall be saved by His life"* (Rom. 5:10). If while we were the objects of the Divine displeasure Christ restored us to God's favor, much more now that we are God's friends will He obtain pardon for our daily transgressions and secure our final salvation. The life of our risen Saviour is the security of His people: *"because I live, you shall live also"* (John 14:19).

"Christ is not only the Mediator of reconciliation to make our peace, but the Mediator of intercession to preserve it. He only took away our sins by His death; He only can preserve our reconciliation by His life. As He suffered effectively by the strength of His Deity to make our peace, so He intercedes in the strength of His merit to preserve peace. He did not only take away, but *'abolished and slew the emnity'* (Eph. 2:15,16). He slew it to make it incapable of living again, and if any sin stands up to provoke justice, He sits as an Advocate to answer the process (1 John 2:2). As God was in Christ reconciling the world, so He is in Christ giving out the fruits of that reconciliation, not imputing our trespasses unto us. Our constant access to God is by Christ. He sits in Heaven to lead us by the hand unto the Father, as a prince in favor brings a man into the presence of a gracious king" (Charnock). The sum of this, and the grand and infallible conclusion to which it all leads is, that nothing *"shall be able to separate us from the love of God which is in Christ Jesus"* (Rom. 8:39).

9. God for us — loving, providing for, protecting, blessing us. If we have been brought into His favor, and if He is the Ruler of the universe, then what will necessarily follow? This: that He will make *"all things work together for our good"* (Rom. 8:28). Nay more: *"All things are yours: whether Paul, or Apollos, or Cephas or the world, or life, or death, or things present, or things to come; all are yours; and you are Christ's and Christ is God's"* (1 Cor. 3:21-23). *"Christ is God's"* is a relation based upon the Mediatorial office. To Him, as the rightful Heir, God has given *"all things"* (Heb. 1:2), and by virtue of our relation to Christ, all things are ours — relatively, and subject to God's government for our good.

10. The beatific vision. On the resurrection morning, the body of the believer will be *"fashioned like unto Christ's glorious body"* (Phil. 3:21), then in spirit, soul and body, we shall be *"like Him"* (1 John 3:2), fully and eternally *"conformed to the image of God's Son"* (Rom. 8:29). Then will His prayer receive answer, *"Father, I will that they also whom You have given Me, be with Me where I am, that they may behold My glory"* (John 17:24).

CHAPTER XXVII

Up to this point we have dealt, almost entirely, with the expository side of our subject. Now we turn to what is more the experimental aspect of it. Some of our readers will consider this the most important and vital part, while to others it will make no appeal, being in their judgment better omitted. Those who read principally for intellectural information must appreciate that which supplies new light on things, explains to them what is obscure, or opens to them a difficult passage of Scripture, and often look with disfavor on that which calls upon them to diligently inquire what use they are making of the light they have received, to what practical ends are they turning their new knowledge. Yet this should be the principal concern of each of us. The interpretation of a passage of Scripture is but a means to an end. The personal appropriation and application of it to my own heart and life is the great desideratum. The value of a book, or of an article, lies chiefly in this: does it help to deliver its reader from the evil powers of this world and serve to assist him in his journey Heavenwards?

Though the other aspects of this grand truth which have been before us may both interest and instruct the mind, yet they will afford little real comfort and lasting peace to the heart until I am personally satisfied that I am reconciled to God, and He is reconciled to me. It deeply concerns each one of us to ascertain whether the wrath of God or the smile of God is upon him, whether the Law curses him or pronounces him righteous. It is a matter of utmost moment for us to determine whether we are the serfs of Satan or the friends of Christ, whether we are in a state of nature or of grace. We are plainly warned in Scripture that *"There is a generation that are pure in their own eyes, and yet is not washed from their filthiness"* (Prov. 30:12), and if I really value my eternal interests then I shall seriously and solemnly inquire, am I one of that deluded company? Am I numbered among those who sincerely believe that they have been cleansed from their sins by the blood of Christ, but are sincerely mistaken? More than a mere inquiry needs to be made: there should be an earnest and definite investigation.

"Examine yourselves whether you are in the faith, prove your own selves" (2 Cor. 13:5), yet that is the very task which the great majority of professing Christians refuse to undertake, and if it is pressed upon them, they see no need for engaging in it, firmly assured that all is well with them spiritually. It is natural for us to think well of ourselves, yet just to the extent that we are influenced by self-esteem will our judgment be prevented from forming a true estimate of ourselves. And while self-love and self-flattery rule our hearts, we shall decline this essential duty of self-examination. Pride produces presumption, so that its infatuated victims are secure in their conceit that they are heirs of Heaven, when in fact they have neither title nor meetness to it. Those thus bewitched cannot be induced to prosecute a course of self-examination, nor will they tolerate a searching and probing ministry, be it oral or written.

What madness has seized those who treat lightly what should become of their souls in eternity! And those who are unwilling for their profession to be thoroughly tested, are as truly numbered in that class as those who make no religious profession. Do you say, There is no need for my profession to be tested for it is a valid one, seeing that for years past I have been resting on the finished work of Christ. But my reader, God Himself bids those claiming to be His people *"give diligence to make your calling and election sure"* (2 Pet. 1:10), and He has given no needless exhortations. O pit not your vain confidence against infinite wisdom. Bare your heart to the Sword of the Spirit: shrink not from a faithful and discriminating ministry. Know you not that Satan employs a variety of tactics seeking to keep a firm hold upon his captives? And one of them is to prevent his deluded victims engaging in this very investigation – lest they should discover that, after all, their hope has rested on a foundation of sand.

"For every one that does evil hates the Light, neither comes to the Light, lest his deeds should be discovered" (John 3:20). Does not that place those who refuse to examine themselves whether they are in the faith and decline to be *"weighed in the balances of the Sanctuary?"* It certainly does. It ranks them among evil-doers. Despite all their religious pretensions, the solemn fact is that they *"hate the Light"* which exposes an empty profession, and therefore they *"come not to the Light"* to be tested by it. And why is this? Because they lack an honest heart, which desires to know the truth about themselves, no matter how unpalatable it is. Therefore it is that they find most distasteful and discomforting those sermons or articles which point out the differences between hypocrites and the sincere, and which show how closely the former may, in many ways, resemble the latter. Even if they began the work of self-examination it would prove so obnoxious as soon to be abandoned, and being under the power of a *"heart that is deceitful above all things"* would give themselves the benefit of the doubt.

But different far is it with those in whom a work of grace has been wrought. They have been made to realize something of the deceitfulness of sin and the awful solemnity of eternity, and therefore refuse to give themselves the benefit of any doubt, being determined at all costs to find out where they stand before God. Of each of them Christ declares *"But he that does truth* (is genuine and sincere) *comes to the Light, that his* (profession and) *deeds may be made manifest, that they are wrought in* (by) *God"* (John 3:21). He longs to know whether he is in a state of nature or of grace, and if his assurance of the latter is based on a conjectural persuasion or well-authenticated evidence, whether his faith in Christ is a natural one or *"the faith of God's elect"* (Titus 1:1), whether his repentance is *"the sorrow of the world"* which *"works death,"* or that *"godly sorrow"* which *"works repentance to salvation not to be repented of"* (2 Cor. 7:10). There is hope for a man who is deeply exercised over such matters; but there is none for those who are complacently satisfied with a false peace.

Readiness to be searched and probed by the Word of God, willingness to go to much pains to learn whether I am treading the Narrow Way which leads unto Life, or whether I am on the clean side of that broad road which terminates in destruction, is a good sign. As there is nothing that a hypocrite dreads more than to have his rottenness exposed, so there is nothing which an honest heart more longs to know than the real truth about his state before God. The earnest prayer of such an one is, *"Examine me, O Lord, and prove me, try my reins and my heart"* (Ps. 26:2). But alas, those who are filled with a carnal confidence feel no need of begging the Lord to *"prove"* them, for they are quite sure that all is well with them. Many, so completely deceived are they by Satan, they imagine it would be an act of unbelief to do so. Poor souls, they *"call evil good, and good evil,"* and *"put darkness for light, and light for darkness"* (Isa. 5:20).

"Examine me, O Lord, and prove me." Is that the cry of your soul, my reader?

If it is not, then there is strong reason to fear you are yet fatally enthralled by Satan. One of the surest marks of regeneration is that such a soul cries frequently, *"Search me, O God, and know my heart: try me, and know my thought: and see if there is any wicked way in me, and lead me in the way everlasting"* (Ps. 139:23,24). Yet it should be pointed out that this must not be made a shelving of our responsibility, a substitute for the performance of our own duty. God has bidden us, *"Examine yourselves whether you are in the faith,"* and every possible effort must be made by us to do so, taking nothing for granted, but resolutely and impartially scrutinising our hearts, measuring ourselves by the Word, ascertaining whether or not we have the marks and evidences of regeneration. Like the Spouse we should say, *"Let us get up early . . . let us see if the vine flourish"* (Song of Sol. 7:11).

"Examine yourselves whether you are in the faith" clearly implies that a knowledge of our spiritual state is possible. As the natural man perceives his own thoughts, knows what views and motives regulate him, and is acquainted with his own designs and aims, so may the spiritual man. "Reflection and knowledge of self is a prerogative of a rational creature. We know that we have souls by the operations of them. We may know that we have grace by the effects of it, if we are diligent. As we may know by the beams of the sun that the sun is visible, if we shut not our eyes" (Charnock). Grace discovers itself in its affections and actions, in its operations and influence on the heart and life. If we observe closely the springs of our actions and *"commune with our own heart"* (Ps. 4:4), we shall have little difficulty in becoming acquainted with the state of our souls. *"For what man knows the things of a man save the spirit of man which is in him"* (1 Cor. 2:11).

In His parable of the Sower and the Seed our Lord likened those who hear the Word unto different kinds of soil which received the Seed, and the various results or yields from them. His obvious design was to supply us with criteria by which we may measure ourselves. If, then, I would properly examine myself, I must ascertain if I am no better than the wayside hearer, who heard the Word and *"understood it not;"* or the shallow-soil hearer, who received the Word with an evanescent *"joy"* and yet had *"no root in himself"* and soon fell away; or the thorny-ground hearer, who suffered the *"care of this world and the deceitfulness of riches"* to choke the Word and render him unfruitful. Or, if by grace I am a good-ground hearer, of whom it is said – not simply that he *"believes the Gospel,"* but – *"which in an honest and good heart,having heard the Word, keep it, and bring forth fruit with patience"* (Luke 8:15). That is the test: not knowledge, orthodoxy, or happy feelings, but FRUIT.

Unless a man knows himself to be a child of God he cannot rationally or lawfully take comfort from the promises which are addressed unto the saints. It is madness and presumption for me to flatter myself that God has declared He will do this and that for me, unless I am reliably assured that I am one of those to whom such delcarations are made. It is the height of folly for me to believe that all things are working together for my good, unless I really love God (Rom. 8:28). On the other hand, if I am regenerate and decline to take comfort from the promises, I forsake my own mercies and allow Satan to deprive me of my legitimate portion. That it is not God's will for His people to remain in uncertainty is unmistakably clear from 1 John 5:13. He moved one of His apostles to write a whole Epistle for the express purpose that they might know they had eternal life, and that they may believe on the name of the Son of God.

Realizing full well that this is the most momentous investigation that any mortal can ever undertake, that sincere souls — conscious of how much is involved — will proceed carefully and cautiously, and making full allowance that an honest heart will be fearful of being deceived in the matter, yet we have never been able to understand why a regenerate soul should find it so difficult to determine whether he is in a state of nature or of grace. We are very much afraid that not a few of God's dear people have been hindered by the teaching they sat under and the general custom which prevailed in the circle where they were. It is indeed deplorable that many Protestants have echoed the dogma of Popery that it is presumptuous for any Christian to aver he knows that he has been made a new creature in Christ Jesus. The N.T. contains not a word in support, but much to the contrary. For a saint to doubt his acceptance by God is not a mark of humility but the fruit of unbelief.

We have been dealing with the Christian's assurance of his state before God in a more or less general way, let us now be specific and ask, How is an exercised soul to ascertain whether he has really been restored to the favor and friendship of God? By what criteria or rules is he to test himself in order to discover whether God is at peace with him? By what evidence may he be rationally assured that he is reconciled to the moral Ruler and Judge of this world? Surely that should not be difficult to determine. Is it possible for a truly converted person, who has passed through a radical change in his heart and life, in his thoughts, affections, and actions, to yet know nothing about it? Surely a person cannot be awakened out of a state of security in sin, to realize what a vile, unclean rebel he is, and to mourn over the same, and yet perceive nothing about it. For one to radically change his selfish and worldly pursuits, to lose relish for his idols, and to live a life of communion with God, and yet be uncertain such is his case, is impossible.

Grace is as evident in its own nature as corruption is, and its operations and fruits are as manifest and unmistakable as are those of sin. Not only so in ourselves, but in our fellow-saints too. In a time like the present it is particularly easy to recognize those who are truly reconciled to God. The few friends of Christ stand out conspicuously among the vast multitude of His enemies. In a day when lawlessness abounds and every man does *"that which is right in his own eyes"* (Judges 21:25), those whose lives are ordered by God's Word cannot be mistaken. They *"shine as lights in the world, in the midst of a crooked and perverse nation"* (Phil. 2:15). Noah *"walked with God"* (Gen. 6:9) though he lived in the midst of the reprobate antediluvians. Elijah was jealous for the glory of God and faithful in maintaining His cause, though his lot was to dwell amid a people who had forsaken God's covenant, thrown down His altars, and slain His prophets (1 Kings 19:14).

It may be easier — we are by no means sure it is so — for one to serve God faithfully in a season of revival than in one of declension, and to journey Heavenwards in the company of a goodly number than to stand alone; but it is more difficult to identify the saints. As the fire evidences the pure gold, so a day either of bitter persecution or of wide-spread apostasy, enables us to discern who are out and out for the Lord, and those who have nothing more than a thin veneer of religion. When many of Christ's nominal disciples went back and walked no more with Him, He turned to the apostles and asked, *"Will you also go away?"* Whereupon Simon Peter acting as their spokesman said, *"To whom shall we go? You have the words of eternal life"*(John 6:68). *"They have made void Your Law, therefore I love Your commandments above gold"* (119:127). Such is the effect upon a true child of God of the defection of his fellows.

But returning to the individual who would ascertain whether or not he is reconciled to God. That problem may be reduced to a simple issue. You are either an enemy of God or the friend of God, plainly manifesting the one or the other in your conduct. It should not be difficult for you to determine in which class you are. *"And you that were sometime alienated and enemies in your mind by wicked works, yet now has He reconciled"* (Col. 1:21). The implication is unescapable. If you have been reconciled to God then you are no longer fighting against Him, and though as yet you are very far from being perfect, or all that you should be, nevertheless, no longer is your mind enmity against Him — ever engaged in wicked works. Nay, if reconciled, the very opposite is the case: you yearn for closer fellowship with Him, you love His Word, honestly endeavor to be regulated by it in all things, and in your measure, are bringing forth good works.

Yes, the issue is a very simple one: to be reconciled to God is for there to be mutual peace between Him and you, and peace is the opposite of war, as love is of hatred. It therefore follows that no soul who is at peace with sin can possibly be at peace with God, for sin is the open enemy of the Holy One. The question to be decided then is, Have I thrown down the weapons of my warfare against the Most High? Have I enlisted under the banner of a new Captain? If I am honestly and resolutely fighting against sin, then I must be reconciled to God: said Christ to His disciples, *"he that is not against us is on our part"* (Mark 9:30). There is no third condition: you are either for or against God, His friend or His foe. God's enemies are opposed to Him, leagued with all that is hostile to Him, doing what He forbids and flouting what He enjoins. If then I desire to please Him, am on the side of His friends, hating what He hates and loving what He loves, must I not be one with Him!

CHAPTER XXVIII

We commence this portion at the point where we left off in our last. Those who are at peace with sin are at enmity with God; but those who are reconciled to God are antagonistic to sin. It cannot be otherwise. Satan and God, sin and holiness, are diametrically and irreconcilably opposed. As the *"sceptre of righteousness"* (Heb. 1:8) holds sway over the kingdom of God and of Christ, iniquity is the dominant power in the empire of Satan, *"he that commits sin is of the Devil"* (1 John 3:8). It therefore follows that all real Christians are opposed to Satan as the common enemy, and evince the same by fighting against sin. Satan's principal work lies in drawing men to sin, and therefore are the saints bidden *"resist the Devil and he will flee from you"* (James 4:7); and again, *"Be sober, be viligant; because your adversary the Devil, as a roaring lion, walks about seeking whom he may devour"* (1 Pet. 5:7). To resist the Devil is to refuse his temptations to fight against sin; contrariwise, to trifle with temptation and commit sin is to render service unto him.

The forwarding of sin is the Devil's main instrument to lead his subjects into more and more of a revolt against their Maker, and the more any yield to his solicitations, the more do they perform his work. To sin is *"to give place to the Devil"* (Eph. 4:27), and to depart from Christ is to *"turn aside after Satan"* (1 Tim. 5:15). Whenever we knowingly sin we join with Satan in his battle against God. We take sides with him and strengthen his cause. How that awful consideration should restrain us and make us tread warily! How it should humble us before God when we have yielded to temptation and thus aided His arch-enemy! Again; the love of God and the love of the world cannot possibly stand together: *"Know you not that the friendship of the world is enmity with God? Whosoever therefore will be a friend of the world is the enemy of God"* (James 4:4). Thus the lines are plainly drawn: if I am a friend of the world, the abettor of Satan, the servant of sin, I cannot possibly be at peace with God. But if I am reconciled to God, then I am in avowed and open antagonism to that evil trinity.

While any soul is at peace with sin, he is certainly not at peace with God, for He is ineffably holy and hates all sin. It was sin which caused the breach between Him and us: *"they rebelled and vexed His Holy Spirit, therefore He was turned to be their Enemy and He fought against them"* (Isa. 63:10). Since sin is the inveterate enemy of God and man it must be fought, or it will destroy us. Therefore His call is *"be reconciled to God."* When a soul really responds to that call he ceases his opposition to God and enlists under the banner of Christ. Christ becomes his *"Captain"* (Heb. 2:10) and he engages to fight against all His enemies. He severs his old allegiance with the world, the flesh and the devil, and binds himself by a solemn bond to live unto God and be the Lord's forevermore. From this time forward can be no truce between corruptions and grace, carnal reasonings and the teaching of Holy Writ. *"Neither yield your members as weapons of unrighteousness unto sin, but yield yourselves unto God"* (Rom. 6:13).

"You have not yet resisted unto blood, striving against sin" (Heb. 12:4). The leading thought of the context is, the need for faithful perseverance in a time of persecution and suffering. In the urging of this the apostle set before them (and us) the grand example of Jesus Christ, and how we should improve the same.

Then he points out that, severe as had been the trials experienced, yet not so fearful as might yet be encountered. They had indeed suffered considerably (10:32,33), but so far God had restrained their enemies from going to extreme lengths. The afflictions already undergone did not discharge them from their warfare. Rather must they continue in this to the point of being prepared to lay down their lives. That warfare consisted of *"striving against sin"* – sin in themselves, which inclined them to take the line of least resistance; sin in their persecutors, who sought to drive them to apostatize.

In Heb. 12:4 the apostle continues to use the figure of the Public Games which he had employed in v. 1, only there he refers to the *"race,"* while here he alludes to the mortal conflict or combat between gladiators, in which one contended for his life against another who had entered the lists against him. In like manner, the Christian has to contend with a mortal adversary, namely, sin, both external and internal. He is called upon to wrestle not with flesh and blood, but against the powers of darkness (Eph. 6:12), and therefore is he exhorted to take unto him *"the whole armor of God."* So too he is to strive against his own indwelling corruptions: *"abstain from fleshly lusts which war against the soul"* (1 Pet. 2:11). Those lusts are violent and powerful, ever seeking to dominate and regulate the soul, antagonizing the principle of grace, endeavoring to overcome our faith and prevent our obedience to God. Sin is a deadly enemy which will slay us unless we daily strive against it with determination of mind and resolute effort.

Here then is one of the principal features which distinguishes the children of God from the children of the Devil. Here is an essential part of the evidence which clearly makes manifest those in whom a miracle of grace has been wrought. Here is the proof that I am reconciled to God. By nature sin is my element and I take to it as ducks do to the water and swine to the mire. By nature I delight in sin: do I not love myself? And in loving myself I am delighting in sin, for sin is part and parcel of my being. I was shapen in iniquity and conceived in sin (Ps. 51:5). If then I now hate my natural self, loathe sin, vigorously resist it, I must be a new creature in Christ Jesus, at peace with God. If I compare myself with what I was in my unregenerate days, is it not obvious that a radical change has taken place! Did I then abhor myself? No indeed, far from it. I was pleased with myself. Did I then look upon iniquity as that *"abominable thing"* which the Holy One hates and takes sides with Him against it? Alas, I did not: I thirsted after it, drank greedily of it, and took pleasure in it.

The natural man may indeed seek to overcome some grosser lust, the yielding to which humiliates his pride. He may seriously endeavor to conquer an unruly temper, that he may not be put to shame before his fellows. But that is a very different matter. One who is truly reconciled to God has voluntarily entered into a covenant to fight against sin as sin, and not merely this or that particular form and outbreaking of it. He is daily engaged in contending with his indwelling corruptions, resisting the Devil, refusing the allurements of the world, mortifying his members which are upon the earth. Here then is the matter reduced to its simplest possible terms, here is the plain but sufficient rule by which you may test the validity of your profession. You know whether or not you really are fighting against sin. We do not say fighting against it as faithfully, diligently, zealously as you ought to be. Nor do we say meeting with that success which you could wish. It is the fact itself we would have you consider: if you are really warring against indwelling sin you must be one with God.

Probably the reader says, Tell us more explicitly what you mean by fighting against sin. Very well. Fighting against sin implies that you hate it, for you do not war against anything you love. Likewise it signifies you earnestly desire to avoid it, keep away from it, have no commerce with it. To countenance sin is rebellion against God; to condemn and oppose sin is conformity to Him. If I hate sin and am engaged in a warfare against it, I shall not trifle with temptation but watch jealously for and seek to suppress the first motions of sin in my heart. When my corruptions clamor for satisfaction I shall earnestly endeavor to deny them. When the apostle averred, *"I keep under my body and bring it into subjection"* (1 Cor. 9:27), he was describing one aspect of his fight against sin. When another of the apostles enjoined, *"Little children, keep yourselves from idols"* (1 John 5:21), he was calling them unto a further part of the same conflict. It was an affectionate appeal for them to avoid, resist, and renounce will worship and whatever could captivate our affections.

This fighting against sin is from evangelical motives. Here too the line is clearly drawn between the regenerate and the unregenerate. Whatever resistance the latter make against sin it is from carnal or legal considerations. That which deters the natural man from the outward commission of evil is either pride or self-respect, because he would retain the good opinion of his fellows, or the fear of consequences. But different far is it with the spiritual man: he would hate and resist sin even if assured there is no Hell awaiting evil-doers hereafter! It is love of God, a desire to please Him, a concern for His glory, a horror of doing that which would sully his profession, bring shame upon the cause of Christ, or stumble any of His little ones. Therefore it is that when Satan gets the better of him and he is overtaken in a fault, he mourns before God. If we are reconciled to God we love Him, and repentance is the first expression of that love – the sorrowing part of it. Those fighting against sin do not *"allow"* or excuse their failures, but grieve over, confess them, and seek to prevent a repetition of the same.

Let us repeat, it is not the measure of our success in this warfare, but the genuineness of our sincerity in it, which is the criterion by which we are to measure ourselves. As one of the old worthies said, "This is the seal which assures us the patent is the authentic grant of the Prince of peace." Or as John Owen put it, "Mortification of sin is the soul's opposition to self, wherein sincerity is most evident." To which we may add, none of our exercises and efforts have any sincerity in them – neither reading, hearing, praying nor worship – unless we are genuinely endeavoring to earnestly and vigorously resist sin. Sin is ever assailing the soul, contending for rule and sovereignty over it. But if a principle of grace is in my heart, then it will constantly challenge sin's right to usurp authority and oppose its assaults. "The subduing of our souls to God, the forming of us to a resemblance unto Him, is a more certain sign that we belong to Him, than if we had with Isaiah seen in vision His glory with all His train of angels about Him" (S. Charnock).

Granted, says the exercised soul, but there is so much in me that is not yet subdued to God, yea which is contrary to Him, and this it is which makes me seriously doubt my reconciliation. I fear that I should be uttering an idle boast and thinking of myself more highly than I ought to, if I declared myself to be engaged in seriously fighting against sin. Dear reader, hypocrites are never troubled over the deceitfulness of their hearts, nor are they concerned at all of being presumptuous, and if you really are exercised over such things, then must you not belong to a totally different class! Vain and empty professors are not exercised about their sincerity, but instead are filled with a self-confidence and sense of security which no expostulations or warnings of man can shake. They are total strangers to the jealous fears and holy exercises of soul which engage those with humble hearts. *"They had rather go to hell on a feather bed than to Heaven in a fiery chariot"* as one quaintly but solemnly expressed it.

Am I reconciled to God, at peace with Him? Yes, if I am daily and sincerely engaged in fighting against sin. But, says the reader, if I am engaged in such a fight, mine is a losing one, for the more I endeavor to resist my corruptions, the more fiercely do they oppose me and thwart my efforts. Yea, so often do my lusts master me, I can only conclude that I am still at war against God. Not so, if you take sides against your lusts and grieve over their prevalence. As it is not the fighting of a number of individuals belonging to two different countries which causes one of those states to declare war against another, but rather its consenting to and maintaining them in their hostility; so it is not the rising up of our lusts against our graces which constitutes an act of war against God, but only when we approve of them, consent to and defend their presumptuous enmity. While we take up and maintain a constant fight against God's enemies – no matter how often we may be worsted in the conflict – hating and disavowing their outrageous uprisings, the peace between God and us holds.

In the chapters on our reception of that peace which Christ effected Godwards on behalf of His people, we showed at some length what God requires from the sinner if he is to become a personal partaker of that peace, and every exercised reader should go carefully over those articles again with one particular design before him – to discover whether he or she has met those requirements. From the lengthy quotation from Goodwin (Feb. issue), it was shown that in preparing us to be reconciled to God it is necessary that we be convinced we are His enemies, and that He accounts us such. Thus, if the reader has never been painfully convicted of his revolt against the Most High, he is in no condition to seek reconciliation unto Him. If I have been made aware that I am a lifelong rebel against Heaven, that all my days have been spent in fighting against God, then I shall be sensible and deeply affected by such a realization. I shall mourn over my wickedness. I shall *"remember my ways and be ashamed."* I shall be *"confounded"* and have not one word to say in my self-defence (Ezek. 16:61-63).

If the Holy Spirit has awakened me from the sleep of self-security, opened my eyes to see my true character in the sight of God, filled me with horror and contrition over my dreadful enmity against Him, then I shall readily respond to that peremptory call, *"Let the wicked forsake his way, and the unrighteous man his thoughts,"* and cease my hostility against the Lord. At first it will appear to me that I have sinned beyond the hope of forgiveness, that it is impossible God should ever be reconciled to such a rebel as I now know myself to be, that nought but the everlasting burnings can be the portion of such a wretch. But later, the same gracious Spirit who revealed to me my horrible plight, acquaints me that God has *"thoughts of peace"* (Jer. 29:11) toward those who throw down the weapons of their warfare against Him. But that seems too good to be true, and for a season the stricken soul finds itself unable to credit the same. To him it appears that a holy God can do nothing but abhor him, that a righteous God must surely exact vengeance upon him, that his doom is irrevocably sealed. Do you know anything of such an experience as that?

When God begins a work of grace in a soul He does not cease when it is but half finished. If He wounds it is that He may heal; if at first He drives to despair, later He awakens hope. When the Law has performed its office – of stripping us of our self-righteousness – then we are prepared to listen to the message of the Gospel, which tells of the garments of salvation provided for bankrupts. The glorious evangel of Divine grace announces that God is not implacable but inclinable unto peace, that His wisdom had found a way whereby the requirements of His holiness and the demands of His justice are fully met so that He can without sullying His honor, yea to the everlasting glory of His matchless name, show mercy to the very chief of sinners. As the soul begins to give credence to that good news, he is persuaded better things of God than his fears allowed, hope is born within him that even his case is not beyond remedy, and the sweet music is borne to his ears,*"Let the wicked forsake his way, and the unrighteous man his thoughts, and let him return to the Lord, and He will have mercy upon him, and to our God, for He will abundantly pardon"* (Isa. 55:7).

But it is in Christ, and Christ alone, that the thrice Holy God meets the sinner in pardoning mercy. Christ is the One who met His claims and endured His wrath on the behalf of all who put their trust in Him. Christ is the alone Mediator whereby transgressors can approach unto a reconciled God. It is the Lord Jesus who is *"set forth a propitiation through faith in His blood"* (Rom. 3:25). And therefore *"He is able to save them to the uttermost which come unto God by Him"* (Heb. 7:25). It is in and through Christ that sinners may enter into covenant with God and by whom He enters into covenant with them, for Christ is *"the Surety"* (Heb. 7:22) and *"the Mediator"* (Heb. 8:6) of the covenant. Christ is the One who came *"to seek and to save that which was lost"* (Luke 19:10), and who declares *"him that comes to Me I will in nowise cast out"* (John 6:37). Have you gone unto Him as a desperately-ill person seeks a physician, or as a drowning man clutches to a life-buoy? You either have, or you have not; and it should not be difficult for you to determine. But am I come to Christ in the right way? Answer, the only right way is to come as a lost sinner, trusting in His merits.

Have you, then, complied with the terms expressed in Isa. 55:1-3, for it is with those doing so that God makes an everlasting covenant. That is but another way of asking, Have you really embraced the Gospel offer, which is made freely to all who hear it? Have you seriously, thoughtfully, broken-heartedly received Christ as your own personal Lord and Saviour? Have you exercised faith in His mediatorial sacrifice? Your faith may indeed have been so weak that you touched but the hem of His garment, yet if it was His garment, that was sufficient. The saving virtue lies not in our faith but in Christ, faith being simply the empty and leprous hand which lays hold of the great Physician. Every penitent believer may be infallibly assured on the Word of Him that cannot lie that his sins were all transferred to his blessed Surety and forever put away by Him; and that he is now made the righteousness of God in Christ (2 Cor. 5:21).

But the honest soul who would *"make assurance doubly sure"* should go further, and test himself by Ps. 50:5, Isa. 56:4-6; Jer. 50:4,5. There we have described the character of those making a covenant with God and who *"take hold of His covenant,"* and it is our wisdom and duty to seriously compare ourselves with those characters and ascertain whether we possess their marks. Have I surrendered to God as my absolute Lord and chosen Him to be my all-sufficient Portion? Have I renounced and relinquished the things which He hates and *"chosen the things that please"* Him? Have I given myself up to Him wholly to love and serve Him, and that not for a brief season only, but forever? Am I now manifesting the sincerity of my surrender by being concerned for His honor and having respect to His Law? Have the resolutions I formed at my conversion been translated into actual practice? — not perfectly so, but by genuine effort nevertheless. If so, then I have good reason to believe that I have savingly complied with His call *"be reconciled to God."*

CHAPTER XXIX

Another criterion by which each of us should carefully measure himself is, Am I now a friend of God? That is a most pertinent and necessary inquiry, for, as was shown under a considerable variety of expressions when defining the meaning of reconciliation, that term signifies the bringing together of two persons who have previously been alienated, the changing of a state of enmity and hostility unto one of amity and friendship. By nature and by practice I was the enemy of God, hating and opposing Him; but if a work of grace has been wrought in my soul then I am now the friend of God, loving and serving Him. As this is a matter of deepest importance, both practically and experimentally, we propose to canvass it in some detail, endeavoring to do so along lines so clear and simple that no exercised soul should have any uncertainty in determining to which class he belongs.

"Abraham believed God and it was imputed unto him for righteousness, and he was called the friend of God" (James 2:23). It seems passing strange that scarcely any of the commentators perceived the force of that last clause, interpreting it quite out of harmony with its setting. Most of them see in God's styling Abraham His *"friend"* an amazing instance of His sovereign grace and condescension, while a few regard the expression in the light of the extraordinary and intimate communion which the patriarch was permitted to enjoy with Jehovah. But what is there in the context which paves the way for any such climax? It was in nowise the design of the Holy Spirit in this epistle to portray the wondrous riches of Divine grace, nor to describe the inestimable privileges they confer upon their recipients; rather was it to expose a worthless profession and supply marks of a valid one. James was not moved to refute the legality of Judaism, which insisted that we must do certain things in order to our acceptance by God, but was repelling Antinomianism, showing the worthlessness of a faith which bore no fruit.

In the days of the apostles, as in all succeeding generations, there were those bearing the name of Christians who supposed that a mere intellectual belief of the Gospel was sufficient to secure a passport for Heaven. There is not a little in the N.T. which was expressly written to refute that error, by an insistence upon holiness of heart and strictness of life being necessary in order to evince a saving faith in Christ. The principal design of James was to show that when God justifies or reconciles a sinner to Himself, He also works in that person a disposition which is friendly toward Him, a spirit and attitude which reciprocates His own benignity. In a genuine conversion an enemy is transformed into a friend to God, so that he loves Him, delights in Him, and serves Him. No one has any right to regard himself as a friend of God unless he has the character of one and conducts himself accordingly. If I am the friend of God then I shall be jealous of His honor, respect His will, value His interests, and devote myself to promoting the same; in a word, I shall *"show myself friendly."*

The apostle's scope is clear enough both from what immediately precedes and follows. In v. 20 he says, *"But will you know, O vain man, that faith without works is dead,"* and in v. 24, *"You see then how that by works a man is justified, and not by faith only."* A bare mental assent to the Gospel is worthless, for it effects no change in the heart and walk of the one exercising it. Fair words on the lips are downright hypocrisy unless they are borne out in our daily conduct.

A faith in Christ which conforms not to His image is not the faith of God's elect. Saving faith produces good works. In vers. 8 to 14 the apostle had insisted that the Gospel requires a sincere respect unto all the Divine commandments, while in vers. 15-25 he shows what a real faith in them brings forth. This he illustrates first by the illustrious case of Abraham. It is to be duly noted that reference is not here made to the initial act of his faith when the Lord first appeared unto the patriarch in Ur of Chaldea, but rather to that memorable incident on mount Moriah recorded in Gen. 22.

Faith is not a passive thing but an active principle, operating powerfully within its possessor. *"Faith works by love"* (Gal. 5:6). Let those words be carefully pondered. *"Faith works:"* it is the very nature of it to do so, for it is a new, living and powerful energy, imparted to the soul at regeneration. *"Faith works by love:"* not by fear or compulsion, but freely and gladly. Such was the faith of Abraham: his faith *"wrought with his works"* (James 2:22), and it wrought by love, for it was love to God which moved the patriarch, in obedience to His behest, to lay his dear Isaac upon the altar; and in this way he attested his friendship to God. "Friendship is the strength of love, and the highest improvement of it. *'Your friend'* says Moses, *'who is as your own soul'* (Deut. 13:6). Friendship is common to and included in all relations of love. A brother is (or ought to be) a friend; it is but friendship natural. Husband and wife are friends: that knot is friendship conjugal. In Song of Sol. 5 we have an instance of both: Christ called His church Sister, and then Spouse; and not contented with both, though put together, He added another compellation as the top of all, *'O My friends'* (v. 11)."

In its first working faith comes to God as an empty-handed beggar to receive from Him, yet if it is a sincere and spiritual faith it will necessarily form the soul of its possessor unto a correspondent and answerable frame of heart unto God; thus if I come to Him for pardon and peace, and receive the same, the reflex or consequence will be the exercise of a filial and friendly spirit in me toward God. Faith is made the grateful recipient of all from God, yet on that very account it becomes the worker of love in the soul. In James 2:21-23 the apostle shows what a powerful working thing faith is: it moulded Abraham's heart into friendship with God. A friend is best known or most clearly manifested in a time of trial. Thus it was in Gen. 22: the Lord there put Abraham to the proof, bidding him, *"Take now your son, your only Isaac, whom you love . . . and offer him there for a burnt offering."* And God so approved of his ready response as to own him as His *"friend"* from this time forward: see 2 Chron. 20:7, Isa. 41:8. And since He only calls things as they actually are, Abraham had truly conducted himself as such.

Let it next be pointed out that Abraham's case is not to be regarded as an exceptional or extraordinary one, but rather as a representative and typical one. As Rom. 4:11 and 16 plainly teaches, Abraham is a pattern and father unto all believers. Those who are his spiritual children (Rom. 9:7,8) and seed (Gal. 3:7,29), *"walk in the steps of that faith of our father Abraham"* (Rom. 4:12) and *"do the works of Abraham"* (John 8:39), and they too are owned by the Lord as His *"friends"* (John 15:14). Observe that in both 2 Chron. 20:7 and Isa. 41:8 it is *"the seed of Abraham Your friend,"* while in James 2:21 Abraham is expressly presented in that passage as *"our father."* Thus, this blessed appellation pertains to all his spiritual seed. For one to be owned by God as His *"friend"* imports that person has a friendly disposition of heart and deportment of life toward Him, as one friend bears unto another. Wherever a saving faith exists it frames the heart of its possessor into a friendlike temper and brings forth a friendlike carriage in our life.

"He was called the friend of God." While that indeed is a title of unspeakable dignity and honor, yet – though scarcely any appear to have perceived it – it is also (and chiefly) expressive of the inward disposition of a saint toward God, describing his love for Him and his bearing toward Him. By our carriage and conduct we exemplify and ratify that character. The faith which justifies a sinner before God is one that works by love and is expressed in an obedient walk, earnestly endeavoring to please God in all things, and therefore the character and carriage of a Christian is appropriately expressed under the notion of friendship. In a truly marvelous way had God befriended Abraham, and the patriarch manifested his appreciation by conducting himself suitably to it. It is the law of friendship to answer it again with friendship: *"A man that has friends must show himself friendly, and there is a Friend that sticks closer than a brother"* (Prov. 18:24), and to Him we must show ourselves supremely friendly, doing nothing to displease or dishonor Him, but exercising subjection to Him, delighting in Him, and promoting His interests.

We will pass now from the general to the particular and consider some of the more obvious characteristics and marks of friendship, together with the duties and offices to be performed as are proper and suited to such a relationship – friendship too combines both privilege and duty, and we should be dishonest if we confined our remarks to one of them only, First of all then, between two friends there necessarily exists a close bond of union, a oneness of nature or at least similarity of disposition, so that they share in common the same likes and dislikes – not perhaps in every detail, but generally and essentially so. There can be no congeniality where there is no singleness and harmony of nature. It is the gift and dwelling of the Holy Spirit within the Christian which is the bond of union, and which capacitates him to hate what God hates and love what He loves. It is that oneness of nature and disposition which causes two persons to have a mutual regard and affection, and to look favorably on one another, in which the very essence of friendship consists. From all eternity God set His heart upon him, and now the reconciled one has given his heart to Him.

One has a very high regard for an intimate and proved friend. That God greatly values and esteems those whom He reconciles to Himself is clear both from His declarations concerning them and what He has done for them. He prizes them above the world and orders all things in its governance for the furthering of their good. *"For I am the Lord your God, the Holy One in Israel, your Saviour. I gave Egypt for your ransom, Ethiopia and Seba for you. Since you were precious in My sight, you have been honorable, and I have loved you"* (Isa. 43:3,4). What a wondrous and blessed testimony is that! *"He delivered me because He delighted in me"* (2 Sam. 22:20). *"How fair and how pleasant you are, O love for delights"* (S. of S. 7:6) is His langauge respecting His Spouse, and She in return declares, *"I sat down under His shadow with great delight, and His fruit was sweet to my taste"* (2:3). So highly does the saint prize God in Christ that he avers, *"Whom have I in heaven but You, and there is none upon earth that I desire besides You"* (Ps. 73:25).

Since real and warm friends highly value and delight in one another it is their chief pleasure to share each other's company, being happiest when together. Thus it is between the reconciled soul and his heavenly Friend: *"truly our fellowship is with the Father and with His Son Jesus Christ"* (1 John 1:3). In nothing can the Christian more fitly evince his friendship with God than by a diligent endeavor to maintain a constant and intimate communion with Him. In addition to the regular tribute of his daily worship, if the soul of the believer is in a healthy condition, he will take occasion to frequently come into God's presence on purpose to have communion with Him. Friendship is best maintained by visits, and the more free and less occasioned by urgent business, the more are they appreciated. David, owned as *"a man after God's own heart"* – the equivalent of Abraham's being called His *"friend"* – said, *"O God, You are my God, early will I seek You . . . To see Your power and Your glory, so as I have seen You in the sanctuary. Because Your lovingkindness is better than life, my lips shall praise You . . . My soul shall be satisfied as with marrow and fatness, and my mouth shall praise You with joyful lips"* (Ps. 63:1-5). That was the language of pure friendship.

Intimate converse and close communications characterise the dealings of one warm friend to another. Things which I would not discuss with a stranger, personal matters I would be silent upon to a mere acquaintance, I freely open to one I delight in. It is thus between God and the reconciled soul. It is so on His part: *"The secret of the Lord is with them that fear Him, and He will show them His covenant"* (Ps. 25:14). *"The Lord spoke to Moses face to face* (without restraint or reserve) *as a man speaks unto his friend"* (Ex. 33:11). Thus Scripture makes this freedom of communication one of the marks of spiritual friendship. So too we find the Lord Jesus saying to His beloved apostles, *"Henceforth I call you not servants, for the servant knows not what his lord does: but I have called you friends; for all things that I have heard of My Father, I have made known unto you"* (John 15:15). Do you, my reader, know anything of this experience? Are you in such close touch with Him as to make this (morally) possible? It is through His Word God now speaks to us: do you know what it is for your heart to *"burn"* while He talks with you by the way and *"opens"* to you the Scriptures (Luke 24:32)?

Yet this intimate conversation is not one-sided, but is reciprocal: the reconciled one finds liberty in opening his heart unto his heavenly Friend, as he does to none other. This is his holy privilege: *"trust in Him at all times; you people, pour out your heart before Him"* (Ps. 62:8). How do you treat your best earthly friend? When you have not seen him for a season, how warmly you welcome him, how freely you express your pleasure at meeting him again, what utterances of good will and delight do you make! Equally free should the saint be with his Lord. He should pour out his heart with joy and gladness. He should unrestrainedly avow his delight in the Lord. He should bring with him a sacrifice of praise, that is, the fruit of his lips, giving thanks (Heb. 13:15). Such will not only be acceptable unto Him, but it will give Him pleasure: it is on these occasions that He says, *"Your lips, O My Spouse, drop as the honeycomb: honey and milk are under your tongue"* (S. of S. 4:11) – such communications are sweet unto Me.

But there are times when one is so sorely troubled and weighed down that his expressions of delight and joy toward a loving friend will be restrained. True, yet that only affords occasion for another attribute of friendship to be exercised, namely, to freely unburden his heart unto him. Thus it is with the reconciled soul and God: he will speak to Him more freely and make mention of things which he would not to his nearest and dearest earthly friend. This is the Christian's privilege: to ease his heart before God. Said the Psalmist,*"I poured out my complaint before Him, I showed before Him my trouble"* (Ps. 142:2), and He deems Himself honored by such confidences. The more communion there is between God and us over our distresses, the more will He discover our secret faults, and the more will we disclose again to Him. The one is a sure consequence of the other. After speaking of our fellowship with God in 1 John 1:3, it is added, *"If we confess our sins He is faithful and just to forgive us our sins."* One great part of our friendship with God is the taking of Him fully into our confidence, as on His part it is to pardon us.

Having confidence in a friend we freely seek his help and advice. When describing a close friend David said, *"we took sweet counsel together"* (Ps. 55:14). And that is how we ought to treat our heavenly Friend, making use of Him, counting upon His favor and help in all our concerns. That is both our privilege and duty: *"in all your ways acknowledge Him, and He shall direct your paths"* (Prov. 3:6) – seek His counsel, give yourself up to His guidance. That little (and large) word *"all"* includes small things as well as great! In this the friendship of God excels that of others. We are loath to trouble an earthly friend about trifles, but we may spread the smallest matter before Him who has numbered the very hairs of our head. In this we honor Him, for it is an acknowledgement on our part that He rules all things, even the very least.

One is very careful in seeking to avoid giving any offence unto a dear friend and doing all in our power to please him. Apply that Godwards and it has reference to our obedience. Therefore do we find Christ saying,*"You are My friends if you do whatsoever I command you"* (John 15:14). That *"if"* is addressed to responsibility and is the testing of our profession. It is by obedience we evidence and approve ourselves to be His friends. Obedience goes much further than resisting sin and abstaining from wicked works: *"cease to do evil, learn to do well"* (Isa. 1:17). It is not sufficient to forbear the commission of sin if we perform not our duty. The fig tree was cursed not because it bore evil fruit, but because it was barren. There are many who, like the Pharisees, pride themselves on negations: I am not profane, immoral, irreligious. But that gives them no title to regard themselves as friends of Christ. Are they actually doing the things He has enjoined – this is the crucial test and characteristic mark of the reconciled.

Observe it is not *"you shall be"* but *"you are My friends if you do."* It is the doers of His Word whom the Lord owns as His friends: they who are as diligent in practicing His precepts as in shunning what He hates. And their obedience is not that of mercenary legalists nor the forced work of slaves, but is the voluntary and joyful response of loving and grateful hearts. An action may have the appearance of friendship when there is nothing of good will behind it. But none can impose upon the Lord – He knows when there is inward conformity to His will as well as outward compliance, when a person's *"good works"* are those of the formalist or of a loving heart. If they are the latter, we shall not pick and choose between His precepts, but *"do whatsoever He commands:" "whatever your soul desires, I will even do it for you"* (1 Sam. 20:4) said Jonathan to his friend. That is indeed the longing and aim of every reconciled soul, but his infirmities and distempers often cause him to go halting.

Another characteristic or mark of friendship is confidence: *"My own familiar friend in whom I trusted"* (Ps. 41:3) said David. Nothing more readily undermines friendship than the harboring of suspicions. It is because we have proved the staunchness and affection of another that we count him our friend, and rely upon him. Thus it is with a reconciled soul and God. He has shown Himself to be graciously disposed unto me, giving me innumerable proofs of His lovingkindness and faithfulness, and that draws out my heart in confidence toward Him. The more I trust in Him and look to Him for help, the more is He pleased and honored by me, and the more do I show myself to be His friend. *"Cast your burden upon the Lord"* is His blessed invitation, for He desires not His child should be weighted down by it. *"Casting all your care upon Him, for He cares for you"* (1 Pet. 5:7). God would have His people act toward Him with holy familiarity, confiding in Him at all time, counting upon His goodness, reposing themselves in His love, making known their requests with thanksgiving, expecting Him to supply all their need. That is both our privilege and duty if we sustain to God the relationship of friends.

Where there is full confidence in a tried and trusted friend we place a favorable construction upon even those actions of his which may puzzle and perplex us. We refuse to impute evil to or harbor suspicions against him. Any fancied slight he has given, any apparent unconcern or unkindness he has shown, anything in his letters which we do not understand, we leave until we again see him face to face, quietly assured that a satisfactory explanation will be forthcoming from him. Thus it is with the saint and his heavenly friend. Some of His dealings sorely try and exercise him, yet he doubts not that He is too wise to err and too loving to be unkind. Some of His dispensations are exceedingly trying to flesh and blood, but a believing soul will *"Judge not the Lord by feeble sense, but trust Him for His grace,"* realizing that *"behind a frowning providence, He hides a smiling face."* Thus it was with Job, *"Though He slay me, yet will I trust Him."* Love *"thinks no evil"* but favorably interprets the most mysterious of God's ways, knowing that He is making all things work together for our good.

There is no real reason why any one of ordinary intelligence should remain in doubt as to his spiritual state. If you faithfully examine yourself and honestly measure yourself by the different criteria we have mentioned in these articles, you should have no difficulty in determining whether you be still alienated from God or reconciled to Him. If you are at peace with Him then you are making common cause with Him, warring against His foes — the Devil, sin, the world. If you are reconciled to God, then you are His friend, evidencing the same by a friendlike disposition and deportment, conducting yourself toward Him, treating Him, as one friend with another. The Lord so add His gracious blessing that in His light each of us may see light.

CHAPTER XXX.

This is an aspect of our subject which will by no means appeal to the empty professor, nor, we may add, to the backslider. The Antinomian is all for hearing about the free grace of God and His unforfeitable gifts, and if the preacher should point out that favors and privileges entail obligations, he is condemned by them for his legality; but if he is to receive his Master's *"well done,"* he will not have the united approbation of a large congregation. It betrays a most unhealthy state of soul when we wish to hear only of what Christ did and procured for sinners, and little or nothing of what He requires from the beneficiaries of the same. God has inseparably joined together privilege and duty, relationship and obligation, and we are lacking an honest heart if we eagerly seize His promises and despise His precepts. It betrays a sad condition of soul if we are not anxious to ascertain *"What does the Lord require of you"* (Micah 6:8).

It is our firm conviction that one of the main causes for such a vast number of empty professors and backslidden believers in Christendom today was the disproportionate and unfaithful preaching of most of the prominent orthodox pulpits during the past century. Instead of giving a conspicuous place to what which tested profession, both doctrinally and practically, nominal saints were lulled into a false sense of security. Instead of insisting that conversion is but the beginning of the Christian life, an enlisting under the banner of Christ to *"fight the good fight of faith,"* in which the Devil is to be steadfastly resisted and a ceaseless warfare waged against indwelling sin, the siren song of *"Once saved, always saved"* was dinned into the ears of those whose walk was thoroughly carnal and worldly. Instead of a searching and probing ministry the pulpit cried *"Peace, peace"* unto those still at enmity with God.

Those who were flattered as being *"the stalwarts of the Faith"* were often most partial in which aspects of the Faith they concentrated upon. Those whose proud boast it was that they *"shunned not to declare all the counsel of God,"* were for the most part men who repudiated human responsibility and detested the word *"duty."* It is handling the Word of God deceitfully to emphasize the expression *"ordained to eternal life"* and to ignore *"good works which God has before ordained that we should walk in them"* (Eph. 2:10). It is withholding that which is profitable unto souls (Acts 20:20) to leave them in ignorance that Christ is *"the Author of eternal salvation unto all them that obey Him"* (Heb. 5:9). It is highly dishonoring to God when we pretend to magnify *"the riches of His grace"* if we fail to insist that His grace effectually teaches its recipients to be *"denying ungodliness and worldly lusts, (that) we should live soberly, righteously, and godly in this present world"* (Titus 2:11,12).

Having dwelt upon the privilege-side of our theme in previous articles of this series, we should be woefully lacking in proportion and completeness if we now failed to consider the duty-side of it. It behoves us to point out God's full rights and just claims upon us, as well as His rich favors and unmerited mercies unto us. It becomes the reader to whole-heartedly welcome our efforts to execute this part of our task. The language of a reconciled soul is, and must be, *"What shall I render unto the Lord for all His benefits?"* How shall I express my gratitude unto that blessed One who has shown me such unspeakable mercy? If the wrath of God is removed from me and I am now taken into His unclouded and everlasting favor, how shall I now most fitly comport myself? Since such measureless love has been so freely lavished upon me, how can I best show forth my gratitude? That is the question we shall now endeavor to answer.

1. By fervent praise unto God. O what thanksgiving is due unto Him for His matchless grace! As it was the supreme demonstration of His love in sending forth His Son to make peace, that should be the principal spring of our thanksgiving. When God bids His people, *"Behold My Servant whom I uphold, My Elect in whom My soul delights,"* whom He gave *"for a covenant of the people, for a light of the Gentiles: to open the blind eyes, to bring out the prisoners from the prison and them that sit in darkness out of the prison-house;"* the use which He enjoins them to make of the same is, *"Sing unto the Lord a new song"* (Isa. 42:1-10). The initial response of one who realizes that his trespasses are no longer imputed to him, but instead that the perfect righteousness of Christ is reckoned to his account, must be *"Bless the Lord, O my soul, and all that is within me bless His holy name"* (Ps. 103:1). So too it should be his daily — as it will be his eternal — response.

"God might have destroyed us with less cost than He has reconciled us; for our destruction there was no need of His counsel, nor fitting out and sending His Son, nor opening His treasures; a word would have done it, whereas our reconciliation stood Him at much charge. It was performed at the expense of His grace and Spirit to furnish His Son to be a sacrifice for our atonement. An inexpressible wonder that the Father should prepare His Son a mortal body that our souls might be prepared for immortal glory" (S. Charnock). The apostle could not consider the will of our Father in this work without interrupting his discourse with a doxology: *"to whom the glory be forever and ever. Amen"* (Gal. 1:4,5); and such should be our response. As the angels rejoiced in the manifestation of the wisdom and power of God in the incarnation of His dear Son, much more should we rejoice at the triumphant outcome of His mission and of our personal interest in the same, joining with them in their *"Glory to God in the highest."*

Who is it, my reader, who makes you to differ from others? Is it not God? Then ascribe glory to Him. If He has made you to differ from others in the exercise of His sovereign mercy, do you differ from them in the sounding forth of His praises. When David considered the works of God's hand in the stellar heavens, he exclaimed *"What is man that You are mindful of him,"* and if we consider what sovereign favor has wrought for and in the regenerate, well may we be overwhelmed with wonder. Pardon of but one sin would make us forever debtors to God, for every sin is a hatred of Him and renders us obnoxious to eternal torments. What then is due unto Him from those whom He has pardoned sins more in number than the hairs of their heads! O the marvel of it, that the one who is by nature a child of wrath should be made an heir of Heaven; that one so vile should be taken into the bosom of the Father! Thanks be unto God for His unspeakable gift.

2. By care to please God. Since He went to so much trouble and cost in restoring us, how our thoughts and affections should unitedly engage in earnestly endeavoring to please Him. The Decalogue is prefaced with *"I am the Lord your God, which brought you out of the land of Egypt, out of the house of bondage,"* as an incentive and inducement for Israel to render cheerful obedience unto Him. *"I am the Lord your God who in Christ has delivered you from eternal death*

and brought you into My everlasting favor" is the tenor of the Gospel – a far weightier motive for the Christian to place himself unreservedly at God's disposal. This it is which will demonstrate the worth and genuineness of our praise: whether it is merely an emotional spasm or the overflowing gratitude of a heart which has been won by Him. If our expressions of thanksgiving and worship are sincere, then the homage of our lips will be borne out by the honoring of God in our daily lives. Whenever I am tempted to gratify the flesh, my reply should be *"How then can I do this great wickedness and sin against God"* (Gen. 39:9); or *"Is this your kindness to your Friend!"* (1 Sam. 16:17). Shall I so evilly requite the One who has been gracious unto me?

The service which God requires from us is that of love, and not of compulsion. We must indeed keep our eyes on the Rule so that our actions may be conformed to its requirements, otherwise God will ask, *"Who has required this at your hand?"* (Isa. 1:12). But there must be something more: the Lord looks on the heart as well as the outward performances. Duties are not distinguished by their external garb, but by the spirit prompting them. A box of ointment with an affectionate regard for the Lord, nay a cup of cold water, is valued and registered. The smallest act of service unto God which issues from gratitude is prized by Him more highly than all the imposing works of men without it. It is at this very point that the saints differ radically from all others. Whatever are the religious performances of the legalist, the formalists, or the hypocrite, they proceed from some form of self-esteem. But that of the believer is wrought by gratitude. It is the love of Christ which constrains him, which moves him to take His yoke upon him, which so motivates him that his chief concern is to keep His commandments and show forth His praises.

If there is good will in the heart toward God it will be evidenced by choosing and doing the things which are pleasing unto Him. There will be a readiness of heart unto obedience, for love prepares and predisposes the heart unto what He requires from us. Good will in the heart toward God expresses itself in the actual performing of what He has enjoined, for the language of gratitude is *"His commandments are not grievous"* (1 John 5:3). When love to Rachel set Jacob a work it was not unpleasant to him, and though it took him seven years, he deemed it not long. So far from a reconciled soul feeling that God is a hard Master imposing a severe task upon him, he is thankful to have the opportunity to manifest his appreciation. When David made such costly preparations for the house of God, he asked *"But who am I?"* (1 Chron. 29:14), considering it a marvel of condescension that the great God should accept anything at his hands. So far from begrudging any self-sacrifice love will mourn that what has been done is so little and so imperfect, realising that nothing can be too much or too good for the Lord – and not only too small to answer God's love, but to adequately express his own.

3. By trusting in God. Since He is reconciled to me and I to Him then it is both my privilege and duty to look to Him for the supply of every need and confidently expect the same. The Christian should habitually view Him as *"the God of peace"* and under that title and relationship implore Him for daily supplies of grace, for it is as such that He works in us *"that which is well pleasing in His sight"* (Heb. 13:20,21). God has promised to be *"as the dew"* unto His peo-

ple under the Gospel (Hos. 14:5), and as the dew descends from a clear sky so does grace from the One who has blotted out our iniquities. We should look then continually for spiritual strength from God in Christ. All our approaches to Him should be begun and attended with a sense that we have been taken into His favor. In all His communications to His people God acts as reconciled to them, and so should we eye Him whenever we come to the throne of grace. As there is not one mercy God shows us but springs from this relationship, so every duty we offer to Him and petition we make of Him should rise from a sense of the same. This should cause us to believe with a holy boldness.

Here is a cordial for us in our sorest problems and trials. What can the greatest difficulty or acutest strait signify when God remains reconciled to the soul in Christ! Providence is ordered by our best Friend. This is the grand stay which Christ has furnished His disciples: *"that in Me you might have peace; in the world you shall have tribulation"* (John 16:33). Is not that a sufficient defence against all the roaring of men and the rage of Satan? Though the world frowns, God in Christ smiles upon you. It was a sense of their reconciliation to God which turned prisons into palaces and dungeons into chambers of praise for those who were persecuted by the ungodly. Here is a shield against fear, security against danger, a treasure against poverty. Under the sharpest affliction the believer may distinguish between God as a loving Father and avenging Judge. Carnal reason and sense will indeed dispute against faith, and while they are listened unto, faith will stagger; but if the heart turns to and is engaged with a reconciled God it will discern under the severest chastisement the rod of mercy, wielded by a love maintaining our best interests.

There should be an expecting of temporal mercies. If God was in Christ reconciling us to Himself, then most assuredly He will be in Christ giving forth all suited benefits. It is entirely inconsistent with His amity to withhold anything really needed by us, for in that case, as one pointed out, it would not then be a *"much more"* as Christ argued, but a much less: *"If you then, being evil, know how to give good gifts unto your children, how much more shall your Father which is in heaven give good things to them that ask Him!"* (Matt. 7:11). Yet it is to be borne in mind that it is only *"good things"* which He has promised to give, and that He alone is the proper judge as to what is *"good."* If God feeds the ravens, certainly He will not permit His friends to starve. If He spared not His only Son, He will not begrudge mere food and clothing. Our covenant God will deny His children nothing which is for their welfare. If we lived in the realisation of that, how contented we would be in every situation!

4. By cherishing God's peace. "The remission of sins past gives not a permission for sins to come, but should be a bridle and a restraint" (Manton). *"There is forgiveness with You that You may be feared"* (130:4). The end of Christ's death cannot be separated: He is no Atoner for those He is not a Refiner, for He gave Himself to *"purify unto Himself a peculiar people, zealous of good works"* (Titus 2:4). As there was a double enmity in us — one rooted in our nature and another declared by wicked works, so there must be a change both in our state and an alteration of our actions. God and sin are irreconcilable enemies, so that where there is peace with one, there must be war with another. Fire and water would sooner agree than a peace with God and a peace with sin. *"There is no*

peace, says my God to the wicked." We should be very tender of God's peace, that no breach fall out between us: *"If I have done iniquity, I will do no more"* (Job 34:32) must be our sincere desire and resolution, otherwise we are but hypocrites.

Peace was broken by the sin of the first Adam, and though it was restored by the last Adam, yet our obedience is necessary if we are to enjoy the fruits of it: *"Great peace have they which love Your Law"* (119:165). Then let us beware of relaxing in our watchfulness or of becoming self-confident in our ability to face temptations. *"He will speak peace unto His people and to His saints, but let them not turn again to folly"* (Ps. 85:8). "When we sought for pardon, sin was the great burden which lay upon our consciences, the wound which pained us at heart, the disease our souls were sick of; and shall that which we complained of as a burden become our delight? shall we tear open our wounds which are in a fair way of being healed, and run into bonds and chains again after we are freed from them?" (Manton). That were indeed crass folly, madness. Backsliders forsake their peace: as it is said of them, *"they have forgotten their restingplace"* (Jer. 50:6). Peace can only be recovered as we repent of our sins and renew our covenant with God.

5. By using our access to God. The most blessed result or consequence of reconciliation is that believers have the right to approach unto God, and therefore it is their privilege to freely avail themselves of the same. *"Having therefore, brethren, liberty to enter into the Holiest by the blood of Jesus...let us draw near with a true heart in full assurance of faith"* (Heb. 10:19,22), that is, with a firm belief in the efficacy of Christ's sacrifice and a firm reliance upon the same. As God was in Christ reconciling, so He is in Him receiving our praises and petitions. As Christ made satisfaction for us by His death, so He provides the acceptance of our sacrifices and services by His merits. Though justification is a transcendent mercy, yet it would not complete our happiness unless we could commune with God. Peace was not the thing God ultimately aimed at – it was but the medium. He would be our Friend, that there might be sweet intercourse between Him and His people. This is an inestimable privilege of which we should make constant use.

But those who would enjoy communion with the Lord must needs be careful to avoid everything which would separate from Him. He is a jealous God and will brook no rivals. If our fellowship with the Holy One is to be intimate and constant, then we must keep a close guard against grieving the Spirit. We must beware of cooling affections, slackening in the use of means and fighting against sin, slipping back into our old ways. If we neglect those duties there can be no real, acceptable or satisfying drawing nigh unto God. Christ has indeed opened a new and living way for His people into God's presence, and has provided them with both the right and title so to do; nevertheless there are certain moral qualifications required of them if they are to really draw nigh unto the Holy One – certainly those who simply offer cold and formal prayers do not do so.

There are many of God's own children who are cut off from conscious access to Him, for their sins have caused a breach (Isa. 59:1,2): *"with the pure You will show Yourself pure; and with the forward You will show Yourself forward"* (Ps. 18:26). Loose walking severs our communion with God, and then He acts distantly toward us: *"How long will You hide Your face from me?"* (Ps. 13:1) has been the sorrowful lament of many a wayward saint. Our folly must be repented of and humbly confessed before there can be restoration unto fellowship with God. If we would draw near unto Him it must be with *"our hearts sprinkled from an evil conscience and our bodies washed with pure water"* (Heb. 10:22) that is, our internal and external man cleansed from defilement, our members kept from evil and used for God. "Universal sanctification upon our whole persons and the mortification in an especial manner of outward sins are required of us in our drawing near to God" (J. Owen).

6. By rejoicing in God. How great should and may be the joy of believing souls! To be instated in the favor of God, to have the Almighty for our Friend, to have the light of His countenance shining upon us. The knowledge of that in the understanding is tidings of great joy, the sense of it in our hearts is *"joy unspeakable and full of glory."* Reconciliation and the realization of it are two distinct things. The one may be a fact, yet through unbelief or carelessness I may lack the assurance of it. But what comfort and happiness is his who has the assurance that he is at peace with God and the testimony that his conscience is sprinkled with the blood of the Lamb! Then, even though the fig tree blossom not, the fields yield no meat, and there are no herds in the stalls, *"yet I will rejoice in the Lord, I will joy in the God of my salvation"* (Hab. 3:18). *"As sorrowful"* over our sins, yet *"always rejoicing"* in the Lord (2 Cor. 6:10) is our bounden duty.

7. By devotedness to God. *"You are not your own, for you are bought with a price. Therefore glorify God in your body and in your spirit"* (1 Cor 6:19,20). That summarises the responsibilities of the reconciled. To conduct ourselves as those who are not only the creatures, the children, but the purchased property of God, in whom He has the sole right. Since He spared not His own Son for us, we should withhold nothing from Him, but present ourselves unreservedly to Him as *"a living sacrifice,"* which is indeed *"our reasonable service."* We must spare no lust, nor indulge anything which is hateful to Christ, but denying self, take up our cross, and follow Him. Let us earnestly seek grace for the discharge of these duties.

CHAPTER XXXI

It might be thought that we had pretty well covered this aspect in the preceding section. Not so; there is another important phase of it which needs to be considered. Sin has not only alienated man from God, but man from man as well. Where there is no love to God there is no genuine love to our fellow-men. By nature we are totally depraved, and as such possessed of a radically selfish, evil, malicious disposition. *"The poison of asps is under their lips, whose mouth is full of cursing and bitterness; their feet are swift to shed blood, destruction and misery are in their ways"* (Rom. 3:13-17). The record of human history consists largely of a solemn demonstration of that fact. Envies and enmities have marked the relationships of one nation to another, one party against another, one individual against another. Frictions and feuds have been the inevitable outcome of a covetous and ferocious spirit among men, were they black or white, red or yellow.

It is only the restraining hand of God which holds men within bounds and prevents the social sphere from becoming worse than the jungle. Every once in a while that restraining Hand is largely withdrawn and then, despite all our vaunted progress, human nature is seen in its naked savagery. The truth is that men today are neither better nor worse than they were at the beginning of this Christian era. Speaking of God's own people during their unregeneracy, the apostle described them as *"serving divers lusts and pleasures, living in malice and envy, hateful and hating one another"* (Titus 3:3). Such are men the world over, though they will not own up to it, nor can they be expected to. Since the natural man is ignorant of his inherent and inveterate enmity against God, it not to be supposed that he is aware of harboring such a spirit against his neighbors. But if all the police were removed from this so-called civilized country, how long would it be before *"hateful and hating one another"* was plainly and generally manifested!

Fallen man not only requires to be reconciled to God but to his fellows, and where the one takes place the other necessarily follows. Reconciliation, as was shown, is one of the fruits of regeneration; for at the new birth a new principle is imparted to its subject, so that his enmity is displaced by amity. *"Everyone that loves Him that begat, loves him also that is begotten of Him"* (1 John 5:1). The reconciliation of a soul to God entails his reconciliation to all saints. Since God has been reconciled to the entire Church (considered as fallen) and its two main constituents (believing Jews and Gentiles) are made one, it follows that each Christian is, fundamentally, harmoniously united to all others. We say *"fundamentally,"* for the work of Christ has federally and legally united them. But that is not all. He procured the Spirit for His Church and He – by the work of regeneration – makes them vitally one in a new creation. *"For by one Spirit are we all baptized into one body, whether Jews or Gentiles, bond or free, and have all been made to drink into one spirit"* (1 Cor. 12:13).

As the Christian's reconciliation to God entails certain clearly marked responsibilities, so also does his reconciliation to all fellow-believers, and these are what we shall now be occupied with. Let us begin with that basic and comprehensive duty, *"Endeavoring to keep the unity of the Spirit in the bond of peace"* (Eph. 4:3). Concerning that simple precept there has been much confusion, both as to its meaning and requirement, with almost endless controversy about church union and divisions. Man, with his usual perversity, has changed that exhortation to *"Zealously attempt to make and enforce a human unity,"* anathematizing all who will not subscirbe and conform unto the same. Romanists have made the greatest outcry about church unity, vehemently contending that it is indispensably necessary that all Christians should submit to the papal authority, and that there is no salvation for anyone dying outside their communion. Thus, a visible and carnal union with an Italian pontiff is preferred to an invisible, spiritual and saving union with the Christ of God.

We do not propose to convass now the various efforts and devices of men since the Reformation to bring into existence organizations for unity and uniformity among professing Christians, both in creed and form of worship, such as State Churches *"by law established,"* denominations which have laid claim to being the *"true Church"* or *"churches of Christ,"* nor the high pretensions of those who rather more than a century ago denounced all sects and systems and alleged that they alone met on *"the ground of Christ's Body"* and *"expressed"* the unity of the Spirit, only to split up in a very short time into numerous factions and conflicting *"fellowships."* No, our object here is not to be controversial but constructive, to give a brief exposition of Eph. 4:1-6, and then point out the practical application and bearing of the same. We cannot intelligently *"keep the unity of the Spirit"* until we rightly understand what that *"unity"* is; may He graciously be our Guide.

"I therefore the·prisoner of the Lord beseech you that you walk worthy of the vocation with which you are called . . . endeavoring to keep" etc. (Eph. 4:1-3). That exhortation holds the same place in this epistle as 12:1 does in that of the Romans, being placed at the forefront of the hortatory section, and we at once observe the verbal resemblances between them in the *"therefore"* by which it is supported, and the *"I beseech you"* the earnestness with which the call is made. Standing as it does at the beginning of the practical division of the epistle, taking precedence of all its other precepts, we have emphasised its deep importance. It was written by the apostle during his incarceration at Rome, but it is blessed to mark that He looked above Caesar, regarding himself as *"the prisoner of the Lord."* Therefore we find his heart was occupied not with his own danger or discomfort, but with the glory of Christ and the interests of His redeemed. He asked not the saints to *"get up a petition"* for his release, nor even to pray for it, but was concerned that they should conduct themselves in a way which would bring glory to his Master.

The *"I therefore beseech you that you walk worthy . . . endeavouring to keep the unity of the Spirit in the bond of peace"* requires that we carefully consult what precedes, for it is the contents of Eph. 1-3 which explains the force of 4:1-3. First, it should be pointed out that the Greek word rendered *"bond"* is not the simple *"desmos"* but rather the compound *"sun-desmos"* – joining – bond. This at once links up with and is based upon the *"fellow-citizens"* of 2:19, the *"being fitly framed together"* and *"builded together"* (2:21,22), and the *"fellow-heirs, and a joint-body, and joint-partakers of His promise"* (3:6 – Greek), where in each case, the reference is to the union of believing Jews and Gentiles in the mystical Body of Christ. It is therefore an affectionate plea that those who in their unregenerate days had been bitterly hostile against each other, should now walk together in love and harmony. The same Greek word occurs in the parallel passage in Col. 3: *"above all things put on charity, which is the joint-*

bond of perfectness" (v. 14), which throws clear light on the verse we are now considering.

"I therefore ... beseech you that you walk worthy of the vocation wherewith you are called," which is unto sonship -- holiness and glory, conformity to the image of Christ. The inestimable privileges conferred upon those who are effectually called by God out of darkness into His marvelous light, obligates its favored recipients to order their lives accordingly. It requires from them a distinctive spirit, a particular disposition and temper, which is to be exercised and manifested in their dealings with fellow-saints. They are to conduct themselves with humility and gentleness, not with self-assertiveness and self-exaltation. They are required to seek the good and promote the interests of their brethren and sisters in Christ, and continually endeavor to preserve amity and concord among them, "to bear with one another in love as to those light occasions of offence or displeasure which could not be wholly avoided even among believers in this present imperfect state" (T. Scott).

For the Christian to walk worthily of his vocation is for him to live and act congruously, suitably for it. Here it has particular reference to the spirit and manner in which he is to practically conduct himself toward his fellow-saints, namely, by endeavoring to keep the unity of the Spirit in the bond of peace. That word "endeavoring" means far more than a half-hearted effort which ceases as soon as opposition is encountered. It signifies "give diligence," laboring earnestly, doing our utmost in performing this task. The nature of this duty is intimated with considerable definiteness by the particular graces which are here specified as needing to be exercised. Had that "unity" consisted of uniformity of belief – as many have supposed, then the saints had been exhorted unto the acquirement of "knowledge" and the exercise of "faith." Or had that unity been an ecclesiastical one which is to be framed or "expressed" on earth, then the call would be to the exercise of "faithfulness" and "firmness," in uncompromisingly resisting all innovations. But instead, it is "with all lowliness and meekness, forbearing one another in love."

Thus whatever is our angle of approach in seeking to define this controversial expression, whether it is from the contents of the previous chapters, the parallel passage in Col. 3:14, or the congruity of the preceding verse, it should be clear that the "unity of the Spirit" which we are to diligently assay to keep "in the bond of peace" has no reference to the formation of an external and visible unification of all professing Christians, in which all differences in judgment and belief are to be dropped and where all worship is to conform to a common standard. The union of Christendom which so many enthusiasts have advocated would, in reality, consist of a unity in which principle gave way to policy, contending earnestly for the Faith once delivered to the saints would be displaced by the uttering of mere generalities and moral platitudes, and the masculine virtues degenerating into an effeminate affection of universal charity. Sheep and goats will never make amicable companions, still less so sheep and wolves. Variety and not uniformity marks all the works of God, whether it is in creation, providence or grace.

The unity of the Spirit is not an ecclesiastical one here on earth, nor is it one which God will make in Heaven by and by. Nor is it the unity of the mystical Body, for that can no more be broken than could a bone in the literal body of Christ (John 18:36). The very fact that it is "the unity of the Spirit" precludes any visible ecclesiastical unity. It is a fact subsisting to faith, without any evidence of it to sight. It is therefore a Divine, spiritual and present unity which is quite imperceptible to the senses. It is that unity of which the Spirit is the Author. It is the new creation of which He makes God's elect members by regeneration. Every soul indwelt by the Spirit is a part of that unity, and none others are. By being made members of the new creation we are brought into *"the joint-bond of peace."* Each soul indwelt by· the Spirit is inducted into a company where enmity has been slain, in which the members are united as the fruit of Christ's sacrifice, and they are here enjoined to act in full harmony with this new relationship.

By virtue of his having the Spirit each Christian is in spirit united with all other regenerated souls, and he is to give diligence in practically observing that fact in all his converse and dealings with them. He is to earnestly avoid falling out with a brother or sister in Christ, being most careful to eschew everything having a tendency to cause a breach between them. He is to love all in whom he can discern any of the features of Christ, whether or not they belong to his own *"church"* or *"assembly."* He is to exercise good will unto all who are members the Household of Faith. He should be slow to take offence, and having himself received mercy, should ever be merciful unto others. God's reconciliation should be our rule in dealing with our brethren: *"If God so loved us, we ought also to love one another"* (1 John 4:11), and since His heart embraces the whole of His family, ours should do no less. If He is longsuffering to usward, we should be longsuffering to themward. *"Be you therefore imitators of God as dear children"* (Eph. 5:1).

Now the only possible way in which the reconciled soul can discharge this essential and blessed part of his responsibility is by exercising those graces enjoined in v. 2. After beseeching the saints to walk worthy of their vocation, Paul described the necessary qualifications for so doing, namely, *"with all lowliness and meekness, forbearing one another in love."* Lowliness of mind or humility is to have a mean estimate of myself, based upon the consciousness of my sinfulness and weakness. Let it be most attentively noted that the exercise of this grace comes first, and that it is not only *"with lowliness,"* but *"with all lowliness."* Nothing so hinders our keeping the unity of the Spirit in the bond of peace as personal pride. Next comes *"meekness,"* which signifies tractability, gentleness, mildness; an unresisting and uncomplaining temper. It is that lamblike disposition which enables one to bear injury from others without bitterness and retaliating in a spirit of revenge. *"Forbearing one another in love:"* suppressing anger and ill feelings, patiently enduring the failings, foibles, and faults of my brethren, as they do (or should) mine.

Those grace of humility, meekness and longsuffering are to be manifested in keeping – recognizing and cherishing – that spiritual and invisible unity which there is between the children of God, loving all in whom they perceive His image doing everything in their power to further one another's interests and to promote harmony and concord. For the glory of God, the honor of Christ, and the good of His people, each believer is under bonds to exercise and manifest a spirit of good will unto his brethren; that is to override all natural peculiarities, all selfish interests, all party concerns. That does not mean a peace at any price, wherein we connive at error or condone the sins of an erring saint, making no effort to recover him. No indeed, the wisdom which is from above is *"first pure, and then peaceable"* (James 3:17). If we perceive a professing Christian walking contrary to the Truth, we are to have no intimate fellowship with him, *"yet count him not as an enemy, but admonish him as a brother"* (2 Thess. 3:15); if he is suddenly overtaken in a fault we should, in the spirit of meekness, seek to restore him (Gal. 6:1).

Rightly did Matt. Henry point out that "The seat of Christian unity is in the heart or spirit; it does not lie in one set of thoughts and form or mode of worship, but in one heart or soul." In other words it lies in the exercise of a gracious and peaceable disposition. As that writer so aptly pointed out, "Love is the law of Christ's kingdom, the lesson of His school, and the livery of His family." If Christ is the Prince of Peace, then surely His disciples ought to be the children of peace, ever striving to maintain amity and harmony. The root cause of strife and dissension lies not in anything external, but within ourselves: *"From where come wars and fightings among you? Come they not here even of your lusts that war in your members?"* (James. 4:1). We should not rudely obtrude our ideas upon others, but rather wait until we are asked to state our views, and then do so with meekness and reverence (1 Pet. 3:15). The cultivation of an amiable disposition and peaceable temper is the best cement for binding saints together.

In verses 4-6 the apostle mentions several motives to prompt unto a compliance with the duty expressed in Eph. 4:1,3. *"There is one Body, and one Spirit, even as you are called in one hope of your calling."* What better grounds could believers have to love and act peaceably toward each other! They are fellow-members of the mystical body of Christ, they are indwelt by the same blessed Spirit, they are begotten unto the same glorious and eternal inheritance. Do they look forward to the time when they shall join *"the spirits of just men made perfect"*? Then let them anticipate that time and act now agreeably toward those they hope to dwell together with forever. *"One Lord, one faith, one baptism."* There may be different apprehensions of that Faith, different degrees of conformity to that Lord, different understandings of *"baptism,"* but that must not alienate the heart of one Christian from another. *"One God, and Father of all,"* whose family all the reconciled belong to; and should not the members of that family cherish one another! Let that sevenfold consideration animate each of us to live in peace and brotherly affection with our fellow-saints.

The unity of the Spirit differs from the oneness of the Body, in that while we may either keep or break the former, we can do neither the one nor the other with the latter. The responsibility of those reconciled to each other is, negatively, to avoid anything which would mar that unity; and positively, to engage in everything that would further it. Pride, self-will, envy, bigotry, fleshly zeal about comparative trifles, are the causes of most of the frictions and fractions among believers. *"Only by pride comes contention."* (Prov. 13:19). That is the most fertile root of all — offence is taken because I do not receive that notice to which I deem myself entitled, or I am hurt because I cannot have my own way in everything. *"A whisperer separates chief friends"* (Prov. 16:28): but he can only do so by one giving ear to his malicious tales! An acquaintance of ours used to say unto those who come to her with evil reports of others, "Please take your garbage elsewhere: I decline to receive it."

"Therefore if you bring your gift to the altar, and there remember that your brother has anything against you; leave there your gift before the altar and go

your way; first be reconciled to your brother, and then come and offer your gift" (Matt. 5:23,24). How emphatically that makes manifest the importance which God attaches to our keeping the unity of the Spirit in the bond of peace! When that unity has been broken, He desires not our gifts. If you have done a brother an injury and he has just cause of complaint, peace has been disrupted, and the Holy One requires you to right that wrong before He will receive your worship. *"If I regard iniquity in my heart the Lord will not hear me"* (Ps. 66:18). God is as much the Father of the offended one as He is of you, and He will receive nothing at your hand until you remove that stumblingstone from before your brother. No worship or service can possibly be acceptable to God while I cherish a malicious spirit toward any of His children.

When a minister of the Church of England gives notice of an approaching *"Holy Communion"* he is required to read unto those expecting to participate from an exhortation containing these words: "And if you shall perceive your offences to be such as are not only against God, but also against your neighbor, then you shall reconciled yourself unto them; being ready to make restitution and satisfaction, according to the uttermost of your power, for all injuries and wrongs done by you to any other; and being likewise ready to forgive others that have offended you, as you would have forgiveness of your offence at God's hand. For otherwise the receiving of the Holy Communion does nothing else than increase your damnation." Alas that there is so little of such plain and faithful warning in most sections of Christendom today, and that Christ is so often insulted by His *"Supper"* being celebrated in places where bitter feelings are cherished and breaches exist between the celebrants.

The following precepts are so many illustrations of Eph. 4:3 and so many branches of the responsibility saintwards of each reconciled soul. *"Have peace "one with another"* (Mark 9:50). *"You ought also to wash one another's feet... love one another"* (John 13:14,34). *"Be kindly affectioned one to another with brotherly love, in honor preferring one another"* (Rom. 12:10). *"Admonish one another"* (Rom. 15:14). *"By love serve one another...bear one another's burdens"* (Gal. 5:13; 6:2). *"Be kind one to another, tender hearted, forgiving one another as God for Christ's sake has forgiven you"* (Eph. 4:32). *"In lowliness of mind let each one esteem other better than themselves"* (Phil. 2:3). *"Comfort yourselves together and edify one another"* (1 Thess. 5:11). *"Exhort one another...consider one another to provoke unto love and good works"* (Heb. 3:13; 10:24). *"Speak not evil one of another"* (James 4:11). *"Use hospitality one to another...all of you be subject one to another"* (1 Pet. 4:8; 5:5).

CONCLUSION

In the course of our explanation of this doctrine we have sought to make a comprehensive view of it as a whole and then to examine in detail its essential components. Truth is a unit, one harmonious whole, but with our very limited powers of comprehension we are incapable of receiving it as such: rather do we take it in *"here a litte, there a little."* That is according as God has constituted us. When endeavoring to master a subject or problem which is presented to the mind, we are obliged to consider singly its several elements and branches. When partaking of material food we do not attempt to swallow it whole, but first break it into fragments and then masticate them. It is thus with the spiritual aliment which God has provided for the soul. Unless we carefully collate all that the Spirit has revealed on the subject, duly ponder each aspect and view it in its true perspective, we shall obtain nothing more than a vague and faulty conception of it.

Though Truth is a unit, it has two sides to it. It had in the communicating of it: it is a Divine revelation, yet it passed through the minds of holy men and is couched in their language. It is thus with its contents, as a whole and all its parts. There is both a Divine and a human side to it, issuing from God, addressed to men: revealing His heart and will, enforcing our responsibility. That necessarily presents a problem to the finite mind, the more so since our mind is impaired by the ravages of sin. As man is constructed, he is unable to take in both sides of the Truth at a single glance, being obliged to view each separately. Unless he does so, a distorted vision will inevitably ensue, for while contemplating but one half he will imagine that he is actually viewing the whole. Now those two sides of the Truth are not contradictory, but complementary. Since God is God, He must maintain His sovereign rights and enforce His authority; and since He has constituted man a moral agent, He deals with him accordingly — having absolute control over him, yet leaving him to act freely.

This twofoldness of truth is exhibited in every doctrine contained in Holy Writ, in every aspect of the Faith, in every branch of the Evangelical system, and it is in the maintaining of a due proportion and balance between them that the competency and helpfulness of any expositor chiefly appears, as it is also the hardest part of his task. Most conspicuously is this the case with the doctrine we have been treated of, for not only is reconciliation itself a mutual affair, but Scripture presents reconciliation as being both an accomplished thing and also as something now being effected — according as it is viewed from the standpoint of what Christ wrought at the cross, or from what is required of the sinner in order for him to personally enter into the good of what the Redeemer there procured. It is specially for the benefit of the young preacher — scores of which will read them — that these closing paragraphs are penned, for unless he is quite clear upon this distinction, his trumpet will give forth an uncertain sound.

When was God really reconciled to the Christian? At the cross or when he savingly believed the Gospel? That question has been discussed earlier, yet we believe that some will welcome a further elucidation. On this subject, as so many, the Puritans are much to be preferred to the best writers of the nineteenth century. "God is never actually reconciled to us, nor we to Him, till He gives us the regenerated Spirit" (T. Manton). "For the preparing us to be reconciled it is nec-

187

essary that we are convinced that we are enemies to God, and that He accounts us such, and that so long as we remain in that state He is also an enemy to us" (T. Goodwin). "There is a double reconciliation here (2 Cor. 5:18,19). First, fundamental, at the death of Christ, whereby it was obtained, This is the ground of God's laying aside His anger. Second, actual or particular, when it is complied with by faith. This regards the application of it, when God does actually lay aside His enmity, and imputes sin no more to the person" (S. Charnock).

Elsewhere Charnock says, "He acts toward the world as a reconciling God towards believers as reconciled. He is reconcilable as long as He is inviting and keeps men alive in a state of probation." The Puritans drew a plain and broad line of demarkation between the impetration or purchase of salvation, and the actual application or bestowing of the same. "By impetration we mean the purchase of all good things made by Christ for us with and of the Father; and by application, the actual enjoyment of those good things upon our believing; as if a man paid a price for the redeeming of captives, the paying a price supplies the room of the impetration of which we speak, and the freeing of the captives is the application of it" (J. Owen). Christ merited and obtained the reconciliation of both sides, yet God is not reconciled to us nor are we to Him until we repent and believe. So it is in justification: Christ wrought out a perfect and everlasting righteousness for all His people, yet God does not impute that righteousness to any of them until they savingly believe the Gospel.

While most of the best theologians of the last century recognized the necessary distinction between the impetration and the application of reconciliation, yet often they failed to frame their postulates consistently therewith. For instance, one of the most eminent of them, and for whose works we have a high regard, stated, "On the ground of God's reconciliation to us, we are exhorted to be reconciled to Him, and the great motive or encouragement is His previous reconciliation." That such language was not simply a slip of the pen (to which all are liable) is clear from what follows in his next paragraph. " 'The chastisement of our peace,' by which peace was procured, 'was upon Him, and with His stripes we are healed.' God was reconciled when that was done, and made justice cease to demand our punishment." It is because such teaching has been so widely received and has led to serious mischief in the evangelical ministry, that its erroneous character needs to be exposed.

To affirm that God is reconciled to sinners, or if you prefer it, to His elect, before they are reconciled to Him, is an unintentional but tacit repudiation of John 3:36: "He that believes not the Son shall not see life, but the wrath of God abides on him." Note it is not "the wrath of God shall come upon him," but it is on him now and remains so as long as he is an unbeliever. In these respects there is no difference whatever between the elect and the non-elect. All are "by nature the children of wrath," under the Covenant of Works, and therefore under the curse and condemnation of the Law. The work of Christ has not changed the attitude of a holy God toward a single soul who continues in love with sin and a rebel against Him. "He is angry with the wicked every day" (Ps. 7:11), and "the wrath of God is revealed from heaven against all ungodliness and unrighteousness of men" (Rom. 1:18). It is not until the sinner repents and savingly believes the Gospel that he passes from one state to another and the frown of God is displaced by His smile (John 3:18; 5:24). Of the elect (1 Pet. 2:10) it is said, *"which had not obtained mercy, but now have obtained mercy"* (2:10).

Here is another declaration from a nineteenth century theologian of high repute, and to whose works we are personally indebted not a little: "God is reconciled: He is no longer angry with the sinner, for he is no longer a sinner in the eye of God and His justice." Had he said, "the penitent and believing sinner," that would be blessedly true: instead he was discussing what Christ's work had accomplished Godwards. In the same paragraph he averred, "All the chosen people are redeemed," which is another statement badly in need of qualification and explanation. Christ indeed *"gave Himself a ransom for all"* – His people (1 Tim. 2:6), and He did so *"that He might redeem us from all iniquity"* (Tit. 2:14), but none then unborn were actually *"redeemed."* The correct way to state it is this: redemption was purchased for all the chosen people by Christ, and *"in due time"* (1 Tim. 2:6) they are made partakers of that redemption by the effectual operation of the Holy Spirit. Believers alone are actually redeemed or emancipated, and it is of them such passages as Gal. 3:13; Eph. 1:7; 1 Pet. 1:18,19 speak.

It is only by attending closely to the exact wording of Scripture and refusing to go one iota beyond its statements, that we are preserved from confusion and error. Christ was made sin for us *"that we might be made the righteousness of God in Him"* (2 Cor. 5:21). It is not said that *"Christ is the end of the Law for righteousness to all His people,"* but *"to everyone that believes"* (Rom. 10:4). *"Though He was rich, yet for our sakes He became poor, that you through His poverty might be rich"* (2 Cor. 8:9). He was *"made a curse for us...that the blessing of Abraham might come to the Gentiles"* (Gal. 3:13,14). Christ *"suffered for sins, the Just for the unjust, that He might bring us to God"* (1 Pet. 3:18). But we are not actually made rich or partakers of the blessing of Abraham, nor brought to God, until we repent and believe. As we must distinguish between the impetration and the application of the atonement, so also must we between the grace of God decreeing and the execution of the decree of His grace. The *"all spiritual blessings"* of Eph. 1:3 include regeneration, yet none are regenerate until effectually called by God.

"We were reconciled to God by the death of His Son" (Rom. 5:10) impetratively, for God has accepted Christ's ransom, yet He does not apply it till faith is exercised by us. Reconciliation, redemption and justification are alike the results of Christ's satisfaction, the blessings which He purchased for His people, but they are only bestowed upon them when they are personally reconciled to God. "God the Father justifies, through the Son, by the Spirit, who works faith to receive the same. But until those things meet together our persons are not properly justified, notwithstanding Christ has wrought out a complete righteousness" (W. Bridge, 1670), nor is God reconciled to us till the Spirit has wrought faith in our hearts. In the light of Rom. 3:25,26 are we not fully warranted in saying that, Christ is set forth a propitiation through faith in His blood that God might be holy, and yet the Reconciler of him who ceases to defy His authority and sues for mercy through the Lord Jesus.

Though the governmental requirements of God demand that the sinner end his revolt before He will be reconciled to him, that by no means implies any doubt of Christ's satisfaction securing its designed effects. The atonement has done very much more than remove legal obstacles which previously stood in the way of friendship between God and men or opened the door for Him to bestow peace and pardon upon all who would accept them, as the Arminian speaks; it has absolutely guaranteed the salvation of all for whom it was made. So far from the word *"might"* in the passages quoted above denoting uncertainty, it is expressive of design and intimates the sure consequence that follows from Christ's sacrifice. As the Westminster Confession of Faith so well puts it, "To all those for whom Christ purchased redemption, He does certainly and effectually apply and communicate the same," where the word *"redemption"* is used – as it often is in Scripture – as including all the blessings which it was the immediate object of Christ's death to procure.

That there is a human side to the Evangelical system by no means introduces an element of uncertainty into it or jeapardises its success. *"God is in one mind and who can turn Him? And what His soul desires, even that He does"* (Job 13:13). The Arminian comes short of the full truth when he says, "All was done on Christ's part which was necessary to make possible the reconciliation and pardon of sinners, and it is now left with them whether they will receive or reject the Gospel offer," and that "since God has constituted man a moral agent, He requires his voluntary cooperation." Christ's sacrifice has made certain the reconciliation and redemption of all for whom it was offered, for it ensured that He would *"see the travail of His soul and be satisfied."* Christ's impetration secured an infallible provision for the effectual application, namely, the gift of the Holy Spirit, who by His invincible operations should regenerate each of Christ's *"seed"* and work saving repentance and faith in them. Though eternal life, repentance and faith are the *"gifts"* of God, they are also the fruits of Christ's atonement, and are conferred upon all in whose room He suffered and died.

Instead of merely opening a door of salvation for the whole of Adam's posterity to enter if they feel disposed to, the atoning work of Christ has effectually secured the actual salvation of all the people of God, for by the wisdom of the Divine counsels and the power of the Spirit they are brought to gladly concur with God's will, and put their trust in the blood of the Lamb. Nevertheless, God still enforces the righteous requirements of His government and treats with men according to their responsibility, sending forth His ambassadors to charge them with their wickedness, bidding them to be reconciled to God, and assuring them of His gracious acceptance upon their eeasing to fight against Him. Before the sinner can enjoy the benefits of Christ's death he must consent to return to the duty of the Law and live in obedience to God, for He will not pardon him while he continues to live in rebellion against Him. The Gospel calls upon men to repent of their sins, forsake their idols, and enter into solemn covenant with God, yeilding themselves up unreservedly to Him, to henceforth live unto His glory.

The work of the evangelist is clearly defined: the O.T. precedes the New, the ministry of John the Baptist went before that of Christ, the substance of Rom. 1-3 is to be preached before the truth of Rom. 4 and 5 is proclaimed. His first duty is to preach the Moral Law, for *"by the Law is the knowledge of sin"* (Rom. 3:20): its requirements, its strictness, its spirituality, its curse, that his hearers may be brought to realize their guilty and lost condition. Coupled with this preaching of the Law must be a presentation of the character of the Lawgiver and His claims upon the creatures of His hand: that He is sovereign Lord, demanding unqualified submission to His will; that He is ineffably holy, hating all sin and iniquity; that He is inflexibly just and *"will by no means clear the guilty,"* and will yet judge every man according to his works. Conviction of sin, by the application of the Law to the conscience, is the first step in the progress by which men are led to take hold of God's covenant. Peace with God, which the covenant established, will be sought and prized by none except those who are conscious of their guilt and dread the displeasure and vengeance of the Judge of all the earth.

The second duty of the evangelist is to preach the Gospel, and that, in such a manner, that he neither contradicts nor weakens what is pointed out in the preceding paragraph – though complementing it. He is to show that the principal design of God in sending His Son here was to magnify the Law, to manifest His detestation of sin, to exhibit His justice; all of which was solemnly seen at the cross. He is then to open the wondrous grace of God in giving His Son to execute His mission and perform His work, not only for the glory of God but the good of sinners. He is to show the amazing thing is that God takes the initiative, that in Christ He makes the advances, that by Christ provision is made for the healing of the breach, and that He sends forth His servants to make overtures of peace, bidding sinners *"be reconciled to Him"* – to be converted, to repent of their sins, abandon their wicked ways, believe in the Lord Jesus Christ, and walk according to His precepts.

It is the duty of the evangelist to show that though Christ is read to be the Friend of sinners, yet He will not be the Minister of sin, but rather maintains the honor and interests of the Father at every point. His call is, *"Come unto Me, all you that labor and are heavy laden, and I will give you rest."* That is, Come unto Me, all you that have in vain sought satisfaction in gratifying self and partaking of the pleasures of sin, and are now weighed down with burdened consciences and a sense of the deserved wrath of God. *"Take My yoke upon you...and you shall find rest unto your souls."* That is, Own My sceptre, surrender to My lordship, walk in obedience to My commandnents, and rest of soul shall be your portion. The One who made satisfaction to God tells us the benefits of it are received only through our believing (John 3:16), and that is an act which principally respects the will. The believe is to *"receive"* Christ (John 1:12) as He is offered in the Gospel: to receive a whole Christ, to be our Prophet, Priest and King.

The work of the pastor or teacher is to further instruct those who have responded to the message of the evangelist. He is to show that as God out of Christ was an offended and threatening God, God in Christ is an appeased and promising God. He is to make it clear that the reason why those who responded to the call and appeal of the evangelist was not because they were in themselves wiser or better than those who reject it, but that it was God who made them to differ (1 Cor. 4:7). That God did so first, by choosing them in Christ before the foundation of the world; second, by giving them as sheep to the good Shepherd for Him to save; third, by causing the Holy Spirit to bring them from death unto life, illumine their understandings, convict them of their lost estate, and make them willing to receive Christ. Thus they have no cause for boasting, but every reason to ascribe all the glory unto the Triune God.

Should the young preacher say, I am not yet quite clear in my mind, especially does the doctrine of election puzzle me as to exactly how I should address the unsaved. Neither election nor particular redemption should in anywise cramp your style. Your commission is to preach the Gospel to *"every creature"* you can reach, and the Gospel is that *"Christ Jesus came into the world to save sin-ners"* (1 Tim. 1:15), and therefore you are warranted in telling your hearers that there is a Saviour for every sinner out of Hell who feels his need of Him and is willing to comply with His terms. Your first business is to show him his need of Christ and count upon the Spirit's making your efforts effectual, assured that God's Word shall not return unto Him void, whether or not you are permitted to see its fruits. But if you are granted the privilege of seeing some comply with Christ's terms, then you may know that they are members of that Church which Christ loved and gave Himself for, and that the Spirit has now vitally united them to Him.

The evangelist's message is that there is salvation in Christ for all who receive Him as He is offered in the Gospel and put their trust in Him. Though Christ purchased reconciliation and justification for all His people, yet they do not re-ceive the same until they repent and believe. God is willing to be on terms of amity with the sinner, yet He will not be so until the sinner submit to those terms. Christ has perfectly made peace with God, so that no other ransom or sacrifice is required, yet none are admitted into it until they make their peace with God. God has appointed a connection – a moral and holy one – between the blessings purchased by Christ and the actual conveyance of them to His people. Though Christ died in order to procure Heaven for them by His merits, He also died to procure for them the regenerating operations of His Spirit to prepare them for Heaven. The test or evidence of our compliance with God's terms is a life of voluntary obedience: *"as many as walk according to this rule, peace be on them and mercy"* (Gal. 6:16) – *"mercy"* toward their defects.

RECONCILIATION BY THE BLOOD OF CHRIST

by

Thomas Goodwin

RECONCILIATION BY THE BLOOD OF CHRIST.

A SERMON.

And (having made peace through the blood of his cross) by him to reconcile all things unto himself; by him, I say, whether they be things in earth, or things in heaven.—COL. I. 20.

THAT ' God was, in Christ, reconciling the world to himself,' is the sum of, and the theme which the gospel dilates upon, 2 Cor. v. 19 ; and the title the apostle gives therefore to the doctrine of the gospel is, ' The word of reconciliation, to wit, that God was in Christ,' &c. ; that is, that God the Father had from everlasting made this his special business, which he hath plotted, and been desirous to bring about ; and that though ' all things are of him,' ver. 18, yet this above all the rest. And that God the Father hath appointed Christ as the means to accomplish it, with full satisfaction made to his justice. ' God was in Christ,' &c.

God the Father's part I have already handled out of another scripture, more proper to that argument, and how far it was advanced by him.

First, By taking up a strong and unalterable resolution, to gather in one the sons of men, scattered from him, Eph. i. 9, 10. It is declared to be ' the mystery of his will, which he purposed in himself, according to his good pleasure ;' and as this text tells us, ' it pleased him.' It had been his full meaning, his everlasting intent and purpose, yea, a matter of the greatest delight to him ; as Jer. ix. 24, shewing mercy, on the earth, not in hell, therein is my delight. This purpose was fed with delight, and therefore vanished not. And the greater men are, the greater delights they use to have ; and this being God's, must needs be a matter of infinite moment and consequence, his heart being in it so much, and he being set upon it.

Secondly, This purpose lay not idle in him, but set him a-work, his wisdom a-work, and out of those his infinite depths, found out and invented a way and means of effecting our reconciliation, even the incarnation and death of his own Son ; before the wound was given, provided a plaster and sufficient remedy to salve all again, which otherwise had been past finding out. For we, who could never have found out a remedy for a cut finger (had not God prescribed and appointed one), could much less for this. It being a case of that difficulty, supposing his justice resolving to have full satisfaction ; which, as it passed all the creature's power to make, so it passed their skill and thoughts to find out how and by whom it might be effected. The devils, they could not imagine any way, no more for us than for themselves, and therefore tempted man, thinking him, when he had sinned, sure enough, and hell gates so strongly locked, that no art could find or make a key to open them, a power to break them open. And Adam, poor man! he trembled, knew not which way to turn himself, and thought God would have flown upon him presently.. The good angels, they know it but by the church, Eph. iii. 10. In this strait aforehand God set his depths a-work to find out one, in and by whom all this might be accommodated, and (to allude to Abraham's speech) 'provided himself a sacrifice' unknown to us.

Thirdly, It hath been shewn that he, to manifest his seriousness in it, called his Son to it; whom,

Fourthly, We have shewn at his entreaty to have been fully willing, and undertook it.

I shall at this time, in handling of these words, give the second part of this story; and that is, to lay open Christ's part, in whom it now lies to be performed. And to this end I have chosen this text, which tells us that all fulness dwells in him for the effecting of it. As,

1. A fulness of fitness.
2. Of abilities.
3. Of faithfulness.
4. Of righteousness, now it is performed.
5. Of acceptation of his person, and what he hath done.
6. A fulness of duration of the merit of what he hath done for ever.

1. First, He had fulness of fitness in him, being fitted so with such a body as hath been described; a fulness of fitness in his person, to be a mediator and reconciler for us.

Now the choice of a fit person, and his fitness, is more especially required and respected in a business of mediation than in anything else, avails as much as wisdom, power, or anything else; for indeed it is the foundation of all, and often for want of a fit person, the force of a mediation is enervated, and avails not, though other sufficiencies concur to effect it. Now to shew this peculiar fitness, 'A mediator,' the apostle says, 'is a mediator not of one,' but of two parties at least, Gal. iii. 20.

The parties here, betwixt whom reconciliation is to be made, are God and man, 1 Tim. ii. 5. Why? Can you then have a fitter person than one that is both God and man? And such a person is Jesus Christ become, that he might be a fit mediator. 'There is,' says the apostle, 'but one God, and but one mediator between God and man, the man Christ Jesus.' There could be but one so fit a mediator. To this end, therefore, the apostle tells us, in Heb. ii. 16, that 'he took the seed of Abraham to himself,' ἐπιλαμβάνεται, took our nature into one person with himself; called therefore a 'tabernacle, which God pitched, and not men,' Heb. viii. 2, and chap. ix. 11, 'not of this building,' of the hands of men. Men must have no hand in it. For this is required to fit a mediator, or an umpire, Job ix. 33, 'that he be able to lay his hand on both;' which phrase notes out,

(1.) That he be an indifferent person between both, ready to distribute with an equal hand, to both their due.

(2.) That he hath an interest, a hand, or prevailing stroke with both; power to deal between both.

(3.) That he be fit to communicate to them, for the benefit of his mediation else is vain. Now all these are in Christ, as thus fitted.

(1.) For the first, Heb. ii. 16, the apostle shewing how he took our nature on him, not of angels; in the 17th verse he gives this as the reason,

'It behoved him,' &c. And why did it behove him? 'That he might be a merciful and faithful high priest in things pertaining to God, to make reconciliation for the sins of the people.' That is, hereby he comes to be a fit, meet high priest. 'It behoved him,' ὤφειλε, which notes out fitness. And why fit? The words shew, there were two parties whose cause was to be committed to him, God and the people's. There were things pertaining to God, who was the party wronged by the sins of the people ; and there was reconciliation or atonement for their sins to be made. God, he was to have his due, though they had reconciliation ; therefore, in regard of the things pertaining to God, *faithfulness* was required ; in regard of things pertaining to the people, *mercy*. If he had been only man, he might have ended it with detriment and wrong to God.

That therefore he might be faithful to him, it was fit he should be God, and so tender of his cause, that he might see such a satisfaction first should be made as was his due, and what pertained to him ; for God put all the glory of his justice into his hand. He had need be God who had such a trust committed him ; God would not trust a mere man again.

And, secondly, he had our souls and salvation committed also to him ; and therefore it was behoveful for us that he should be man, to be merciful and pitiful to us ; that he might be sensible of the pains human nature was to be put to, and so, out of experimental kindly pity, moved to make an atonement.

(2.) Secondly, Hereby he was one that was peculiarly fit to deal with both, and to have a hand and stroke in both, and both with him.

For now, as Zech. xiii. 7, he is become ' the man, God's fellow ;' and so, more than man. He had not else been meet to deal with God ; it had been robbery in a mere man to have arrogated such an equality, which yet was not in him, Phil. ii ; for as God says, Jer. xxx. 21, who but he could ' draw nigh to me,' so near as thus, to mediate ? Who durst attempt, or presume, or engage his heart to do it ? But him, being my fellow, ' I will cause to draw nigh unto me ;' and there is no unfitness, no disparagement in it, which, if he had been but a creature, would have been.

And, secondly, he being the man, God's fellow, we may draw nigh to him, and he to us. For why, as in the same Jer. xxx. 2, ' he comes out of the midst of us.' So also, Heb. iv. 14, 15, see what a fit high priest, by this, he is made for us, so as we may boldly draw near, ver. 16, to the throne of grace ; that is, seeing we have a great high priest, not simply a high priest, but a great high priest, no less than Jesus, the Son of God, who may draw nigh to God for us.

But you might say, This is too high a priest, too great for us to draw nigh to ; therefore he adds, ' But yet he is not an high priest which cannot be touched with the feeling of our infirmities,' that is, is a man as we are, and therefore subject to the same feeling of pain and miseries, which (as God) he is not ; and therefore we may come boldly to him and make our moan, &c., as in the 16th verse.

(3.) And, thirdly (which is a reason beyond all this), by this peculiar fitness of his, he is fitted to communicate the benefit of his mediation to us, which without it he had not done ; and therefore this fitness of his is a matter of great consequence and moment.

Now the benefit we were to receive by his mediation, was to have righteousness from him, so as to appear in God's sight without sin, and so to be brought into favour, and that so great as to be the sons of God. Now, in that the Son of God took our nature, he was fitted to do this ; for,

That we might have his righteousness communicated to us, it was fit that our nature should be a fountain or cistern of it first, else what peculiar claim could we make to it more than other creatures? Heb. ii. 11. this reason is given, 'He that sanctifieth, and they that are sanctified, are one,' that is, ἐξ ἑνὸς, *ejusdem naturæ*. Had they not been so, he could not so fitly have been made righteousness and sanctification to us; and therefore (says he, John xvii. 19), 'For their sakes sanctify I myself,'—that is, my human nature, which he calls himself, as one person with himself, for his Deity was sanctified from everlasting—'that they might be sanctified,' that is, partakers of the same righteousness that I have. And this is one reason he gives in Heb. ii. why, ὥφειλε, 'it behoved him,' ver. 10, that so he might sanctify us, by first sanctifying our nature; for it was fit that that nature which had sinned should be sanctified, 'to condemn sin in the flesh,' as the apostle reasons, Rom. viii., and so now it is fitly imputed to us, as done for us; and therefore a redeemer in the old law was to be a kinsman, he had right of redeeming only, Lev. xxv. 25 and Ruth iv. 4–7, and therefore the Hebrew word *Goel* signifieth a redeemer and a kinsman. And Christ therefore, that he might have right of redeeming and sanctifying, and they a right in his redemption, it was fit they should partake of one. Wherefore, ver. 14 of Heb ii., 'Forasmuch as the children were partakers of flesh and blood,' &c., he also, that so he might be of a kindred to them, and rightfully call them brethren, ver. 11, and to make them sons of God, as himself was, John i. 12.

And hence now, by reason of the want of this very fitness, the benefit of his mediation, so as to convey righteousness, is not intended to angels; and therefore it is exclusively added, ver. 16, 'He took not on him the nature of angels;' they had not this benefit by it, because not their nature. So as this fitness is a thing God much looked at and respected; for though of never so great a value in itself, yet doth good but to those for whom he was then so properly and peculiarly a fit mediator, namely, men.

In a word, take this for a sure rule, that though the intention of the merits of Christ did arise from his sufficiency and abilities to mediate, yet the extension from his proper fitness; and therefore to none but as * men, whose nature he partook of.

First, We see he hath fulness of fitness in him; let us now see if he hath fulness of abilities and sufficiencies in him for this great work, which is a distinct thing from the former; for in the old law the next akin was always most fit to redeem, but it may be not always able.

2. Secondly, Christ hath a fulness of ability to effect this great business, to make a perfect mediation every way satisfactory. And surely if he hath all fulness in him to this end (as in Col. i. 19), he therefore wants no ability and sufficiency hereunto to make a perfect saviour, as he is called, Heb. v. 9. And this may be demonstrated from what went before.

For, *first*, God called him to this great work. Now, if he had not been fully able to undertake and go through with it, God would never have pitched upon him. Men may call one to a place who may prove insufficient, because they often know not what men's abilities are when they call, neither can they give abilities by calling; but God calls none but he knows their sufficiency already, or in calling makes them such.

Now, God knowing Christ's sufficiency, called him to it, Ps. xlv. 7. Because he hated iniquity and loved righteousness, therefore he anointed him to be a head; because he was therefore able to fulfil all righteousness,

* Qu. 'us'?—ED.

and not to sin; that is, he was armed with power to execute the office of priesthood for ever, and overcome all difficulties; and therefore he is said to have been made a priest, with power of an endless life, and not after the law of a carnal commandment, as other priests were. Their office, he says, was weak, and not able to bring things to perfection, as it was not able to satisfy God; but he with the power of an endless life; because Christ had power enough to survive the encounter of his Father's wrath, and live for ever; to go through-stitch with the work and bring it to perfection, and not *succumbere* or sink under it.

And, *secondly*, in that God called him, he undertook to make him able. Besides that God knew Christ able, and therefore called him, it may be further said, that in calling him he undertook to make him able. Men, if they find not men able for places when they call them, cannot give abilities; but God doth give abilities by calling: Isa. xlii. 1, 4, 'Behold my servant whom I uphold; mine elect' (or chosen one), ver. 6, 'whom I have called in righteousness' (says God); that is, I have called him to this office, and that in righteousness, put him not upon it unwillingly; and him I chose of all that ever were or shall be, and he is my servant in it, and therefore certainly I will uphold him in it; and therefore (as it is ver. 6) he promiseth that he will hold his hand up that he sink not, even as Christ held up Peter from sinking, and will keep him so (as ver. 4). 'He shall not fail,' or fall short to accomplish the work of mediation, in the least tittle; 'nor shall he be discouraged,' or (as it is in the original) 'not be broken;' and he was to undergo that which would have broken the backs of men and angels, and pushed them to hell. But he shall not be broken, but backed with all the power that God hath, 'who made the heavens,' &c., as it follows, ver. 5.

And, *thirdly*, you heard how Christ was willing to undertake it, and therefore surely knew himself able to go through with it, for otherwise he would never have undertaken it. A wise man will not undertake an enterprise that he is not able to manage or go through with, and Christ much less, who is the wisdom of his Father, Col. ii. He will not do as a foolish builder, that begins and sets upon a work which he is not able to finish. What wise man will enter into bond for another for more than he is worth himself, and so lie in prison for ever? No wise man will, much less Christ; therefore surely he was able.

And, *fourthly*, in that he is God as well as man (as you have heard), therefore surely he must needs be able. If it had been possible his Father should forsake him, as he complained he did afford him no succour, no support, but leave him to himself; nay, do his utmost against him, and make known the power of his wrath, as indeed he did; why, he is able to uphold himself, for 'the fulness of the Godhead dwells bodily in him,' Col. ii. 9. Mark it, he hath not only some gifts of the Godhead, or virtue from the Godhead dwelling in him, and so supporting him, but the fulness of the Godhead itself; and this not lodging there as a friend or sojourner, but knit to and residing in him, as a householder, for ever, that will be sure to keep possession for ever; and so nearly knit, as that Godhead and manhood make one person *bodily*, that is, personally; as *anima*, by Hebraism, signifies person. So human nature and God make one person. Therefore he, having power, must put it forth to the utmost to preserve human nature from sinking in this business; and all must sink if it sink.

Now, one of his names, Isa. ix. 7, is, that he is 'the mighty God.'

Why? First, he must fulfil all righteousness: 'It becomes us' (says

Christ) 'to fulfil all righteousness,' of moral law and ceremonial, Mat. iii. 15. Why, and that is least of all, for this angels in heaven perform; and Christ, if he had been but a mere man, filled with all grace as he was, John i. 16, would have done that, having the Spirit so without measure, John iii. 84. Only this, if he had been a mere man, it had not been a righteousness sufficient and able to mediate for us, for it would but have justified himself; there must therefore be a further ability than any creature hath to go to this. But he being God also, and therefore Lord of the moral law, as he is said to be Lord of the Sabbath, and so not subject to the law; that he should take on him the form of a servant to the law, and be made under the law, who made and gave it, Gal. iv. 4, and become obedient to every tittle of it, as he did; this made that active righteousness of his of infinite value, able to mediate for us. Therefore he is called 'Jehovah our righteousness.'

Secondly, As he must be able to do and fulfil the law thus, so to suffer also; for, Heb. ii. 10, he is made a perfect Saviour through suffering; and then says Christ, 'I shall be perfected,' and 'without shedding of blood there is no remission,' Heb. ix. 24. He cannot save a man unless he die, but must enjoy heaven alone: John xii. 24, 'Unless a corn of wheat fall into the ground and die, it remains alone;' so Christ, if he had not died. And being God he could not indeed, but being man. He would easily enough do that (you will say), nothing easier than to die. But yet, if his death be a mediating death, he must be able to offer up himself in death; be his own sacrifice, altar, priest; and borrow nothing, and all at once; and that no creature could. But now being God also, he was able to offer up himself, needed no other priest, Heb. ix. 14. 'Through the eternal Spirit he offered up himself;' yea, and find a sacrifice also himself, offering up his body, Heb. x. 10; and 'his soul also an offering for sin,' struggling under the wrath of God, Isa. liii. 10; yea, and be the altar himself, Heb. xiii. 10.

But, thirdly, there is a business of greater difficulty yet behind, that exceeds the power of any creature, yea, of all, which will draw out the power of God indeed; and that is, that he must rise again as a conqueror over death, overcome hell and God's wrath, and not lie wrestling under them to eternity, for till then God's wrath would not be satisfied; for if he had lain by it, and been kept in prison, then it had been a sign the debt was not paid. If ever therefore he will justify us by his death, he must overcome and rise again, or else we should 'be still in our sins,' 1 Cor. xv. 18; and this no creature could ever do. God's wrath would have held them tugging work to eternity, and they could never have risen again, nor stirred. He that overcomes that must be as strong as God himself; yea, and he must do this himself, by his own power too. It were not enough to be raised up, as Lazarus was, by the power of another. That will not serve. For that power that raised him must first satisfy and overcome God's wrath, and break open the prison doors.

Now, if another power than his own had done it, that party had been mediator, and not he. But now he being God, he is able to do all this, and to do it himself also. For being God, that power was able to raise him up, and to loose the pains of death; and it was impossible he should be held of them. They were the pains of death, namely, the wrath of God, which would have sped all the creatures in the world; and which pains would not have let him go till they were loosened and overcome; for, if possible, they would have held him, but being God, it was not possible.

He will take hell gates, as another Samson, and throw them off the hinges, and carry them away, and swallow up death in victory: 'Destroy this temple' (says he, John ii. 19), 'and I have power to raise it up;' I, myself. The body could not raise itself indeed, therefore if he had been mere man he could not have done it; but that Spirit, the eternal Godhead, could, 1 Pet. iii. 18. He was able, you see, to this work of mediation.

3. Thirdly, Christ had faithfulness in him not to fail in the performance, Heb. iii. 2. It is said, ' He was faithful to him that appointed him.' God did appoint (as ye heard) and trust him, and therefore he failed not in his expectation; for God otherwise had not pitched upon him. And the reasons which may evince he would be so are,

First, He being God, and having passed his word to his Father, he could not but be faithful and true in it; for with God 'is no variableness, nor shadow of turning,' James i. 17. And plead inability he could not, and his Father that had appointed him would not release him: Heb. vii. 21, 'He swore, and would not repent, that he should be a priest.'

Secondly, It concerned himself to be faithful in the performances, for otherwise, as the case stood, he himself must have lain by it; as a man that is surety for another (as Heb. vii. 22, 'He was made a surety'), he made it his own debt; and we could not, nor were able, and he therefore undertook it; and therefore it concerned him to discharge it, and to pay the utmost farthing.

Thirdly, God, upon this ground, took his word and bond, and had let thousands of debtors go free, and saved millions under the Old Testament, upon his bare word; ere ever he came to do it, Heb. ix. 15, he is there called ' the mediator of the new testament, that by means of death, for the transgressions under the old testament,' &c. Many a man's sins then were put upon his score, and God should be a great loser by him; and therefore it was necessary he should discharge those debts: Rom. iii. 25, he says, that ' God had set him forth to be a propitiation, to declare his righteousness,' or faithfulness, 'for the remission of sins that are past, through the forbearance of God.' There seem to be two arguments: 1. That God had pardoned and forborne many sins, before he came into the world, he had been at great expenses of mercy; and he should be a loser if he came not to be a propitiation for them. 2. Upon Christ's promise to him, he had made a promise of Christ to the world; and therefore, to shew his faithfulness and truth, he sent him. To make good his Father's faithfulness, he must needs be faithful.

Fourthly, When he came down from heaven, and took our nature upon him, he left his glory as a mortgage or pawn for to make his promise and bond good, never to take it up again and look his Father in the face in glory till he had performed it; for so much that speech of his implies, John xvii. ver. 4 and 5, 'Now glorify me with the glory I had with thee before the world was.' That same *now* having reference to finishing the work in the 4th verse, implies that till then he was not to reassume it.

4. Therefore, fourthly,

He hath done it, and fully performed it; so his own words are in the same John xvii. 4, ' I have finished the work which thou gavest me to do;' and hath all fulness of righteousness dwelling in him, to make peace and reconcile us, Col. i. ver. 20. For,

First; Whereas God had a bond against us, Col. ii. 15, till that was discharged we must lie by it. He hath discharged that debt, paid an equivalent ransom to it, *ἀντίλυτρον*, 1 Tim. ii. 6, and cancelled that bond,

Col. ii. 13. And whereas we were to die, bodies and souls, he offered both his body, Heb. x. 10, and also his soul as an 'offering for sin,' Isa. liii. 10, and 'poured it out to death,' v. 12, whereof the two elements of bread and wine are signs and seals to us, though both conveying one and the same whole Christ, yet represented to us as having his body broken in the bread, and his soul poured out in the wine ; the life or soul lying in the blood, it signified the suffering of his soul, which sacrifice being offered up by the eternal Spirit (that is, the Godhead), who was both priest and altar, Heb. ix. 14, therefore sanctified the gift or sacrifice, as the altar did, Mat. xxiii. 19, and therefore, being the blood of the Son of God, it cleanseth from all sin, 1 John i. 7. Yea, and so perfect a satisfaction is it, that he needed to do it but once : Heb. x. 14, 'By once offering he perfected for ever them that are sanctified ;' that is, purchased a perfect peace and final discharge, and that so perfect, that God doth herewith not only rest satisfied, but also finds a sweet smelling savour, Eph. v. 2, so as the scent of sin cannot come up into his nostrils.

Secondly ; He hath fulfilled all the active righteousness of the law ; for so indeed it 'became him,' who is our high priest, 'who is holy, harmless, undefiled,' &c., Heb. vii. 26. So when he was to lay down his life, and pay the last sum and part of the payment, he says, John xvii. 4, 'I have finished the work thou gavest me to do ;' and John viii. 29, I do always the things that please thee ;' and, 'I came not to destroy the law, but to fulfil it,' even every *iota* of it. For (says he, Mat. iii. 15), speaking of the necessity of his being baptized, which was a branch of righteousness, 'Suffer it to be so, for it becomes us thus to fulfil all righteousness,' namely, necessary for justification, which I add, because some parts of the law he had no occasion to fulfil : as not the duty of a husband to a wife, nor of a father to a child, because they were not compatible with his condition and office of mediatorship ; and which are rather duties of a particular state and condition of life, than of the nature of man in general, which he undertook for. That therefore, as we say, it was not necessary he should in his passive obedience take on him the several personal infirmities and diseases which befall men, but only those which are common to man's nature, as hunger, sleep, &c., which he did ; so is it in his active obedience also. It was not necessary thus particularly to fulfil every such branch as is but personal ; though all those he did perform more eminently, in a more transcendent manner, as the duties of a husband and a father to his spouse and children, the church.

Thirdly ; And besides, as in his passive obedience he underwent the substance of those pains we were to undergo, but was not bound to all the circumstances, as of eternity, and of the place in hell, &c., so, nor in his active obedience was he bound to perform the occasional duties, which are but circumstances to man's nature, or diversified by several conditions in this world. It was enough he performed the sum and substance, of loving God and man in that eminent manner he did ; love being, for substance, 'the fulfilling of the law.'

And thus it was impossible but that he should fulfil the whole law. Had he been mere man, then indeed there might have been room for a supposition, that being a creature, he might have failed ; but being God, he could not, James i. 13, and therefore not fail in performing any part of it. Which obedience and fulfilling of the law being performed by one who, till he took man's nature on him, was no way subject to it ; and then also was lord of the law as of the Sabbath, may be accepted for us, and we saved by it ;

so as 'the righteousness of the law' is said to be 'fulfilled in us,' Rom. viii. 4, 5.

And that he hath fully performed both these is evident by this: that now he sits at the right hand of God, which is the demonstration brought by the apostle, Heb. x. 12, that he hath done whatever was requisite to perfect and consummate our peace and reconciliation, as ver. 14. For, says he, after his offering that his sacrifice, ' He sat down at the right hand of God,' or 'the Majesty on high.' Now, it is certain he had never come thither if he had not paid the debt; God would never have suffered him; for he must have lain in prison till he had paid the utmost mite. But now being got out of prison, as Isaiah speaks, chap. liii. 8, and set down on God's right hand there in heaven, surely he hath paid the debt, and if he could have broke loose and got thither, yet in heaven he would not stay, unless he had performed it; thither would the wrath of God pursue him, and there arrest him and seize on him. For when Adam had sinned, paradise could not hold him; nor would heaven hold Christ, if he owed God anything; therefore, says Christ, John xvi. 10, bringing it as an evidence of his righteousness all sufficient, and to convince the world of it, ' I go to my Father, and ye shall see me no more;' if it had been otherwise, his Father would not have received him, but sent him down again.

Fourthly; And by this his both active and passive obedience, through the acceptation of his person, who performed it, he hath completed the work of reconciliation with his Father, which, consisting of peace and good will (that is, being pacified towards us, and receiving us into favour again) as the parts of it, these two main parts of obedience serve to procure and consummate both. His blood procureth peace; so Col. i. 20, ' Having made peace through the blood of his cross;' that is the first. But yet, because when peace is made, the party may say, Though I am at peace, and pardon the traitor, yet I can never love him again or receive him into favour, as I was wont; therefore his active obedience, through the favour of the person performing it, procures the manifestation of good will also, to make us complete and perfect friends. Therefore to reconcile in that Col. i. 20 is made more than simply to make peace. Peace is but the foundation of it; for ' *having* made peace to reconcile us,' &c., says the text; and the blood of his cross goes to make peace; this other serves to restore us to his lost favour, to make us accepted, and all through him. Therefore there lies the emphasis, as you may observe it in that Col. i. 20, ' By him I say;' it comes in twice there.

5. Therefore, *fifthly;* add to all this, there is a fulness of acceptation of the person with God who performed all this. For he that brings creatures into favour must be more beloved than a creature; and in matters of mediation, the chief thing lies in the graciousness of the mediator, with his interest in the party offended; and if either his love or money will procure full friendship for us, he will use both. His money (you see) is paid, he hath laid it down, a sufficient price; and besides, he is infinitely beloved of his Father, so as for his sake he cannot but accept it, and love us again through him better than ever. For, Prov. viii., he is his old friend, and ancient companion, ver. 30, even before the world was, his only begotten Son, not by will but nature, the very substantial image of his person, Heb. i. 3: in whom therefore he cannot but delight, and be well pleased, as he himself from heaven hath said, ' This is my beloved Son, in whom I am well pleased;' not with him only, but in him with others; for therefore he bids us hear him and believe him; and if it had not been that he is well pleased with us in him,

it had no way concerned us. Therefore, in Eph. i. 9, we are said to be 'graciously accepted in him, as the beloved one of his Father,' as it is there. And though he secretly bore good will to us before, yet in that his beloved, he hath *made* us graciously accepted, made way for owning us, and shining graciously upon us, in and through him, whereas without him, he would never have afforded us one good look.

And though in Adam we were beloved, having his image in us in him, yet infinitely more in Christ: Rom. v. 17, 'We receive abundance of grace, and righteousness, and life in Christ;' and therefore, says Christ, John x. 10, 'I came that they might have life, and that they might have it more abundantly.' It is a degree of comparison, and therefore with that former state of life we once had; they shall have all that life (and God's favour is our life) they once had, and more abundantly. In that Rom. v. 17, he speaks comparatively with our estate in Adam, and seems to make this the fruit of that abundance of grace and righteousness that we receive, above what in Adam we should, that we shall reign in life, be kings in heaven, to which place his righteousness would not have brought him, but served only to continue that life and degree of favour he was received into. But in him we are beloved with the same love Christ himself is: John xvii. 23, 'Thou hast loved them, as thou hast loved me;' and therefore, ver. 27, adds and makes this a further favour granted at his request, that they might be where he is, whither else they should not have come. For he ascended to prepare that place for us, and then heaven was opened, and not till then; when he said, 'This is my beloved Son, in whom I am well pleased.' We are therefore not only made friends again in heaven, but further received into a greater degree of favour than ever, and to a higher place in court.

6. But now because, in the *sixth* place, it may be said, that though for his sake we are made friends as good as ever, yet we may fall out again, a breach may come, and so the enmity become greater than ever; he may use us kindly for a while for his sake, but yet, upon some provocation, he may cast us off again, and remember all our former sins.

Therefore, sixthly, know that there is eternity and perpetuity annexed to this his mediation, to make it yet more full; and so full as nothing now can more be added; Heb. x. 14, 'By one offering he hath perfected for ever them that are sanctified.' His offering, though but one, yet it was a perfect one, wanting nothing; once was enough; it is of everlasting force and merit, for it perfecteth for ever. And it is not thus only in itself, but in the fruit of it to those who enjoy it, it perfecteth them for ever who are sanctified by it. There is no danger of justification, if sanctification hold out, that being the condition on our part; and therefore shewing the eternal efficacy of that one offering, he says, it perfects them who are sanctified; even that being the covenant on his part to perform in us, as well as justification is; and therefore he adds, ver. 15, 16, 17, 18, 'Whereof the Holy Ghost is a witness to us: for after he had said, This is my covenant; I will write my laws in their hearts; he says, and their sins and iniquities I will remember no more.' The sum whereof is this, that justification is eternal: 'Their iniquities will I remember no more.' And therefore sanctification is eternal also, and both he puts upon the merit of that one offering, that righteousness which hath influence into both, being eternal also, and perfects for ever; and therefore, Dan. ix. 24, he is said to finish and put an end and a seal to sins, and to make reconciliation for iniquity, and to bring in everlasting righteousness; that is, such a righteousness as shall, through the strength and eternity of its merits, for ever put an end to sins, and to make a reconciliation as eternal as itself is, and us friends for ever. For it is such a righteousness, that as it is of that breadth to cover millions of worlds of sins, so of that length, that no times to eternity could wear it out where it is once imputed.

And indeed the reason why it is of that length is, because it is of that sufficiency, though it be but one offering, yet it perfects for ever when it is once imputed; and till the guilt of .sin can come to be of more force than the merit of his righteousness, it cannot cease to be imputed when once it is imputed. And therefore it is not said, that by reason of it, sins are remembered no more, but iniquities also, in both the forementioned places. So that when Christ ceaseth to be righteousness, then may we, when once he is made righteousness to us.

And to this end further, besides the everlastingness of his righteousness, he himself on purpose lives for ever to keep us in favour, and his righteousness in memory, and our sins in forgetfulness: Heb. vii. 24, 'This man,' says he, 'because he continueth for ever, hath an unchangeable priesthood; wherefore he is able to save to the utmost them that come unto God by him, seeing he ever liveth to make intercession for them.' He is able to save to the utmost; that is, the utmost of sins, be they what they will; to the utmost of times, though continued never so long. No guilt can reach so far, and to such greatness, from which he is not able to save; and he makes this as one reason of it, because he himself lives for ever, and lives on purpose to put remembrance and force into his mediation, 'He liveth to make intercession.'

He is not one that will be silent whilst he lives, never hold his peace till he have peace. 'If any man sin,' after the imputation of that righteousness, 'we have,' saith he, 'an advocate with the Father.' If sin and the devil, who is sin's advocate, plead against us, yet we have Christ our advocate, who never took any cause in hand wherein he was foiled; and this with the Father, both his and ours, who is therefore ready to hear his children pleaded for by such a Son. And if the blood of dead Abel cries, shall not the blood of living Christ speak louder? If the sin of Adam, now he is long since dead, would to eternity continue to condemn men born of him (if it might be supposed generation might last to eternity), one man after another, and never have any stint; and shall not the righteousness of him 'who is alive for evermore,' Rev. i. 18, be of force to dispel the guilt of all the sins, that can be supposed to be committed, even to eternity?

See how the apostle argues it, Rom. v. 10, 'If, when ye were enemies, ye were reconciled by his death, much more shall we be saved by his life.' He argues from the less to the greater; and the comparison is double. 1. His death and life are compared together. And, 2, our state before reconciliation and after. If after we had gone on many years in a state of enmity and rebellion, and yet were made friends through the strength of his mediation; and all that enmity forgotten and pardoned; then being made friends, it is easier for Christ to keep us so, and to get our sins still pardoned to the end of our days. And if his death was of force enough to reconcile you then, much more, being now alive, and so able to put life into the merit of his death, will he be able to keep God and you friends; and therefore, says he, in the 6th chapter 9th verse, having said at the 5th that 'we are planted into the likeness .of his resurrection,' he makes the likeness and similitude to hold in this, 'knowing that Christ, being raised from the dead, dieth no more; death hath no more dominion over him. For in that he died, he died unto sin once' (he had not died but for sin, and then needed die but once for it) ; ' but in that he liveth, he liveth unto God. Likewise,' says the apostle, ver. 11, ' reckon ye yourselves also dead unto sin, and alive unto God through Jesus Christ.' Make account that when Christ is out'of favour, then you may be ; when he is damned, you may. But he liveth ever, so shall you ; for by that one death ' he hath perfected for ever them that are sanctified.'

Use. Now the common use or corollary from both these, what God has done, and what fulness dwells in Christ, is this, that certainly there is peace and reconciliation to be had and obtained with God by sinners and enemies to him ; and this, my brethren, is the pitch,* the marrow of the gospel ; such news, that as soon as it burst out, heaven and earth rang with joy again. The angels could not hold, but, as being ambitious to be the relators of it, posted down to earth to bring the first news of it : Luke ii. 18, 14, ' Peace on earth, good-will towards men.' Though you can hear it, and be no more moved than the seats you sit upon, yet when it was first preached it brought in men by troops, as voluntaries, more than the law had done : Luke xvi. 16, ' The law and the prophets were till John : but since the kingdom of God' (that is, the gospel) ' is preached, and every man presseth into it.' But now, alas ! we that are daily used to the tidings of it, how little are we moved with it ! How few come in upon proclamation made of it ! And therefore we are fain to make it the greatest of our business to preach the law, and 'come with that great hammer to break your bones in pieces first, that we may then preach the gospel, as it is Isa. lxii., to the captives, and to bind up the broken-hearted, and so to make ourselves work ; and this we count our misery. Yea, and this we profess before you all this day, we tremble most when we come to preach it ; for we are afraid that men should still go on, and lie in their sins, which if they do, they had well nigh as good have been in hell, as in the church to hear it, because God may be provoked to swear against them that they shall never enter into his rest.

Yet because a necessity is laid upon us, not to preach only, but to preach the gospel, and that all that are brought home to God must have the knowledge of it, I return to enlarge and press the use mentioned, and shew the connection of it with what hath been delivered, and how it flows from it.

Reconciliation, I say, surely may be obtained.

First ; Because God the Father so strongly purposed and intended it for some, therefore surely it may be had, for he will never go back or alter any resolution he hath so peremptorily taken up ; yea, though he had not made known that his purpose to us his creatures, for ' he is not as man that he should repent ;' he should be conscious to himself of imperfection if he did : and he swore (as I told you), and would not repent from everlasting, and now he hath made known this which he purposed in himself, Eph. i. 9.

Secondly ; His delights were in it, and therefore are in it still, his greatest and strongest delights. Though we poor, frail creatures alter our delights daily (for indeed our delights do arise out of alteration and variety), yet he can never alter his ; but what he delighted in once he delights in still ; and surely if the thoughts of making us friends aforehand possessed his heart so deeply and so long, much more now, when he shall come to the performance and execution of it, and to reconcile us actually ; to see that done, the thoughts of which so pleased him. Do we think that such thoughts, so deeply set, and fed with delight, can vanish or be forgotten ? Surely no. It is the day he longs for, which he hath seen a-coming and rejoiced in,

* Qu. ' pith ?'—Ed.

and said in himself, ' When will it be ?' Jer. xiii. 27.   And in the shewing
mercy and dispensing it, ' I do delight,' says he, Jer. ix. 24.   No request
therefore or suit pleaseth him so, or agrees more with his heart, than suing
for mercy and pardon, and to be friends with him ; he is grieved when he
is hindered by our impenitency from enjoying his delights.   And then,

Thirdly; He spake to his Son himself, unbespoke to by us, and made
known his mind to him, and called and anointed him to this work, and with
the greatest vehemency, when he swore concerning him, that he should be
a priest ; and having expressed so much seriousness, as then he did to him,
when he swore and said he would not repent, Heb vii. 21.   For his gifts
and calling, and oaths, are without repentance.

And, *Fourthly ;* In that his Son did as willingly undertake it, and now
hath also undergone it, and a covenant having passed between them, he is
much more engaged to accept it.   For to what end did he trouble his Son
to come down from heaven, and to take our shame and frailties, and to die?
What, in vain ? as the apostle elsewhere argues, Gal. ii. 21.   What, to
spend his strength for nought ? as Isa. xlix. 4.   A shame it were to take
such a journey to no purpose.   No ; God made him a promise, Isa. liii.
10, 11, that he should ' see his seed, and see the travail of his soul, and he
should be satisfied ; for my righteous servant shall justify many ;' and this
because he underwent so much grief and sorrow so willingly, as it is in the
former part of the chapter ; and the joy of this was it made him undergo it
so willingly : Heb. xii. 2, 'For the joy that was set before him.'   And that
his joy was this, that he should ' prolong his days,' and though he died in
the travail, yet he should see the travail of his soul ; and as a woman, though
she be in great pains, yet her joy is ' that a man-child is born into the
world ;' so it is with Christ, that many should be justified by him, as it
follows there, for nothing else will satisfy Christ.   And that he should ' divide
the spoil with the strong,' ver. 12, ' because he poured out his soul to
death' ; that is, he triumphed over hell and death, and in the conquest
spoiled principalities and powers, and obtained heaven and everlasting
righteousness, by which he himself was not made the richer.   God
therefore allows him to divide it, and give it away to others.   And God con-
sidereth also how that in this work he was his servant : ' My righteous
servant ' (saith he) ' shall justify many ;' and he was *his* servant, did *his*
business in it ; and should he have no wages nor reward ?   Yes, the only
reward which he seeks for is the salvation and justification of his elect, and
those God hath given him.   Isa. lxii. 11, when Zion is saved, and his salvation of them cometh, it is added that ' his reward is with him, and his
work before him,' that being the reward of his work ; and Isa. xlix. 4, when
Christ complained that in regard of Israel, that is, the Jews, ' I have,' in a
manner, ' spent my strength in vain,' so few of them are called, that my
reward and work is with my God to give me wages.   What is that ?   Ver. 6,
' I will give thee for a light to the Gentiles, and that thou mayest be my
salvation to the ends of the earth ;' and ' I have heard thee in an acceptable
time ;' and ' I will give thee for a covenant to the Gentiles, to say to the
prisoners, Go free.'   This is God's answer to him there.

Fifthly ; It is the duty of Christ, if I may so speak with reverence, to
bring men in, John x.   And as to him, so to us, he hath manifested so
much, by all means possible, to assure men of his willingness to be reconciled to them, if they will be so to him, to assure us he hath engaged himself by all means possible.

And unto all these secret engagements in his own heart, and to his Son, we may now add, all the professed publications of his mind herein to us, which he hath made upon all occasions, and by all means possible. As,

First; He hath published this news by all three persons. First; himself to Adam in paradise; and renewed it again and again, with his own immediate voice from heaven, 'This is my well beloved Son, in whom I am well pleased,' which we heard (says Peter), and is no fable.

Secondly; Christ, who is 'the faithful and true Witness,' Rev. i. He came from the bosom of his Father; and as he died, 'so he preached peace,' Eph. ii. 17; and it was one of the first texts he preached on: Luke iv. 18, 'The Spirit of the Lord is upon me, because he hath anointed me to preach the gospel; to preach deliverance to the captives.'

Thirdly; The Holy Ghost bearing witness. 'God hath exalteth'him, to give repentance and forgiveness of sins, Acts v. 31, 32, and so Heb. x. 16. These are the three witnesses in heaven, 1 John v. .7, and their record is this, 'That there is life to be had in his Son:' ver. 11, 'And if we receive the witness of men, the witness of God is greater;' and he that believes not this makes God a liar, because he believes not the record that God gave of his Son.

And, fourthly; He hath published it also by all creatures reasonable, and to all creatures reasonable.

(First.) The angels, they came and preached 'peace on earth, good will towards men,' Luke ii. 14.

(Secondly.) To men he hath given gifts powerful and full of glory, Eph. iv. 8, &c., and a commission, most large and gracious, to tell men that 'God was in Christ reconciling the world,' 2 Cor. v. 20. Yea,

(Thirdly.) And he hath maintained this ministry in all ages, all times ring with the news of it. The world is as full of these ambassadors now as ever. And these lie as lieger ambassadors, to treat with men about this peace; to proclaim that he is fully willing, and upon that ground to beseech men to be reconciled; and so long as lieger ambassadors lie in a place, and are not sent for away, so long the treaty of peace holds.

(Fourthly.) He hath done this by them in all places; he has bidden them 'go and preach it to all the world, to every creature,' Mark xvi.; and accordingly his disciples did preach it, and had done it in Paul's time, Col. i. 6. And this openly; 'Wisdom cries without, utters her voice in the streets, and cries in the chief places of concourse,' Prov. i. 21. Christ cries his riches at the cross; cares not who hears it, yea, would that all should know it, and he would not have it spoke so openly and generally, if he were not most serious in it: and 'if it were not so, he would have told you.'

(Fifthly.) He hath declared it by all means else that may argue seriousness.

[First.] Not by bare word of mouth, but you have his hand for it; he hath left his mind in writing this book, which is dropped from heaven; the title of it is, 'The word of reconciliation,' 2 Cor. v. 19, the main argument of it being reconciliation; and if there be any truth in it, then certainly in this doctrine of reconciliation. In this book we find proclamation sent forth after proclamation, book after book, line after line; all written to this end, that we might have hope and strong consolation, as the apostle witnesseth.

[Secondly.] He hath added the seals of the sacraments, and an oath to it also; and that was not made or slipped from him at unawares, as oaths from men use to do; but advisedly, with the greatest earnestness and deliberation that might be, Heb. vi. 17. God willing (the text says) more abundantly to manifest this his intent, and the immutability of this his counsel of reconciling the world to himself through Christ (which is the promise mentioned in the former verses made to Abraham), confirmed that promise with an oath, that by two immutable things (his word and oath), we might have strong consolation and hope.

[Thirdly.] He hath pawned heaven and earth, the covenant of day and night, in mortgage, to forgive iniquity through his Son's death, Jer. xxxi. 34–36, and chap. xxxiii. 20, 'This is my covenant' (says God there), 'that I will forgive their iniquity, and remember their sins no more,' ver. 34 and ver. 36 : 'If those ordinances depart, of sun and moon,' &c., ver. 35, 'and if you can break the covenant of day and night,' ver. 20th of 33d chap., 'then may this covenant of mine be broken.' Day and night, we see, continue still, and therefore this covenant holds good still.

(Sixthly.) And lastly ; If all this will not persuade men of this his willingness to be reconciled to them, and shew them mercy, manifested so seriously so many ways (wherein it is impossible for him to lie, as the apostle speaks), yet at last, let his actions and courses, which he hath taken from the beginning of the world, speak for all the rest. He hath been reconciling the world in that sense : that is, he hath been bringing friends and pardoning many, in all ages, from the beginning of the world. As first, Adam and Eve, the ringleaders, the heads of the rebellion, who drew all the rest of the world into that enmity, were yet reconciled. Kings usually hang up the heads and chiefs in treason, for examples of their justice, though they pardon others ; yet them did God reconcile to himself, as examples of his mercy to all that should come of them. And it is observable, that the first thing he did, after the world was fallen, was preaching this gospel, and shewing of mercy in pardoning them. He began to do that soon ; he meant to be always doing that to the end of the world, which he delighted in. His heart appears to be most in this work, when he began it so soon. What should I reckon up the rest that followed that ? Abraham, David, &c., the time would fail me. The Romans were enemies, and they were reconciled, Rom. v. 8, 10 ; the Ephesians, Eph. ii. 12, 14 ; the Colossians were 'sometimes enemies, yet now reconciled,' Col. i. 21 ; yea (and God be blessed), Christ is yet, according to his own promise, that he would be with us to the end of the world, reconciling the world to himself still. God hath some true friends now in the world, that are truly reconciled to him, that walk in the streets by you, live amongst you ; and he will have thousands when you are gone. And what are these but as flags and patterns of mercy and reconciliation, hanged out by God to toll others in ? Eph. ii. 7.

And yet, because notwithstanding all this assurance of God's willingness to be reconciled, there are certain tacit objections and stumbling-blocks which lie in poor distressed souls' minds, which block up their access to God for this peace, I will therefore remove some discouragements, which are apt to arise in men's minds when they hear this news of peace and good will. For as when God would speak peace to his people, Isa. lvii., and brings them into the land of Canaan again, he bids them (ver. 14), 'Cast up, and take away the stumbling-blocks ;' so when we would persuade men to come unto God, we must make the way clear, and shew how there is an abundant entrance made into the kingdom of Christ.

First, the consciousness of their own rebellions strike such terror into their consciences, as they dare not come into his presence, nor look him in the face ; but for that consider what we have been speaking of this while.

Is it not a matter of reconciliation? Now, if there were not sin nor rebellion in thee, there needed not a reconciling: Christ might have been spared this labour. Nay, consider that if this were any real hindrance, there should be no saints in heaven but Christ and his holy angels; for all those saints, who now behold his face with joy, were sometimes enemies as well as thou. For when the text says, He reconcileth all things in heaven, it implies that all those saints who are now in heaven were enemies and rebels once; for else what needed any reconciliation?

But some will further say, Ay; but I have been a deadly, desperate, hateful enemy, and opposer to himself, his children. Why, consider, that these Colossians were enemies in their minds, in evil works, as deeply and as strongly contrary as any others.

Ay; but I have been a transcendent enemy, an arch rebel; and though he may be reconciled to others, yet never, I fear, to me. Well, suppose thy heart and thy life have been never so full of enmity and rebellion against him, yet consider the text tells us, that 'Christ hath all fulness in him to reconcile;' and till thou canst be fuller of sin than he of righteousness, there is enough to pardon thee: 'He is able to save to the utmost,' be the case never so bad, the matter never so foul.

Ay, but thou wilt say, I have been so for these many years, I have lived in enmity, and in that state long, twenty, thirty, forty, fifty years; and it is an old grudge God may. have against me. Consider that this fulness dwells in Christ; it hath resided longer in him, and in God's acceptation, than sin hath done in thee; yea, it will dwell in him for ever, it is an everlasting righteousness.

In a word, suppose thy sins are never so many and so grievous, yet consider that his thoughts of pardoning are more, for they have been from everlasting, as I shewed out of the 40th Psalm, 5th verse, 'They cannot be numbered.' And also that the plot of this business is to make grace and mercy abound; it is Christ's trade to purge sin, Mal. iii., and the more sin the more work you bring him. He is a physician, who healeth freely and simply, to shew his skill and. pity, and for no other end; and therefore the older the worser, the more festered the sore is, he is the willinger to heal it; for he shall have his end in healing it more, shew the more skill, the more mercy; therefore, though it may seem to discourage thee, yet it doth not discourage him; when thou comest to him, thou art the welcomer if thou wilt but come to him. It was his business he came for, to save sinners; and suppose thou beest the chief, as Paul was, 1 Tim. i. 15, and a blasphemer, as he, ver. 13, yet is it 'a faithful saying, that Christ came to save sinners,' &c., 'even the chiefest of them.'

But you will say, That was extraordinary, and no way exemplary for me. But the words shew the contrary; for he says it was a truth worthy of all acceptation, as therefore concerning others as well as himself, let them be as great sinners as he: 'And to me first' (says he, ver. 16), 'that I might be a pattern' (of mercy) 'to all that should believe.' Yea, to all that should be afraid and discouraged to believe, by the greatness of their sins; and in that God began with him, he meaneth not to end with him, he puts him in the forefront of the bill, 'to me first,' to bring others the faster in. Some one in heaven must be the chiefest of sinners, and who can tell but that it may be thee?

But when these objections are answered, and sins proved to be no bar between pardon and them, yet then they plead that it may be that they are not elected, as Paul and others were, for whom God intended all this-

and therefore it may prove an uncertain suit; for if they be not elect ones also, they shall miss of it, though they should seek and seek never so earnestly. If I knew certainly indeed that peace were to be had for me (my person) in particular, there was some life to stir in it.

For answer to this. Not to meddle with the controversy of the universality of Christ's death and God's love, in this place and at this time. But let all this be granted.

First, Let me deal with you upon that supposition, that it might prove uncertain in regard of particular election; and convince you what strong incentives there are for you to seek it, all this supposed.

I. Unless thou didst certainly know that thou shouldst certainly miss of it, and until God declares thou art none of the number, so long there is hope concerning this thing; there is an *It may be*, which is as much as we find many promises expressed in, as Zeph. ii. 3; so Joel ii., he exhorts them to turn to him with their whole heart, for he is gracious, &c. 'And who knoweth if he will turn and repent, and leave a blessing behind him?' If it be no more, God expects you should turn upon this; this hope may quicken you, and stir you to cast yourselves upon his free grace, seeing it is in him; to refer yourselves to his mercy, depending upon him in the use of all means. 'Let us turn' (say the poor Ninevites, who therefore will rise up in judgment against thee), 'for who can tell but the Lord may repent of the evil?' And God did so, Jonah iii. 9, 10. There might be a door of escaping—and they were thought prisoners, yet of hope, Zech. ix. 12—and venture they would for a pardon, though they did not know certainly that they should obtain it. But,

II. Suppose yet further, more unlikely than likely that thou shouldst speed in thy suit; yet considering it is a case of absolute necessity to seek out for reconciliation and peace, there is a strong ground to move thee to seek out for it, and spend the utmost of thy endeavours to attain, and think it an infinite mercy that it is not declared to be absolutely impossible for thee.

In case of absolute necessity, we see men weigh not impossibilities; but do put themselves and all their endeavours upon a venture, though the business be very uncertain.

For example, men being pressed to the wars, though it be usually certain that some shall die, and those in all probability who fight in the forefront, or venture upon some desperate piece of service, yet it being necessary for them to undertake that service which is commanded upon pain of life, and there being some possibility they may escape, it may fall out so; in this case they are content to hazard and venture themselves; therefore also why not much more in this case shouldst not thou, though there were more unlikelihood that thou shouldst not obtain, than that thou shouldst? To give another also, 2 Kings vii. 3, 4. Two* lepers, they reasoned with themselves, 'If we enter into the city, then the famine being in the city, we shall die there; if we sit here, we die also. Come, let us fall into the camp of the Aramites: if they save our lives, we shall live; and if they kill us, we are but dead.' Thus, in a case of necessity, they chose that part which, though it had many improbabilities in it, yet which might fall out otherwise, there was an *if* might be made of saving their lives; and yet the most unlikely one, for they did not know but that the Aramites might be resolved to cut off all the Jews, and spare not a man alive; and if they meant to spare any, yet of all others (they might well think) they would cut off them; because,

* Four.—Ed.

being lepers, they were unfit for service and employment, and might infect the camp.

And suppose this were thy case, that of all others thou wert most likely not to obtain mercy, that thou a persecutor and contemner of grace, &c., shouldst in all probability be cut off, yet there being some possibility, in a case of such necessity, come in and venture thyself. And the necessity is greater in thee; for the lepers there might be supposed some miraculous way of preserving them, but for thee no other at all; God hath no other. And the death the leper should die, both one way and the other, would be alike; but if thou seekest not, thou wilt die a worse death. But,

III. In this case of reconciliation, there is (supposing the doctrine of particular election) both a certainty that God intends it for many, and as equal and indifferent a likelihood in view that it is intended for thee as for any other. Which, besides that great necessity to enforce thee, may add much encouragement and hope to thee. For thou heardest before, that none of thy sins are any bar at all; and if any sin must hinder, no sin but that against the Holy Ghost. Though there be many signs of election, yet none of absolute reprobation but it. No former dealings of God with thee, nor any dealing of thine with him, though never so base and injurious; no circumstance in any sin, either that it hath been so often and so long lain in, and committed after such vows, mercies, convictions, deliberations, can exclude thee. Nay, none of these do argue thee further off from mercy than another that is in the state of nature with thee, there is nothing can be said concerning thee but it might have been said of some whose portion reconciliation hath been; as the apostle saith, 'No temptation hath befallen you but what is common to men;' so nothing can be objected against thee but hath been and is common to those who have obtained mercy. No leprosy makes thee unfitter or unlikelier to be saved than another. So that lay but these two together.

1. That it is certain some in all ages shall find mercy, and that thou are as fairly capable and as nigh as another.

2. There is no qualification in the statute to exclude thee: thy country, sex, age, parts, hinders nothing; for God did look to none of all these when he chose men; Acts x. 34, 'He is no respecter of persons;' so as thou mayest say as they, Acts xv. 11, 'I believe that, through the grace of Christ, I may be saved, as well as they;' for grace is free, and respects nothing in the person, one way or other, to whom it intendeth favour.

And therefore I, seeing nothing against it, as well as nothing why I should, I am as near it as another, and therefore will stand for it. 1 Kings xx. 31; when they, having heard the kings of Israel were merciful kings, and had spared others in the like case that they and their master Benhadad were in, and saw nothing in their condition had not been pardoned to others by them, they, upon this ground, say, 'Let us put ropes about our necks, peradventure he may save thy life.' It was but a peradventure, and a greater one than can be supposed in thy case; for they had heard only in the general, 'the kings of Israel,' but whether this king Ahab were of such a disposition they knew not, and yet they adventured upon it to seek him. But thou heardst that this great God is a God gracious, merciful, &c., and that he hath pardoned thousands in the like condition.

IV. In the fourth place, thou art not only thus equally capable of it, as well as another, but there is a probability, a likelihood God doth intend thee, because thou hast heard that he is a merciful God, and willing to be reconciling by his own appointment.

The news of it is especially directed to thee by himself; and he hath bidden thee to stand for it, and come in for it. For the word of reconciliation which we preach is made known but to a few; and those to whom it comes, it comes out of special mercy, and by God's direction, rather to one place than another, rather to one man than to another; as why was Paul forbidden to go into Bythinia? Acts xvi. 7, and called to go into Macedonia? and bidden (Acts xviii. 10) to stay at Corinth and preach? but because, as it is there, 'I have much people in this city.' When the plague comes to a place any man lives in, whenas other places are free, he fears lest God may intend to take him away by it, rather than others in other places, and still looks on himself in bed, if he hath no token on him. So when the gospel comes to the place thou livest in, and not the sound of it confusedly, but the knowledge distinctly of it to thy ears, thou hast cause to think it exceeding probable that God doth intend thee for salvation, and the kingdom of God is come nigh thee. It is a great probability of election that the gospel comes to thee, 1 Thess. i. 5, and an especial sign he means to save, and hath chosen those to whom he makes known this mystery of his will, of reconciling and gathering men to himself, Eph. i. 9, &c. Those servants of Benhadad had no intimation of mercy from Ahab himself, or by his direction; but thou hast from God. The mystery hid from all ages, and now from most of the world, is revealed unto thee, and he hath directed us to thee in an especial providence. He hath not proclaimed this pardon to all prisons, but to a few; and therefore, thou being in those prisons to which these proclamations of mercy are sent, hast cause to seek out for it, and much encouragement also to do it. Especially,

V. Fifthly, this gospel, offering great salvation as annexed to this peace and reconciliation made with God; the lepers thought only to save their lives, and so did Ben-hadad; he was out of hopes haply of having his kingdom again; this, added to that indifferent capableness of thy attaining it, and the probability annexed to that, should exceedingly quicken thee to seek out for it; for in case of preferment, as when a great office is void, a living or fellowship, which will certainly be bestowed on some, when a man shall hear of such a thing, and have a hint of it from the party that bestows it, and be told by him that he is as fair for it as any other, and as capable, that there is no clause in the statute to exclude him and shut him out, and that he hath as good means to make for it as any other; how would and doth this use to quicken men to use their utmost endeavour, to lay out their money, and put in for it? when yet they know there are many suitors, and that the place can be bestowed but upon one.

Now this is the case in hand; the gospel offering great salvation; 'so great,' as he can no otherwise express it; Heb. ii. 3, 'But how shall we escape if we neglect so great salvation?' And this thou art as fair for, canst make as good means, if thou comest to Jesus Christ, as any other. This the apostle intimates, 1 Cor. ix. 24, speaking of his endeavour to be partaker of the gospel, and the salvation in it: 'Know ye not that they which run in a race run all, though but one receive the prize?' yet all will venture, and therefore why not thou? Will not this practice of men, in case of a corruptible crown, as he calls it, though there be an uncertainty in it, condemn our neglect of seeking an incorruptible crown, as ver. 25, and stop our mouths for pleading, that few can attain, and some may miss it?

VI. Sixthly, consider God's manner of revealing and making known this reconciliation to be had (suppose but by a few); yet it is indifferently to be propounded to all, as expecting that all should be stirred up at the hearsay of it, with the hopes of it, and endeavours after it, Luke x. 5. Christ bade them say to every house they came at, 'Peace be to this house;' and God looks that every one to whom this news should come should look out for peace, as a thing belonging to him, Luke xix. 42; yea, commands all to whom it comes to stand for it, and to use all means to attain it, 1 John iii. 23, and Acts xvii. 30, and will condemn men if they neglect to do so, Heb. ii. 3; and not only so, but beseecheth you to be reconciled, to come and seek it at his hands. And if one that had a great preferment in his gift should do so, would it not mightily encourage you with hopes to attain it, if he should send to thee to stand for it?

VII. But yet further, in the seventh place, if this news which thou hast heard, of willingness in God to be reconciled, &c, thou either art affected and moved to come in, or not affected; one of these must fall out. If not affected at all to listen after it, thou hast no cause to complain thou shalt not obtain it; for can any complain he cannot attain that which he hath no heart to, nor mind to attain? But if thou beest affected with it, and hast a heart desirous to obtain it; if thy heart be set on work to seek out for it; if he hath enamoured thy heart with his Son, and given thee a high esteem of reconciliation with him, and given thee a restless spirit after it, this is a strong presumption, more than a probability, that it is intended for thee, that thou art a son of peace, Luke x. 6. 'For if it be hid, it is hid to them who are lost,' 2 Cor. iv. 3.

VIII. In the eighth place, if thou wilt seek it, and dost continue to seek it, there is a certainty that thou shalt obtain it; and it is a false connection to say, that there being few elected, therefore it may prove uncertain though I seek it.

Now, that there is a certainty annexed to seeking, is plain by what Paul says, 1 Cor. ix. 26, 'I therefore so run, not as uncertainly;' that is, I so run, that I shall be sure to speed. He had said in the 24th verse (as I shewed before), that as in the Olympian games many run, yet but one receives and wins the crown, and yet many will run though it be so uncertain; but, saith he, in endeavouring after salvation in the gospel, of which he there speaks, if you will but endeavour to run as you ought, with your utmost might, you shall be sure to attain, as many as will take pains to do so, and use all means, as he speaks there; some, indeed, fall short through lazy running; but, says he, 'So run that ye may attain;' that is, there is a running and a seeking which will certainly obtain; I therefore so run, and so running shall obtain; not as uncertainly, but so as I shall be sure to win the prize. And so Christ also hath said, 'Seek, and ye shall find; knock, and it shall be opened unto you;' and he backs this by a strong convincing demonstration to assure us of it, Luke xi. 5, If one comes to a friend at midnight, and desires some necessary thing of him, though he be one who hath no list to rise, ver. 7, nor regarded the relation of friendship at all in it, ver. 8, but says he has all his children already in bed with him, ver. 7, yet for his importunities' sake, he would rise in the end. Then I say unto you, says Christ, 'Knock, and it shall be opened;' though the door seems shut against thee, though thou shouldst think God intended not friendship to thee, and had (as it were) all his friends about him already, yet he would hear in the end; and ver. 10, he confirms it by experience, that there was never yet any turned away, 'But every one that asketh, receiveth; and that seeketh, findeth.' There was never any yet that did so and was turned away empty.

And indeed, if you use the means, and seek constantly, who should hinder you? Or how is it possible that you should come to miss of it? Neither God the Father, nor God the Son, who yet are the parties through whose hands reconciliation runs.

1. Not God the Father; for he having committed the word of reconciliation to us, to make it known to every man indifferently, with command from him, yea, with earnest beseeching to persuade men to be reconciled to him, 2 Cor. v. 20. If any soul upon this news comes, and hath a mind to prove, is taken with his friendship, can never be quiet without it, and useth all means to attain it, God is as truly bound to dispense peace to that soul as if he had named him from heaven; for we do all this ' in God's stead,' as 2 Cor. v. 20, and as ambassadors do in his stead beseech you; and herein we are lawful ambassadors; so as it is, as if God by us did beseech you, and we exceeding not our commission; God will make it good, as kings use to do the treaties of their ambassadors in the like, when they do things in their names and according to their instructions. God the Father's warrant we have to go to his Son, and he condemns us if we do not.

And, 2. Jesus Christ will not be your hindrance; for he hath said, John vi. 37, ' Whosoever cometh unto me, I will in no wise cast out.' And we have reason to think him willing; for it was the end of his death, that he might see his seed and be satisfied. Christ needed not have purchased it for himself, who was and is ' God blessed for ever;' and therefore is not desirous to keep it to himself; it is no profit to him to have it lie by him: he had rather it should be put out, and that others should share in it. And who should? The good angels have no need of it, and the bad ones are incapable; therefore for us poor sons of men it is ordained, called therefore man's righteousness.

And, besides, he was God's servant (as was said) in that great work. When, therefore, I come to him with his father's warrant and command (which you heard you have), it is as if you should come to the lord treasurer with a ticket from the king for so much money; he must dispense it, for it is the king's money, as this *God's righteousness*, and so called; and he is but the king's servant, as Christ also was. And it is also his office; for why else was he appointed priest? (as she said, Why art thou a king, if thou wilt not do me justice?) for Heb. v. iii., If one brought a sacrifice to the priest, he was bound to offer it by the law, otherwise he failed in his office; and so is Christ to present thee to his Father, if thou comest to him: John x. he says, His sheep he must bring; he looks at it as his duty.

Only this he will say to thee, that as his Father hath appointed him a priest, and he is but a servant in this dispensation of righteousness, yet his Father hath appointed him a king, a head, a husband to thee, to submit to; and that he will require of thee, or thou shalt have no benefit by his death; as thou hast a patent for righteousness, he hath a charter for sovereignty over thee, and obedience from thee; which is the second thing you are to be convinced of.

www.ingramcontent.com/pod-product-compliance
Lightning Source LLC
Chambersburg PA
CBHW022356280326
41935CB00007B/211